Please remember that this is a library book,
and that it belongs only temporarily to each
person who uses it. Be considerate. Do
not write in this, or any, library book.

Learning and the
Educational Process

LEARNING WITHDRAWN
AND THE
EDUCATIONAL
PROCESS

JOHN D. KRUMBOLTZ, *Editor*
Stanford University

Selected Papers from the Research Conference on Learning and the Educational Process held at Stanford University June 22–July 31, 1964

Conference Directors: Lee J. Cronbach and Richard C. Atkinson of the Committee on Learning and the Educational Process of the Social Science Research Council

Supported by the Cooperative Research Program of the Office of Education, United States Department of Health, Education, and Welfare

RAND MᶜNALLY & COMPANY
Chicago

RAND M^cNALLY EDUCATION SERIES

B. Othanel Smith, *Advisory Editor*

Broudy and Palmer, *Exemplars of Teaching Method*
Broudy, Smith, and Burnett, *Democracy and Excellence in American Secondary Education*
Elam, ed., *Education and the Structure of Knowledge*
Farwell and Peters, eds., *Guidance Readings for Counselors*
Foshay, ed., *The Rand McNally Handbook of Education*
Haines, *Guiding the Student Teaching Process in Elementary Education*
Kimbrough, *Political Power and Educational Decision-Making*
Lewenstein, *Teaching Social Studies in Junior and Senior High Schools*
Litwack, Holmes, and O'Hern, *Critical Issues in Student Personnel Work*
Norris, Zeran, and Hatch, *The Information Service in Guidance*
Parker, ed., THE RAND M^cNALLY CURRICULUM SERIES
    Ford and Pugno, *The Structure of Knowledge and the Curriculum*
    Wellington and Wellington, *The Underachiever*
Peters and Farwell, *Guidance: A Developmental Approach*
Peters, Shertzer, and Van Hoose, *Guidance in Elementary Schools*
Rollins and Unruh, *Introduction to Secondary Education*
Smith and Ennis, eds., *Language and Concepts in Education*
Trump and Baynham, *Focus on Change: Guide to Better Schools*
Vassar, ed., *Social History of American Education*, 2 vols.
Zeran and Riccio, *Organization and Administration of Guidance Services*

Also published by Rand McNally
Gage, ed., *Handbook of Research on Teaching—A Project of the American Educational Research Association*

FOREWORD
By the Conference Directors

LEE J. CRONBACH and RICHARD C.
ATKINSON, Stanford University

This collection of papers is an outgrowth of a six-week summer conference held at Stanford University in 1964. Since the conference itself was part of a movement significant to the prospective readers of this volume, a brief discussion of its background is in order.

During the past half-dozen years, many agencies have sought to encourage basic research in educational learning. This movement has been timely for two reasons: (1) the developers of new curricula are posing questions about the nature and means of learning that go far beyond what the findings to date can answer; and (2) recent psychological concepts and techniques have opened up to exploration areas that were nearly untouched in the older literature. At the same time, the national interest in improving education has created an enormous demand for new ideas and a corresponding increase in funds to support research.

What has been lacking is a supply of research talent proportionate to the problem itself. Few people have been able to keep abreast of the many developments from empirical research, and those who know that side of the problem are little informed about the contemporary issues and innovations in education. Yet both must be known to the person who seeks to help in educational reform. Conferences arranged by such agencies as the National Research Council, the National Science Foundation, and the United States Office of Education, usually in cooperation with universities, have done much to bring curriculum developers into communication with educational researchers and psychologists. Various consultative relationships have emerged that provide some help from behavioral scientists to the curriculum workers, and themes arising in the curriculum movements are beginning to receive attention in the research laboratories. But this communication among established investigators can accomplish only a little compared to the work that needs to be done.

The Social Science Research Council appointed a committee in 1962 with the charge of stimulating basic research that would shed light on educational learning. The committee has proceeded in various ways to identify particularly significant problems on which research should focus and to bring these to the attention of researchers. But in the forefront of every discussion has been the personnel problem. Research pertinent to education, if it is to be other than trivial, requires a breadth of background and a flexibility of approach that is not readily acquired. The committee therefore planned the 1964 Summer Conference, for which funds were provided through a contract between Stanford University and the Cooperative Research Program of the United States Office of Education. Supplementary funds to cover certain special expenses were provided by the Carnegie Corporation of New York.

We, as members of the SSRC Committee, directed the conference, but its detailed planning and conduct, and its eventual success, must be credited to the team of instructors. There were four group leaders: John B. Carroll of Harvard University, Lawrence M. Stolurow of the University of Illinois, Fred L. Strodtbeck of the University of Chicago, and John W. Atkinson of the University of Michigan. Paired with these men, respectively, were these instructors: Ellis B. Page of the University of Connecticut, Richard C. Anderson of the University of Illinois, Louis M. Smith of Washington University, St. Louis, and Robert Moulton of the University of California, Berkeley. The forty participants, selected from a much larger group of applicants, were an outstandingly promising group of young research workers in education, psychology, and sociology. During the summer the instructors aided them in reviewing their past work and laying plans for the new studies they could embark upon. They were stimulated to think of new questions and new procedures by presentations of theoretical perspectives and of specimen work made by the instructors, by the other participants, and by consultants. These distinguished consultants included both curriculum developers and research specialists.

Professor Krumboltz has selected from the program of talks and lectures a representative group that shows what is stirring in this field. This collection by no means presents all the topics and ideas that were in the air. It is restricted both by space limitations and by the fact that some excellent presentations were informal and could not at this time be put into formal manuscripts. This book does not pretend, therefore, to offer a systematic coverage of the leading lines of research that will in due time bring us to a new understanding of learning and motivation in the schools. But it is a fine sampling of those approaches and of some of the significant findings that have already come to light. We are grateful to the authors for their participation in the conference and for their willingness to prepare their manuscripts for the larger audience this book will reach.

PREFACE

Learning and the Educational Process is intended to stimu-
late the thought of any person seriously interested in research
approaches to the problems in education. It consists of ten papers
prepared by an outstanding group of researchers in education,
psychology, sociology, and language. The authors of these
papers have suggested new concepts, reported findings from a
number of provocative research lines, and offered research suggestions and leads for others to follow.

The book will probably be of most value to the following
types of individuals:

1. Instructors of graduate students in education or educational psychology who wish to select a supplementary
   text which will provide their students with an advanced
   presentation of some recent trends in research relevant to
   education.
2. Graduate students in education (or other behavioral
   sciences) who may wish a relatively detailed overview of
   some representative lines of research relevant to education
   to suggest ideas which may be useful in planning their
   own doctoral research projects.
3. Professional educators who wish to examine a number of
   ways in which research on learning problems can contribute to educational practice.
4. Psychologists, sociologists, and educational researchers
   who are interested in some integrated accounts of recent
   work that is significant for theory and basic research on
   learning and motivation as well as for practice.

A preview of a few major ideas in the book may help to
clarify its nature and possible usefulness. Robert Gagné begins
with an exposition of the importance of stating educational
objectives in terms of observable human performance. A useful
element for describing behaviors he defines as the "task"—the
smallest unit of performance which has a distinct and independent purpose. Six categories of tasks are specified which have

relevance to education and which may facilitate research on the conditions for their learning.

J. W. Atkinson then provides an integrated summary of the research he and others have conducted on achievement-oriented activity. He describes his theory of achievement motivation and the predictions which can be made from the theory. The tendency to avoid failure is as important as a motivating influence as the tendency to achieve success. Then an impressive series of studies are marshalled to test the predictions arising from his theory. He argues that his formulation accounts for the data better than the Law of Effect.

D. E. Berlyne continues the discussion of motivation by stressing the work on "intrinsic" rather than "extrinsic" motivation. He points to the evidence that people engage in exploratory behavior without extrinsic reward, that people receive pleasant affect from mild deviations from expectations, and that people vary consistently in such traits as "intolerance for ambiguity." Curiosity seems to result from conceptual conflict which can be produced through various discovery methods involving surprise, doubt, perplexity, and bafflement. Berlyne believes that the value of discovery methods may lie not so much in the effort of independent discovery as in the arousal and subsequent relief of curiosity.

However, the importance of appropriate extrinsic motivation, especially for lower-class children, must not be overlooked, according to Fred Strodtbeck. He argues that middle-class homes typically provide an environment in which children learn to manipulate verbal symbols in order to obtain a share of the family resources. In lower-class homes, however, no amount of verbal skill is successful in adding to physical or psychological welfare. To provide the lower-class child with this experience in use-of-words-for-material-welfare, Strodtbeck advocates that the schools provide more opportunities, resources, and power with which the underprivileged child might bargain.

The language difficulties of lower-class children are further pointed up by Walter Loban in his longitudinal study of language development. The less verbal children tend to come from the lower socioeconomic classes and tend to speak with fewer complete sentences, fewer complex words, more word mazes, and fewer subordinate expressions. However, the difference in speed of response between the high and low verbal groups appears negligible.

This finding in speed of response is of interest in relation to Jerome Kagan's identification of the impulsive-reflective dimension—a tendency of children to respond to complex stimuli after a consistent interval of time. The tendency to respond quickly or slowly generalized across several types of problem situations as well as an informal interview situation and had significant relationships to reading, the occurrence of various kinds of errors, and other personality variables such as persistence. The possible implications of developing reflectivity in the schools are explored and several questions requiring research are raised.

Evan Keislar and Larry Mace provide a useful analysis of some major tasks in learning a foreign language and examine the effects of various sequences of these tasks. Among their findings is the conclusion that training in speaking followed by training in listening produces better comprehension than either the reverse sequence or concurrent training. Other results and the discussion of their implications raise a number of provocative research questions.

An intriguing series of experiments by Ernst Rothkopf explore "mathemagenic behavior"—the behaviors that produce learning from written materials. Like Keislar and Mace, Rothkopf varied the sequence and placement of various elements, but in written English stories. He found among other things that immediate repetition of a fact, even when the phrasing was varied, produced less learning than delayed repetition but more generalization to rephrased test items. The problem in preparing written documents is how to keep the reader working until he has mastered the desired training objectives.

As a general approach to solving instructional problems Lawrence Stolurow argues that it is misleading to examine what master teachers do and that instead we should construct appropriate teaching models. He illustrates by describing SOCRATES, a computer-based systematic approach which models the teaching process and tests the appropriateness of the models. Implications of the evidence on interaction effects involve the importance of immediate feedback with low-ability students, self-directed study only for high-ability students, and minimum amounts of information feedback for average-ability students. A number of research questions are suggested by this approach.

Finally, John Carroll pulls many of the pieces together in emphasizing the need for studies of long-term learning outcomes. Curriculum evaluation must be conducted by assessing the extent to which each curriculum accomplishes its own set of objectives, not by experimentally comparing curricula on the same objectives. Carroll proposes a model for school learning which differs from Stolurow's and includes the variables of aptitude, perseverance, opportunity to learn, quality of instruction, and ability to comprehend instruction. In Carroll's view the study of these variables in long-range curricular evaluations will provide us with the kind of information we need to improve educational effectiveness.

The diverse views and lines of attack expressed in this book do not always agree with each other, but it is hoped that the dissonance they may produce will result in constructive efforts at resolution.

J.D.K.

January, 1965

TABLE OF CONTENTS

Chapter 1

EDUCATIONAL OBJECTIVES AND HUMAN PERFORMANCE

ROBERT M. GAGNÉ, *American Institutes for Research*

There is something that seems incongruous in the two topics of my title—educational objectives, and human performance. The combining of these ideas seems to be analogous to certain other strange concatenations, like sunspots and the stock market, or like soybean prices and the length of ladies' skirts. It will be my task, therefore, to reduce this incongruity—to explore the relations between these two topics. Why or how do educational objectives have anything to do with human performance, and vice versa?

The phrase "educational objectives" means different things to different people. The boy in the fourth grade may say: "Why do I have to study mathematics?" He may be asking a very fundamental question, and it is difficult to know what answer will satisfy him. Shall we say to him:

1. You need it in order to learn more mathematics, or to learn science?
2. You need it in order to balance your checkbook when you grow up?
3. You need it in order to be successful in almost any job?

4. You need it in order to become an informed and responsible citizen?
5. You need to appreciate the beauty of numbers?
6. You need it in order to think logically in solving problems?

Any or all of these answers might occur to a thoughtful adult. And if the student then asks: "How do you know?" it is apparent that a response could be given with somewhat differing degrees of confidence, depending upon the choice of a first answer. It is not difficult to demonstrate that trigonometry enters into the solving of problems about velocities of physical particles; it is surely more difficult to show the beauty of number relationships to someone who hasn't experienced them. Some educational objectives, in other words, are much more nearly immediate than others. Some pertain to longer time periods of the individual's life than do others, and some relate to more comprehensive aspects of his human existence than do others. The first step toward seeking relationships between human performance and educational objectives, then, may be to restrict the scope of the problem somewhat.

THE BROAD GOALS OF EDUCATION

The broad goals of education have been formulated by a number of distinguished national groups and commissions (National Education Association, 1964; Rockefeller Brothers Fund, 1958) as well as by outstanding scholars of the educational scene (Gardner, 1960). It will not be possible to deal with these extensively in the present context—only with a relatively small component of them. Suffice it to say here that there is a relatively high amount of agreement about these broad goals. It appears that there are three major emphases, which I summarize here in my own words.

1. Education has the purpose of making it possible for the individual to participate in and to share with other people a variety of aesthetic experiences.
2. A second major goal is the development of responsible citizenship.

3. The development of individual talents to the end of achieving satisfaction in a life work or vocation is a third goal.

However these three goals may be expressed, and my expression of them is surely not the best, it is difficult to disagree with them. They do in fact seem to represent goals of education with which a vast majority of informed people in the United States would agree.

To the student or practitioner of education, the questions raised by these statements of goals are difficult ones indeed. How do we know that what is being done in the education of the young gets us as far toward these goals as possible? How does one know that a particular content or a particular educational method will be optimally effective in reaching these ultimate objectives? The answer has at least two different parts to it. First, we need to understand and to specify to the best of our ability what is meant by "participating in aesthetic experiences," and what is meant by "responsible citizenship," and what is meant by "satisfying vocational activity." In other words, we need to be able to inform ourselves how we can tell when these things *have been achieved* by individuals. And second, we need to analyze, or break down into smaller components and stages, the progression toward these goals. We need to be able to see what it is about what the student can achieve in the eleventh grade which will relate to what he does as a voter, or as a father, or as a productive scientist.

Having acknowledged the problems posed by these broad goals, I can now state that it is not my intention to deal with them further here. Instead, I shall restrict my attention to the third and most frequently mentioned educational objective, pertaining to the acquiring of intellectual competence which will ultimately fulfill a vocational aim. I am interested in discussing mainly the objectives of instruction which attempt to provide the individual with ever increasing power to deal with and master his environment—the kind of instruction which we think of as including such subjects as English and mathematics and languages and science. This should not be taken to mean that I consider these the only important parts of the curriculum—far from it. But one has to start somewhere. Furthermore, I shall be concerned, as you will shortly see, with the problem of how to analyze or break down broadly stated objectives into smaller pieces, so that they can be dealt with more readily.

HUMAN PERFORMANCE

What about the other phrase in my title, *human performance?* What is that, and what does it have to do with educational objectives? Performance may be defined in several ways. The definition I wish to use here is an observable human accomplishment. "Behavior" is what brings performance about, but performance, as defined in this context, is the *outcome* of behavior. We can observe an individual close a door; that is a performance, and the proof of it is the outcome—the door is closed. Or, we can observe an individual solving a mathematical problem; the performance is the solution.

The fundamental reason why human performance is related to education is that it must be used to define what happens, or what is supposed to happen, in the educational process. Education is for learning, we say. Yet it is of great importance to keep in mind just what learning means, and how we know when it has taken place. We *infer* that learning has occurred when there is a difference in *performance* of the student from time X to time $X + 1$ (which difference for other reasons we cannot attribute to growth). On one day we observe that Johnny cannot add two-place numbers; on a subsequent day he can. There is a change in his performance, and we say he has learned. On one day a student cannot tell us where or what Ghana is; on the next day he can. Again, the change in his performance is what provides evidence of learning.

Occasionally, educational language appears to depart from this principle. For example, there is the phrase "learning experience." I should not want to deny that there may be such a thing. But one cannot tell whether learning has occurred until a difference in performance is observed. It will not suffice for the student to report he has learned something, or for the teacher to report that a learning situation has been provided. I have heard several separate reports recently from educational experimenters who undertook to give a test *before* the lesson as opposed to afterwards, just to see what would happen. Besides a certain amount of teacher shock, what happened was that half the students were able to complete the test nearly perfectly *before* instruction had begun! For this group of students, if the lesson had been given without the test, would there have been a "learning experience"? At any rate, if one compared their performance before and after, it would be quite clear that there had been no learning. Human performance is the fundamental class of data one must have in order to infer learning. It is, therefore, of equally basic importance to education.

ISSUES IN DEFINING OBJECTIVES
BY HUMAN PERFORMANCE

Since observable human performances form the basis on which the inference of learning is made, it would seem to be a corollary that these same performances should constitute the objectives of education. If one could specify all the performances he expected of a high-school graduate, for example, this would serve two purposes: it would tell us what the student is able to do at the end of high school, and it would also tell us what he is able to do before he goes to college. The first could be used to compare with what he could do when he entered high school, and thus provide an idea of how much learning has occurred; the second could provide a base line for the changes in performance we hope will occur during his college attendance. It is indeed difficult to see how one can assess learning without such "before and after" observations of human performance.

Yet the defining of educational objectives in terms of human performance is not a universally accepted practice. There are two quite different sorts of objections raised to such a procedure.

ACCOMPLISHMENT VERSUS DIRECTION OF CHANGE

First, there is the argument that objectives should state what is to be *attempted,* not what is to be *accomplished.* In line with this idea, one sometimes finds objectives stated in some such way as this:

The student should acquire a developing awareness of the
magnitude of the solar system and the universe; or
The child should become increasingly confident in extemporaneous oral expression.

It is difficult to know what to say about such statements except
that they are weasel-worded. Why is it not possible to say exactly what one wants the student to do in showing his awareness
of solar system magnitudes? Why is it not possible to state what
kind of extemporaneous oral expression one expects the child to
perform? The answer may be, of course, that the latter kind of
objectives can indeed be stated, but not all students will attain
them. Unfortunately, this is probably true under present circumstances. It would be good, though, if we could amend the statement to read: "Not all students will attain them *with the same
speed*." Then they would still remain objectives which any intelligent person could identify, rather than descriptions which
if not deliberately hedging are at least ambiguous.

LONG-RANGE UNANTICIPATED OUTCOMES VERSUS INTERMEDIATE SPECIFIED EVENTS

A second kind of objection to clearly stated objectives is a
much more serious one. It runs like this: "I can't be sure exactly
what the student should be able to do at the end of some period
of instruction. In fact, I am not interested in this. What I am
interested in is how he will perform five or ten or even twenty
years hence. If he studies science, this should mean that he will
make wise decisions about science as an adult. If he studies
English, this should mean that he will make wise choices of
literature as an adult." In other words, the tenor of this objection
is that it is not possible to state immediate objectives of instruction because some of them cannot be anticipated. How does one
know what a student will be able to do following some unit of
instruction when he might just do something which even the
curriculum designer has not thought of yet? Better keep one's
eye on far-reaching or long-term objectives, and say what one
hopes he will do when he gets to college, or even when he
finishes college.

I have said that this kind of objection is the more serious, and the reason is that it is held with such emotional vigor by some influential people. This is the only reason I can see that it is more serious, because actually it is intellectually insupportable. If one is actually interested in performances which will appear ten years hence, there is nothing wrong with that. Two courses of action are then available. The first is to perform some longitudinal studies to determine what differential factors are in the current educational backgrounds of people who behave desirably and people who behave undesirably at some future time. Alternatively, one could experimentally introduce certain differences in the education of groups of present students, and follow them up after five or ten years to see what kinds of decisions they make. Both of these techniques are of course well known to behavioral scientists, and successful studies have been and are being done to find answers such as these.

But such studies take time, and some curriculum designers are naturally impatient to get on with the job of "improving" education. It is then up to them to make some reasonable guesses about *what kinds of capabilities learned now* will have the desirable effects wished for ten years hence. It is of course necessary to recognize that these *are* hypotheses. But that is no reason not to state them explicitly and in terms which meet the criteria of ordinary operational definitions. What would we think of a biologist who behaved this way toward the growth.of plants? Suppose he said: "I am really only interested in the flowering of this plant, which may happen ten weeks from now. In the meantime, I think it would be wrong, possibly even dangerous, to say what I think the necessary stages which precede this flowering may be. I will say that the plant must be watered properly and exposed to sunlight, but beyond that I will not go. It is really the future flowering I am interested in—the events between now and then are entirely up to the plant." What ridiculous behavior this would be for a scientist to display! Is there a way of justifying similar behavior when it is said with reference to the intellectual development of a human being? I think not.

If we must make hypotheses concerning the precursors or determinants of some ultimate performances in advanced stages of education, or in adult life, by all means let us do so. But there is no reason not to make these hypotheses explicit. In fact I should call it presumptuous not to do so. What can I make of such a statement as that which informs me that my son is going to study astronomy in the seventh grade? Is it because thereby one of his college requirements will be met? What in fact will he be able to do after he has studied astronomy? It is not that I am playing the carping parent when I ask these questions. These are serious questions, because I really do not know what hypotheses are guiding such instruction. If these were made explicit, if they were in fact stated in terms of human performance, it *might* become apparent whether my son needs to study astronomy in the seventh grade, as opposed, perhaps, to something else.

And what about the idea that there may really be some unanticipated outcome from studying astronomy, or probability, or geography, at some particular age and in a way which encourages problem solving? Well, of course there may. I shall be just as pleased as anyone if this is the case. But I return to an earlier point—unless it can be demonstrated that learning has occurred, the expectation of some *other* outcome seems slim indeed. And if one expects that learning is going to occur then this means there must be a demonstrable change in performance. There may be some other unexpected kind of change, but there *has* to be some particular kind of change that can be specified. And that brings us back to human performance, since that is where the observable change will appear. There would seem to be no valid reason why such performances cannot be described.

REASONS FOR
DESCRIBING EDUCATIONAL OBJECTIVES

By this time, or perhaps long before this, the question may have occurred to you, "Why describe educational objectives, anyhow? Why bother?"

The fundamental reason is one that I have already given, and it is primarily aimed at those who are trying to understand education, to study it as a process, or to improve its quality. Nowadays, let it be noted, such persons are not only "professional educators"; they are university professors of physics and chemistry and mathematics and English; they are experimental and educational psychologists and sociologists; and they are also many intelligent public-spirited citizens whose profession does not lie directly in the educational realm. What these individuals need to understand is perhaps the most fundamental fact about *learning*, namely, its definition. Learning is a change in capability which is inferred from differences in an individual's performance from one time to a later time. Learning has·some mystery about it, for many people. But the most important fact about it is embodied in this definition, which relates it integrally to human performance.

There are, however, other reasons for defining educational objectives, which have some practical implications for education itself. Perhaps no one has written more sensibly and persuasively on this subject than has Tyler (1949; 1950). In a relatively recent paper (1964), he describes some reasons which I shall mention here in my own words:

1. Definitions of objectives are necessary to guide the behavior of the teacher. While many teachers are able to recognize educational goals and translate them into effective conditions for learning, some teachers have not carried their thinking beyond the stage of selecting the content to be presented. The danger here is that the teacher will not recognize effective ways of reaching the necessary objectives if in fact he has not formulated these objectives for himself.

2. Defining objectives for the student is an inadequately exploited educational technique. Tyler reports that unless students know what the objectives are, they are likely to resort to memorization and mechanical completion of exercises in textbooks or workbooks, rather than carrying out relevant sorts of learning activities. When one tells the student what he is expected to do after he learns, this is not "giving him the answer." Rather it is providing him with a goal which he himself can use to organize his own learning activities. Of relevance here is a study of Mager and McCann (1961), who found that when a group of engineers were told the objectives of their learning they succeeded in reaching them in much less time than under other instructional conditions.

3. Another purpose of defining objectives has often been

emphasized by Tyler and others: unless the objectives are known, it is impossible to know what the student's capabilities are at any given moment. This reason for objectives has often been stated in terms of the requirements for measurement, or "testing." But "testing" is also sometimes an emotional word, and it may therefore be thought that this is an unpersuasive reason for defining objectives. Whatever emotionally toned arguments there may be about "testing," one thing is perfectly clear. It is impossible to carry on the enterprise of education without assessing each student's attainments. Quite possibly, students need to be assessed much more frequently and perhaps less elaborately than they have been up to now. But it makes no sense to undertake to *teach* something which the student either knows already or, alternatively, which he cannot possibly learn because he does not have the prerequisite knowledge. We must know what the student is capable of doing at any given moment in his educational progress. And this means we must have statements of objectives which define what we expect him to be able to do.

There are, then, several important reasons for seeking to define educational objectives in terms of human performances. These objectives are used to tell us whether the inference of learning can be made. They are used as specifications of the kinds of questions to ask the student in assessing his current capabilities. They become important guides for the teacher's behavior in selecting appropriate instruction. And they could probably be used to greater advantage than they are at present in informing the student of goals to be achieved.

THE PROCESS OF DEFINING OBJECTIVES

How does one go about defining objectives in terms of human performance? There are, after all, many action words, verbs, in the English language, and these can be used to construct a great variety of descriptive sentences. How can one decide what the components of a good description are?

It is at this point that I see many important parallels between the work of those who have struggled with the question of educational objectives as such, and a quite different area of work in which people have been struggling equally hard to describe performance as it occurs in human occupations and jobs (cf. Miller, 1962a; Miller, 1962b). These two different problems seem to have many things in common as long as one agrees that they both must be concerned with human performance.

First of all, it is evident that a description of human performance must contain a good "strong" verb, a verb referring to observable human action. This point has been elaborated in a delightful book by Mager (1962). As a first approximation, or as an approximate way of speaking, it seems reasonable to try a statement of an objective in some such terms as "understands probability." The trouble is, however, that this may mean several different things, and not just one thing. Does it mean that the student can "state a verbal definition of probability"? Does it mean he can "predict the probability of a hit for a batter with a batting average of .240"? Does it mean he can "compute the probability of tossing a penny to obtain nine heads in a row"? Or perhaps all of these? Actually, the answer to people who insist on using such verbs as "understand" in statements of objectives is very simple. It consists of another question: How would you be able to tell that the student understands? The answer to this second question has a high probability of containing a verb referring to observable human action.

How detailed or specific does an acceptable definition of an objective need to be? One degree of nonspecificity is represented by such a statement as "solves problems in algebra." But this is not very helpful because it doesn't tell us what kinds of problems, and there are, after all, many possible kinds. Another degree of specificity is suggested by the statement "computes the normality of a chemical solution." Still more specific would be a statement like "identifies nouns or noun-phrases in English prose sentences." Each of these statements describes performance with a verb which implies that objective observation is possible. Yet they obviously differ considerably in their degree of specificity, in the fineness of detail they contain. They therefore suggest the question of how finely performance should be described.

Here is one of the striking parallels with the work of investigators who have been trying to find the right level of description for human performances in jobs. These people too have long been plagued with the same kind of question. For example, one can describe the job of policeman, if one so chooses, as "enforcing the law." Yet it would be immediately recognized that such a statement is in one way or another highly inadequate in conveying to another person what a policeman does. Accordingly, researchers in this field have generally agreed that one must describe performance in somewhat greater detail. In these terms, a policeman's job is considered to be composed of *tasks*, such as "checks the locked condition of doors on his beat"; "disperses sidewalk crowds"; "provides information on locations of major traffic arteries"; and so forth. As a part of a job, a task may be defined as the smallest component of performance which has a distinct and independent purpose. Describing a policeman's job in any greater detail (e.g., "puts left foot in front of right foot") would be meaningless because the purposes of such detailed performances are not evident. The task is, then, an extremely useful unit of description, which can be rather readily identified for any job, old or new.

It seems to me that the problem of describing educational objectives is a very similar one. Again we are up against the problem of how detailed to make a description. If the statement is too broad, like "writes English compositions," we are dissatisfied because we recognize a great lack of information. On the other hand, if a statement is too detailed, like "identifies the infinitive forms of irregular French verbs," we are unlikely to see its purpose; we are inclined to say, "What does anyone want to do *that* for?" What is needed, apparently, is a level of description that is comparable to the *task*. In other words, it must be the *smallest unit of performance which can be identified as having a distinct and independent purpose.* "Punctuating sentences" is a performance that has a distinct purpose. "Differentiating the varieties of 'stop' marks" does not have a clear purpose; it is therefore too detailed as a statement of an educational objective.

Here I must refer again to Tyler's recent statement regarding this problem of level of specificity of definitions of objectives (Tyler, 1964). The most useful degree of specificity, he says, is at the level of generality of behavior that one is seeking to help the student acquire. One of the main indications of this is that the description identify a performance which can be valued in and of itself as being of effective use in the individual's life. This view, I think, corresponds closely to the one I have tried to state in somewhat different terms. Tyler is emphasizing two points about a useful level of description for behavioral objectives: (1) they should express a *purpose* which makes sense within the larger context of the person's life goals; (2) this purpose should be *distinguishable* from others. Tyler's criterion would lead us to seek statements of objectives such as "reads a French newspaper," rather than "reads French"; "solves problems requiring the use of sine, cosine, and tangent," rather than "understands trigonometry"; "makes a quantitative description of dispersion of errors in observations," rather than "knows statistics."

I am inclined to think, therefore, that investigators of educational objectives and investigators of performances in human work have come to independent conclusions which resemble each other to a marked degree and that it is something other than chance which has brought this about. Both lines of investigation lead to the idea that one must seek descriptions in terms of observable human performance and that the most useful degree of specificity is achieved when the performance described is the smallest entity of human activity that has a distinct and independent purpose. In other words, those who have struggled with the problem of describing educational objectives have ended up by specifying human performances at a level which other people, engaged in different studies, have called *tasks*. It should not be surprising that task statements serve both these purposes, since they have to meet a common requirement of being maximally communicative to everyone, not just to the technical specialist.

ANALYSIS OF HUMAN PERFORMANCES

If educational objectives are stated as tasks, and the level of greater generality is avoided, we can expect communication about education, its goals and its procedures, to be most effective. There will be little remaining obscurity about what is to be learned. And as I have previously stated, this can probably have salutary effects on the process of education itself insofar as clarity of purpose is conveyed to both teacher and student. In addition, the improvement in communication to educational administrators within school systems, and to parents and the larger public as well, is another highly desirable outcome to be expected.

For the person who wishes to study the process of education, to analyze it, to perform research upon it for the purpose of understanding and improving it, statements of educational objectives as human performances are an absolutely essential starting point. For one thing, they help to keep in sharp focus the fact that *learning of the individual student* is the central purpose of education, and that all other questions, such as those of homogeneous groupings, guidance services, class scheduling, library facilities, and the other practical questions of school administration, are simply contributors to that central purpose. In addition, objective statements of performance provide the empirically observable foundations to which all speculations, hypotheses, and innovative hunches about educational improvement must be referred. The number of differences of opinion about educational procedures which can be rather simply resolved if both parties agree to base their arguments on performance objectives is surprising, even startling.

It is also true that for the individual who wants to do certain kinds of research in education, statements of performance objectives are *merely* a starting point. Having achieved good objective statements of human performance, one must go farther than this. There must be, for purposes of investigation, an *analysis* of these objectives. The entities with which one must deal in educational research are even finer, more detailed, performances. A number of problems illustrate this need for further analysis:

1. In *designing a curriculum*, it becomes very evident that certain objectives depend on other ones. In other words, there are such things as subordinate objectives; there are performances which are prerequisite to other perform-

ances. If one states an objective as "reading prose material composed of the 1000 most frequent English words," for example, it is immediately evident that the child must learn some other things first. He cannot simply plunge into a book written in basic English before he has mastered other performances such as recognizing words, sounding phonemes, and recognizing printed letters. Similarly, a student of physics cannot meet the objective of "computing the resultants of forces" unless he has previously acquired the performance of "determining the lengths of sides of triangles using trigonometric relationships." Practically all educational objectives have prerequisites, and such an analysis of objectives must be done if an effective sequence of instruction is to be designed. Some of my own work with colleagues in the University of Maryland Mathematics Project (Gagné, 1963; Gagné & Bassler, 1963; Gagné, Mayor, Garstens, & Paradise, 1962) demonstrates this point with reference to some topics of junior-high mathematics. When one conducts such an analysis, he *begins* with a task, a statement of an objective having a distinct purpose. But the statements of performances which result from the analysis are considerably more detailed than this. Their purposes can usually not be understood by themselves, but only as prerequisites to the more generally stated objective with which the analysis was begun.

2. Closely related to this reason for breaking down educational objectives into finer units is the need for *assessing student progress*. If it is true that there are really prerequisites in continuous learning (and not just the ones suspected of being phony that often appear in college catalogs), then the need to test whether a student has met these prerequisites before going on should be an important educational procedure. It appears doubtful if this function of assessing student performance on prerequisites is being done very carefully and systematically in most schools today. To do it properly, it is necessary not only to state objectives but also to analyze them. Tests which are based on such detailed performance statements

can be truly diagnostic of the progress of students within the framework of a curriculum.

3. One of the most important reasons for analyzing objectives is to determine some important facts about the *conditions for learning* them. Statements of objectives do not in themselves provide all the information that is needed to make it clear how they need to be taught, even though they do perform the very important function of communicating in unambiguous terms what the accomplishments that follow learning are to be. To clarify what is needed for learning, the original objective must be broken down into more specific statements of performance. Suppose, for example, one has decided upon the objective of "constructing utterances in German which are understandable to a German-speaking person." The statement itself gives few clues to how this performance is going to be learned. Does one learn to do this by acquiring German words and German grammar? Should a learner learn to say the words first, then acquire their meanings, and finally learn the structural features of the language? How much can he learn by listening to a recorded German speaker? All of these questions are of course familiar to teachers of foreign languages. They are faced and solved in a variety of ways in American schools. But they obviously demand an analysis of the objective for their answer, if one is concerned with the proper conditions for efficient learning.

THE CONSEQUENCES OF ANALYZING OBJECTIVES

Here, then, are three important reasons for making a more detailed analysis of educational objectives stated in terms of human performance. They are, as I have said, primarily important to the individual who wishes to understand the educational process by the use of analytic and experimental methods. They do not contribute to an immediate purpose of communicating facts or ideas about education, but to a more long-term purpose of explaining how the process of education works.

REDUCTION OF COMPLEXITY

If one persists in analyzing educational objectives into finer units, what are the consequences? Doesn't one end up with large masses of detail that become difficult to grasp and to do anything with? In some sense, this is true. If one is determined to analyze human performances, he must be prepared to deal with great numbers of individual facts. The fundamental reason for this, of course, is that human performance *is* complex; the variety of unitary actions that can be performed by human beings, in a variety of settings, is tremendous. Dealing with the "fine grain" of human performance is perhaps something for which a modern computer could be used, although I am not aware that that particular usage has been previously suggested.

However, in another sense, the analysis of objective statements of human tasks (or objectives) does *not* have the consequence of making things more complicated, varied, and difficult to deal with. Instead, a marvelous possibility becomes evident: all of this tremendous variety of human performance begins to fit together into categories, which can then be dealt with and thought about as *classes of events,* rather than as separate and distinct ones. The advantages of thinking about performance events as classes are the same as those which occur in other scientific disciplines. The biologist is able to study the properties of skin and muscle and bone and blood in some common ways because they are composed of a class of entities called *cells;* the chemist is able to deal with a great variety of acids, bases, and salts in solution because they form a class of *electrolytes.* In quite a similar way, it is possible to identify classes of human performance and to use them as tools in thinking about the previously mentioned problems of curriculum design, of student assessment, and of the conditions for efficient learning.

It is at this point that those who are concerned with analysis of tasks, or objectives, must, I think, make contact with psychology. For here is the science which attempts to formulate the fundamental principles of behavior that make a set of classes possible. Those who began with task statements for jobs and human work arrived at this conclusion as they continued their analysis of human performances (Gagné, 1962; Miller, 1962a;

18   Learning and the Educational Process

Miller, 1962b). There are many reasons to think that the analysis of educational objectives will similarly draw upon the principles of psychology to derive useful classes of performance which can serve the purposes already mentioned.

The basic principle which appears to be of use in deriving classes of human performance may be called the *principle of stimulus processing*. This is the principle that the stimulus inputs to the human organism undergo a limited number of kinds of transformations into outputs, or human performances. If one examines human behavior in an analytic fashion, as psychologists have been doing for many years, it becomes evident that there are several different kinds of these stimulus-performance transformations. Without necessarily knowing their exact sites or mechanisms, it is nevertheless possible to distinguish them from each other. These different kinds of transformations of stimuli into human action form a class of events which may be collectively called varieties of stimulus processing; in other words, varieties of behavior.

CATEGORIES OF BEHAVIOR

If one employs the principle of stimulus processing to differentiate classes of human behavior, he arrives at not a great many classes—more than one or two, but probably fewer than twelve. In other words, rather than there being a tremendous variety of entities to be considered, there are only relatively few classes of behavior, and these can serve many purposes of reasoning about the variables which produce human performance. I have described these more extensively elsewhere (Gagné, 1964a, Gagné, 1964b), but it will be possible to state them briefly here, using as examples the kinds of performances familiar to the education scene. Six classes of behavior which are of some importance to education are these, beginning with the simplest:

  1. A simple *connection*. The young child learns to say "mama" when his mother gives the stimulus "mama." Not different in principle is the American adult learning to pronounce the German word *ich* in response to some appropriate stimulus.

2. A *chain* or *sequence*. The child is able to draw a square. Or he may recite verbatim and in sequence the names of the letters in the alphabet or the names of the numerals from one to ten. Verbal associations, such as those involved in translating a foreign word, may be an important subcategory.

3. *Identification*. The student may learn to distinguish among stimuli of different physical appearance. A young child having a set of leaves on his desk may learn to distinguish them by means of the verbal labels "elm," "maple," "oak," "poplar," and so forth. A student of astronomy learns to identify certain stars and certain constellations. He distinguishes them, one from the other, by giving them different names, or perhaps by pointing to them.

4. A *concept*. A great many performances established by school learning involve the use of concepts, which are *classes* of objects or events. Early instruction in mathematics, for example, consists in teaching such concepts as the numbers one, two, three, and four, the concept of set and member of set, the concepts of joining and separation, and so on. A student of biology learns to use the concept "cell"; a student of chemistry the concept "gas"; a student of physics the concept "force."

5. A *principle*. A principle is a chain of concepts; in its simplest form, if A, then B. Many such principles are typically called "facts," such as "Water boils at 212° F," or "Birds fly south in the winter," or "The atomic weight of oxygen is 16." Obviously, a great many subordinate performances of school learning belong to this class.

6. A *higher-order principle, or general principle*. A higher-order principle results from the combination of two or more simpler ones. These are the generalizations that enable the student to think about an ever broadening set of new problems. They may, and hopefully do, result from problem-solving behavior on the part of the student. As performances, they make possible the solving of novel problems by application of the principle to new situations. A student may be able, for example, to apply New-

ton's second law to a specific problem involving an automobile rolling downhill. Or a student of English may be able to select some metaphoric language to express an idea in a composition.

Each of these classes of performance may readily be identified in the things that a student is able to do after he has learned something. They represent, in a sense, the unitary steps in accomplishment that he takes on the road to the attainment of each more generally stated educational objective.

THE IMPLICATIONS OF BEHAVIOR CATEGORIES

Each of these stimulus-processing categories, or "behavior categories," carries some definite implications for certain important procedures of education.

First, the establishment of each of these categories of performance requires a different set of conditions for learning, and thus makes a difference in the method of instruction used to bring it about. It is not possible for me to discuss these differences in learning conditions extensively here, as I have done elsewhere (Gagné, 1965). But surely it is quite evident that the conditions one has to arrange in order to bring about the correct pronunciation of an umlauted "u" are quite different from the conditions one must set up when the learner is to be engaged in learning to use the proper order of words in a German sentence. Similarly, it is evident that learning to identify a triangle requires considerably different conditions for learning than does learning to formulate a definition of a triangle ("three line segments joining three points which are not on the same straight line"). One of the most important implications resulting from the *analysis* of performance objectives, then, is that the researcher, and the designer of instructional methods, are able to deal with classes of behavior which are quite independent of specific content, but which demand a common set of procedures for the arrangement of conditions of instruction.

Second, each of these performance classes implies something different with respect to the sequencing of instruction within a topic to be learned. For example, a principle cannot be learned unless the concepts which make it up have previously been mastered. The child who is expected to learn to perform according to the principle "The sum of three and five is eight" must have previously acquired the concepts "sum," "three," "five," and "eight." Learning a principle, in other words, requires some prerequisite performances. The same is true for the other behavior categories. Establishing the proper sequences within the topics of a course of study is a matter of considerable importance to the effectiveness of education.

Third, the classes of performance which are analyzed out of educational objectives suggest the possibility of "diagnostic" assessments of student progress along the way to a more comprehensive goal. This idea appears to be related to the differentiation of types of tests described in *Taxonomy of Educational Objectives*, by Bloom and his colleagues (1956). These investigators distinguished the testing categories of knowledge, comprehension, application, analysis, synthesis, and evaluation and suggested that these may be arranged in a hierarchical order. Although there is not a one-to-one correspondence of these categories with those I have outlined, there are definable relationships between them, and the similarity of the basic idea is apparent. Classes of performance which represent different kinds of behavior—different kinds of stimulus processing—must be differentially tested. Each requires a different kind of test item to reflect what is being measured. Each in turn has a different meaning for student progress, depending upon the sequence of instruction that is being followed to reach the educational objective.

A SUMMARY VIEW OF EDUCATIONAL OBJECTIVES

Let me now summarize some of the major points of what I have tried to say.

For those goals of education which ultimately pertain to productive occupational goals, and probably for others as well, clear statements of educational objectives can have some very important and desirable effects. Primary among these is unambiguous communication among educators, students, parents, and the public. Clear statements require definitions which refer to human performances, since the fundamental events which are the focus of interest are those of learning, and learning means a change in human performance. The advantages of clear communication to educational change and improvement are many. They include not only an increase in general understanding and support for innovations, but also more direct and immediate uses in the educational process itself in affecting the techniques of teachers and the goals and motivations of students.

Those who question the desirability of defining objectives in performance terms seem to have advanced no valid arguments to support such a position. There is no conflict between statements phrased in terms of performance and the use of more abstract nouns like "comprehension," "understanding," or "appreciation." It is simply a matter of answering the further question: "How shall I be able to tell when 'understanding' has occurred?" There is also no conflict with the idea that some of the outcomes of education must surely be projected into the future, or that some may be unanticipated. Again there is a further question to be answered, which is something like this: "What are the changes in present performance without which such long-term or unexpected outcomes could not occur?" Each of these questions leads one back to a dependence on statements about human performance as expressions of educational objectives.

Clear statements of objectives need to represent some particular level of specificity. I have suggested that this level is what researchers in another related field have called the "task" level, defined as the smallest unit of performance having a distinct and independent purpose. For greatest communicability, educational objectives need to have some evident relation to useful life activities.

For many purposes of educational research, such performance statements provide an essential starting point, but only a starting point. Further analysis is necessary into finer and more detailed entities of performance. Order can be brought into this mass of detail with the use of the principle of stimulus processing, by means of which one is enabled to classify the great variety of performances in which human beings engage. The employment of such a classification of behavior makes possible the drawing of systematic implications for three important aspects of the educational process: the definition of conditions for effective learning, the design of proper sequences of instruction, and the assessment of student progress. All of these rest upon the basic relationship between educational objectives and human performance.

REFERENCES

Bloom, B. S., (Ed.), Engelhart, M. D., Furst, E. J., Hill, W. H., & Krathwohl, D. R. *Taxonomy of educational objectives:* Book 1. *Cognitive domain.* New York: Longmans, Green, 1956.

Gagné, R. M. *The conditions of learning.* New York: Holt, Rinehart & Winston, 1965.

Gagné, R. M. Human functions in systems. In R. M. Gagné (Ed.). *Psychological principles in system development.* New York: Holt. Rinehart & Winston, 1962.

Gagné, R. M. Learning and proficiency in mathematics. *Math. Teacher,* 1963, **56**, 620–626.

Gagné, R. M. Problem solving. In A. W. Melton (Ed.), *Categories of human learning.* New York: Academic Press, 1964. (a)

Gagné, R. M. The implications of instructional objectives for learning. In C. M. Lindvall (Ed.), *Defining educational objectives.* Pittsburgh: Univer. of Pittsburgh Press, 1964. (b)

Gagné, R. M., & Bassler, O. C. A study of retention of some topics of elementary non-metric geometry. *J. educ. Psychol.,* 1963, **54**, 123–131.

Gagné, R. M., Mayor, J. R., Garstens, H. L., & Paradise, N. E. Factors in acquiring knowledge of a mathematical task. *Psychol. Monogr.,* 1962, **76** (Whole No. 526).

Gardner, J. W. National goals in education. In *Goals for Americans.* The Report of the President's Commission on National Goals. Englewood Cliffs, N.J.: Prentice-Hall, 1960.

Mager, R. F. *Preparing objectives for programmed instruction.* San Francisco: Fearon, 1962.

Mager, R. F., & McCann, J. *Learner-controlled instruction.* Palo Alto, Calif.: Varian Associates, 1961.

Miller, R. B. Analysis and specification of behavior for training. In R. Glaser (Ed.), *Training research and education.* Pittsburgh: Univer. of Pittsburgh Press, 1962. (a)

Miller, R. B. Task description and analysis. In R. M. Gagné (Ed.), *Psychological principles in system development.* New York: Holt, Rinehart & Winston, 1962. (b)

National Education Association, Project on Instruction. *Schools for the sixties.* New York: McGraw-Hill, 1964.

Rockefeller Brothers Fund. *The pursuit of excellence: Education and the future of America.* Panel Report V of the Special Studies Project. Garden City, N.Y.: Doubleday, 1958.

Tyler, R. W. Achievement testing and curriculum construction. In E. G. Williamson (Ed.), *Trends in student personnel work.* Minneapolis: Univer. of Minnesota Press, 1949.

Tyler, R. W. The functions of measurement in improving instruction. In E. F. Lindquist (Ed.), *Educational measurement. Washington,* D.C.: American Council on Education, 1950.

Tyler, R. W. Some persistent questions on the defining of objectives. In C. M. Lindvall (Ed.), *Defining educational objectives.* Pittsburgh: Univer. of Pittsburgh Press, 1964.

Chapter 2

THE MAINSPRINGS OF ACHIEVEMENT-ORIENTED ACTIVITY

JOHN W. ATKINSON, *University of Michigan*

The psychology of motivation must provide a useful way of thinking about the several factors that combine to produce interest in the various activities which constitute the curriculum in education. We have passed the day when there is any consensus that motivation, conceived merely as drive, must be present and reduced for learning to occur. But no one disputes that a student must be sufficiently motivated to attend school, at least, if he is to get an education, and sufficiently interested in what is going on in the classroom to pay attention once in a while if educational curricula are to have any of their intended effects on him.

The sources of interest in schoolwork and in those activities outside of classrooms which educational institutions try to encourage may vary substantially from one person to the next. For one, attention to the task at hand may be a matter of compliance with the wishes of an authority; for another, a way of gaining the warm approval of nurturant teachers and parents; for another,

Results of previously unpublished studies reported in this chapter were obtained during the course of recent research on "Determinants of Human Choice" (GS-9) sponsored by a grant from the National Science Foundation.

the expression of curiosity; for another, an avenue for expressing an interest in meeting the challenge of intellectual tasks and performing as well or better than others; for another, the first practical step toward some long-term goal; for another, the competitive challenge may produce debilitating anxiety. The combination of all of these constitutes what we habitually refer to as motivation for learning in school. It is still an open empirical question whether one kind of interest in schoolwork enhances learning more than another and whether learning is influenced in any substantial way by the strength or degree of interest. These questions, as important as they are, have yet to be systematically explored.

Why have not these and other related questions pertaining to motivation in education already been answered definitively? They have not been answered because one or another of the essential ingredients for a *coordinated* attack upon this domain of ignorance has been lacking. First, there must be some methods of study which promise results commensurate with the time and effort involved in research. Second, there must be a conceptual scheme or theory which provides some fruitful initial guidelines for empirical investigation. Finally, and perhaps most important, there must be a critical mass of individuals with a common enthusiasm for the problem, a language they share for discussion of it, some common research tools and skills, and a strong dedication to that intentionally cooperative enterprise of discovery and communication we call science. All three are required for the sparks to fly in any domain of empirical inquiry.

Today there could be an integrated rather than a sporadic attack on many interrelated problems of motivation in education. Some useful techniques of study are available to replace the conventional wisdom, and so, also, are the enthusiastic and competent researchers. Perhaps the attack has already begun. Most needed to give it impetus and direction are a common understanding of the problem of motivation and a conceptual scheme which will provide a more enlightening initial guide than traditional psychological concepts of motivation generated in the study of lower animals. Those who are primarily concerned with the learning process frequently assume that the *kind* of motivation sustaining problem solving and practice is irrelevant as long as there is *some* motivation. I believe that this assumption is one of those shared oversimplifications derived from our common scientific heritage—the inadequate and nonfertile theory of drive.

The progress made in several programs of experimental study of human motivation since 1950 deserves the special attention of researchers in the field of education. One such program is Berlyne's work on curiosity (see Chapter 3). The others are the work on effects of anxiety on performance, which originated at Iowa (Spence, 1958; Taylor, 1956) and at Yale (Sarason et al., 1960), and the analysis of achievement motivation centered at Michigan and Harvard (Atkinson, 1958; Atkinson, 1964; Atkinson & Feather, 1965; McClelland et al., 1953; McClelland, 1961). These programs of research on anxiety and achievement motivation represent the beginning of an integration of what Cronbach (1957) has called "the two disciplines of scientific psychology"—the study of individual differences and the study of basic process. The two programs have produced fruitful tools for research—the self-report tests of anxiety and the method for content analysis of imaginative behavior to assess the strength of achievement motive and other important social motives. And each has produced a fund of experimental findings describing how these components of motivation affect human learning and performance.

My immediate aim is to draw attention to a conceptual scheme which has evolved in the fifteen-year program of research on achievement motivation, particularly as it applies to analysis of the problems of aspiration and persistence in problem-solving behavior. These are central aspects of the problem of motivation in education. I hope to encourage some of you to begin to think a certain way about these issues—not because I believe this theoretical scheme or model represents the truth in any final sense, but because I believe it provides a very adequate memory aid and initial guide. It summarizes most, if not all, of what we know about the dynamics of achievement-oriented behavior, and it suggests new and nonobvious hypotheses about motivation which constitute potential tests of the scheme itself. Since the theory is testable—that is, it states what should happen under certain conditions that can be arranged in experiments—we shall soon discover its shortcomings and be led on to some new and more useful concepts. I want to encourage your interest in the scheme, then, because I think you will find it a useful tool to use as an opening wedge in the conceptual analysis and empirical study of some of the stubborn motivational problems in education.

My plan is to review the basic concepts of the theory of achievement motivation, then to survey some of the evidence obtained in experimental and field studies which have employed the thematic apperceptive method for assessment of n Achievement[1] and the Test Anxiety Scale developed by Mandler and Sarason. The conceptual scheme represents an effort to integrate the results of the two programs of research. Later, I will turn the discussion more directly to questions of motivation in education, some of which have already been explored and others suggested by the scheme.

A THEORY OF ACHIEVEMENT MOTIVATION

The contemporary guide for research on achievement motivation bears a striking resemblance to the resultant valence theory of level of aspiration advanced about twenty years ago in the writings of Lewin, Escalona, and Festinger (see Lewin, et al., 1944). It extends, elaborates, and refines their earlier ideas and, at the same time, brings into the discussion systematically the basic concept of psychogenic need or motive advanced in the writings of Murray (1938) and McClelland (1951) as a useful one for description of how individuals differ in disposition to strive for certain general goals. The ideas of the theory are based primarily on the results of experiments in which individuals are classified as relatively High and Low in n Achievement in terms of the frequency of imaginative responses suggesting their concern over performing well in relation to some standard of excellence. These responses appear in stories they have told or written in response to pictures or verbal cues in a standard thematic apperceptive test situation. The scheme represents a specification of

---

[1] n Achievement is an abbreviation for the personality disposition termed "need for achievement."

the nature of the interaction between personality and environmental determinants of behavior which Lewin proposed in the programmatic equation, $B = f(P, E)$.

THE TENDENCY TO ACHIEVE SUCCESS

First, it is assumed that the strength of the tendency to achieve success (T_s), which is expressed in the interest of an individual in some task and his performance, is a multiplicative function of three variables: motive to achieve success (M_s), conceived as a relatively general and relatively stable disposition of personality; and two other variables which represent the effect of the immediate environment—the strength of expectancy (or subjective probability) that performance of a task will be followed by success (P_s), and the relative attractiveness of success at that particular activity, which we call the incentive value of success (I_s). In other words, $T_s = M_s \times P_s \times I_s$.

The concept of motive here represents individual differences in liking for success in general. The concept of expectancy, which refers to degree of belief that some act will be followed by some consequence, and the concept of incentive value of the expected consequence or goal are the basic building blocks in the kind of theory advanced earlier by Tolman (1955) and Lewin (1938) and by contemporary workers like Rotter (1954) and others in the field of decision-making (see Edwards, 1954).

According to this kind of Expectancy × Value Theory, one can influence motivation by manipulating cues which define an individual's expectations concerning the consequences of his actions and/or the incentive value of the consequences (or goals) produced by action. Following the early proposal of Lewin, Escalona, and Festinger, it is assumed that the incentive value or attractiveness of success is greater the more difficult the task. This idea is now stated as a relationship between the incentive value of success (I_s) and the strength of expectancy or subjective probability of success (P_s): viz., $I_s = 1 - P_s$. In light of evidence obtained when the reported probability of success at a task is related to some independent estimate of the incentive value of success, it would appear that the notion $I_s = 1 - P_s$ has more the status of a general description of con-

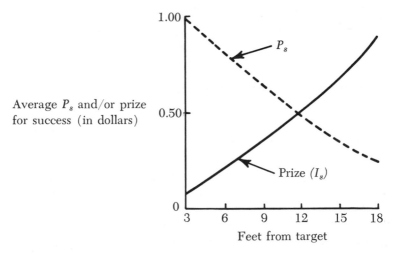

FIGURE 1. Estimated probability of success (P_s) and prize recommended for success (I_s) by 20 college students in ring-toss game (after Litwin, 1958, with the permission of the author).

ditions which exist, for whatever reason, in the domain of achievement-oriented activity than the status of a theoretical assumption. Consider, for example, what happens in a ring-toss game when each subject in one group is asked to stand at various distances from the peg and indicate how many times out of ten he thinks he can hit the target from that distance and each subject of another group is asked to recommend a monetary prize for hitting the target from various distances. Figure 1 shows that the average estimate of P_s decreases with distance, and the average monetary prize proposed, which we assume to be symbolic of an individual's estimate of his reaction to success at that distance, increases with distance. The result is similar when immediately after success at tasks which differ in difficulty, subjects are asked to rate the degree of their pleasure in success (Brown, 1963).

The major theoretical implications of these two assertions, $T_s = M_s \times P_s \times I_s$ and $I_s = 1 - P_s$, are shown in Figure 2. Curves representing the strength of the tendency to achieve success (T_s), as a function of expectancy of success (P_s), are shown for two hypothetical individuals who differ in strength of achievement motive (M_S). The tendency to achieve is more strongly aroused by tasks having intermediate probability of success than either very easy or very difficult tasks. When difficulty is held constant for a group of individuals, tendency to achieve will be more strongly aroused when the motive is strong than when it is weak. And, finally, the behavioral differences attributable to differences in strength of tendency to achieve in individuals who differ in strength of achievement motive are most pronounced when the task is one of intermediate difficulty. The differences in strength of the tendency to achieve success at very easy and very difficult tasks as a function of strength of motive are not, as you can see in Figure 2, very substantial.

Figure 2 summarizes the results of a number of studies which show stronger preference for intermediate risk or moderate difficulty among persons scoring high in n Achievement and generally high level of performance of these persons in achievement-oriented situations. Since many of the experiments undertaken before we arrived at this theoretical scheme did not specify the degree of difficulty of the task, it is little wonder that they do not always show large differences between the performance levels of high and low n Achievement groups. We should

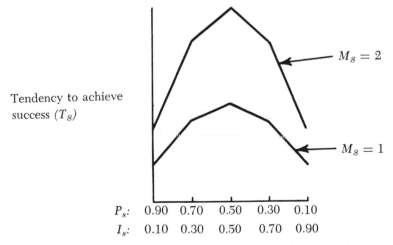

FIGURE 2. Theoretical implications of assuming that $T_S = M_S \times P_s \times I_s$ and that $I_s = 1 - P_s$.

expect little correlation between the n Achievement scores of individuals and their performance level when the task is easy or very difficult, given our present only moderately reliable tool for assessment of the personality variable.

It is my belief that the current theory of achievement motivation is better than the method of assessment and that the time is ripe for a renewed attack on the problem of developing better techniques for assessing differences in strength of achievement motive. The pendulum swings in scientific work. The thematic apperceptive method led us to this conceptual scheme and still is the most useful and valid technique for assessment of differences in achievement motive and other social motives. But now, with some theory to guide our effort, we can turn again to the problem of developing more reliable diagnostic tools, hopeful of better results than those of earlier trial-and-check efforts to do the same thing (see McClelland, 1958a). The virtue of a theory is that it specifies what particular behavioral indicators we might use, and under what conditions, to assess relatively stable differences in the theoretical term M_S.

THE TENDENCY TO AVOID FAILURE

For some years, our studies focused only on the behavioral consequences of differences in achievement motive until the unsolved problems and accumulated evidence in them, as well as in the independent programs of work employing the Manifest Anxiety Scale and the Test Anxiety Questionnaire, made it patently clear to us that whenever performance is evaluated in relation to some standard of excellence, what constitutes the challenge to achieve for one individual poses the threat of failure for another. The tendency to avoid failure associated with anxiety is as fundamentally important a factor in achievement-oriented action as the tendency to achieve success. We treat this tendency, which is conceived as an inhibitory tendency that functions to oppose and dampen the tendency to undertake achievement-oriented activities, as the source of the conscious experience of anxiety. The tendency to avoid failure is also considered a multiplicative function of a motive, an expectancy, and an incentive. We speak of the motive to avoid failure (M_{AF})

and refer to a disposition which is separate and distinct from the achievement motive. It might be thought of as a capacity for reacting with humiliation and shame when one fails. This is considered the source of individual differences in the anticipatory emotional reaction called anxiety or fear of failure. The tendency to avoid failure (T_{AF}) is aroused and expressed when there is an expectancy that some act will lead to failure (P_f), and it is also influenced by the incentive value of failure at that particular activity (I_f). That is, $T_{AF} = M_{AF} \times P_f \times I_f$. The incentive value of failure is negative, signifying that it functions like shock for a rat. It is a noxious event to be avoided. It is assumed that the negative incentive value of failure, i.e., the repulsiveness of failure, is greater the easier the task. No one feels very bad when he fails at a very difficult task, but to fail when a task appears easy is a source of great embarrassment. This idea is summarized in the assertion, $I_f = -P_s$. The previously unpublished evidence we have obtained by asking subjects to estimate expectancy of success and to recommend a suitable monetary penalty for failure at tasks which differ in difficulty (Figure 3) suggests that here again we are dealing with a description of

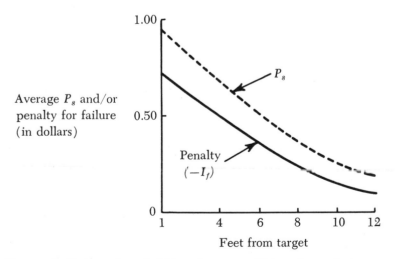

FIGURE 3. Estimated probability of success (P_s) and penalty recommended for failure $(-I_f)$ by 37 college students in a target practice game.

the conditions that exist in achievement-oriented activities and not a theoretical assumption.

It should be apparent that the implications of these two assertions about the tendency to avoid failure, $T_{AF} = M_{AF} \times P_f \times I_f$ and $I_f = -P_s$, are described in curves looking very much like those already presented in Figure 2 except that the behavioral implications are just the opposite. That is, if you will look again at Figure 2 but imagine that the two curves are labeled "tendency to avoid failure when M_{AF} equals 1 and 2," we can say the following things. The tendency to avoid failure, which produces inhibition and decrement in performance, is most strongly aroused when the probability of success (and so, therefore, also of failure) is intermediate. (We assume that the sum of the subjective probabilities of success and failure is approximately equal to 1.00.) The tendency to avoid failure is stronger generally the stronger the motive to avoid failure, which in our experiments is assessed by means of the Mandler-Sarason Test Anxiety Questionnaire. And finally, as with the achievement motive, we expect the effect of differences in disposition to anxiety to be more apparent in tasks of intermediate difficulty than in very easy or very difficult tasks. This follows from the assumption of a multiplicative interaction between the personality disposition and the situational determinants.

THE RESULTANT ACHIEVEMENT-ORIENTED TENDENCY

We study achievement-oriented behavior today assuming that all individuals have acquired a motive to achieve (M_S) and a motive to avoid failure (M_{AF}). That is to say, all persons have some capacity for interest in achievement and some capacity for anxiety about failure. Both are expressed in any situation when it is apparent to the individual that his performance will be evaluated in reference to some standard. One of these motives produces a tendency to undertake the activity; the other produces a tendency to avoid undertaking the activity. There is what we traditionally call an approach-avoidance conflict. It is suggested by the conceptual scheme that we might better begin to think of this as a conflict between an *excitatory* tendency and an *inhibitory* tendency. It is assumed that the two opposed tendencies combine additively and yield a resultant achievement-oriented tendency which is either approach (excitatory) or avoidant (inhibitory) in character and of a certain strength depending upon the relative strength of motive to achieve success and motive to avoid failure in the individual. That is, the resultant tendency equals $T_S - T_{AF}$. Figure 4 shows the resultant tendency when the achievement motive is dominant within the individual. Figure 5 shows the resultant tendency when the motive to avoid failure is dominant. Such a person should inhibit all achievement-oriented activity. Given a choice between alternatives which differ in difficulty, he should choose none of them unless there are other extrinsic positive incentives to undertake these activities which overcome his resistance.

THE ROLE OF EXTRINSIC MOTIVATION

If, for example, there is intrinsic interest or curiosity in a task, or a tendency to seek approval or to comply with an authority—all arbitrarily described as sources of "extrinsic" motiva-

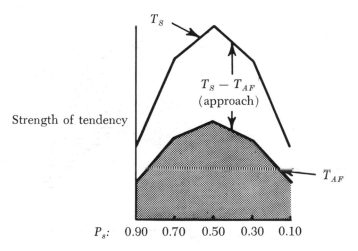

FIGURE 4. Resultant achievement-oriented tendency $(T_S - T_{AF})$ when the motive to achieve is dominant in the individual, i.e., $M_S > M_{AF}$.

tion when we have focused attention on the achievement-oriented process—then the tendency to avoid failure which would otherwise inhibit performance completely may be overcome by a stronger approach (excitatory) tendency. Except in very rare cases, there are always a number of different "extrinsic" components in the positive tendency to undertake activities that are viewed, by an observer, as achievement-oriented activities. In Figure 6 we see the effect of a constant amount of "extrinsic" excitatory tendency added to the resultant achievement-oriented tendency when the latter is negative, i.e., avoidant in character. The *difference* between the curves represents the *final strength of tendency* to undertake activities which differ in probability of success. You will note that the final strength of tendency is *weakest* in the intermediate range of difficulty. Thus the anxiety-prone person, when given a choice among activities which differ in difficulty, should prefer to avoid all of them, but should, if constrained, undertake either an easy task or a very difficult one because the final strength of his multidetermined tendency is then stronger than at the point of maximum challenge and threat where the subjective probability of success is near .50.

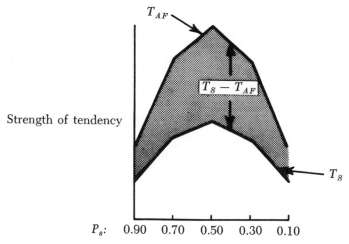

P_s: 0.90   0.70   0.50   0.30   0.10

FIGURE 5. Resultant achievement-oriented tendency ($T_S - T_{AF}$) when the motive to avoid failure is dominant in the individual, i.e., $M_{AF} > M_S$.

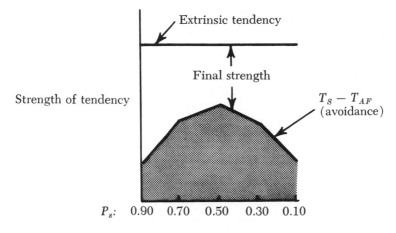

FIGURE 6. Effect of constant extrinsic tendency to undertake an activity when the motive to avoid failure is dominant in the individual, i.e., $M_{AF} > M_S$.

IMPLICATIONS CONCERNING ANXIETY

A basic idea in this analysis is that a person who is dominated by a strong inhibitory tendency, the tendency that is expressed in anxiety when he is constrained to undertake achievement-oriented activities, may sometimes *appear* to have a very high level of aspiration. He may undertake what appears to the observer a very difficult task. But we conceive this as a defensive reaction, a mere going through the motions of achievement activities. He does it at all only because of other non-achievement-related sources of motivation. He is engaging in a compromise between the tendency to avoid failure and the sum total of his extrinsic motivation. If not constrained by extrinsic incentives, he would not undertake any activity when his performance might be evaluated. His tendency to avoid failure, by itself, does not tell us what he *will do* but what he *will not do*. His anxiety does not instigate avoidance behavior. His avoidant activity would take the form of complete inhibition of achievement-oriented activity were there not other sources of positive motivation which overcome his inhibition. The price this fellow pays for achievement-oriented action is the experience of anxiety, which I assume to be directly proportionate to the strength of the resistance, the inhibitory tendency, that is overcome.

These are some implications of the scheme concerning anxiety and avoidance. They represent a departure from the widely accepted view that anxiety is a source of excitation of responses and anxiety-reduction constitutes reinforcement. An Expectancy $\times$ Value formulation of the determinants of action suggests that "anxiety" is the consequence of inhibition overcome, a symptom that a negative outcome is expected for the action being performed. When the individual performs an act with no anticipation of a negative consequence, there should be no anxiety. Thus we have a rationale for using a self-report test concerning anxiety in achievement situations to assess the strength of the motive to avoid failure. We assume that the amount of anxiety experienced by a person in a competitive situation is proportionate to the strength of his tendency to avoid failure. This inhibitory tendency must have been overcome by stronger positive tendencies, including the tendency to achieve, or else the individual would never have been present in the kind of achievement test situation about which he is later questioned on the Test Anxiety Questionnaire. When he reports how much anxiety he has experienced in test situations, he is telling us about the strength of his resistance to achievement-oriented action. From this we infer the strength of his motive to avoid failure. We cannot assess this motive very well through content analysis of the emitted behaviors which constitute a TAT story for the very reason that on a so-called projective device the subject is not constrained to undertake those preferably avoided activities in thought or to report them verbally. Perhaps if we explicitly instructed subjects always to tell achievement-related stories we could produce imaginative content *in all subjects* expressing the strength of the motive to avoid failure.

EVIDENCE CONCERNING ASPIRATION AND PERFORMANCE

Before discussing the theory in reference to changes in motivation produced by success and failure, let us consider some evidence that concretizes the static predictions of the theory.

N ACHIEVEMENT AND PERSISTENCE

Table 1 shows results presented by French and Thomas (1958) relating the level of performance and persistence at a fairly difficult problem-solving task to strength of n Achievement in Air Force personnel. A number of studies have shown that n Achievement and Test Anxiety are uncorrelated in young college men when both tests are administered under neutral conditions. This means that the average strength of motive to avoid failure can probably be assumed equal in the high and low n Achievement groups of this experiment. Given the measured difference in strength of n Achievement, the resultant achievement-oriented tendency should be stronger in the high n Achievement group.

N ACHIEVEMENT, TEST ANXIETY, AND PERFORMANCE

Results of a more recent study employing a measure both of n Achievement and of Test Anxiety are shown in Table 2. The main point of this study was to show the influence of achievement-related motives on all three of the traditional dependent performance variables in one study: direction of behavior (in the measure of level of aspiration or risk preference), performance level (the score obtained on the final exam in a college course), and persistence (time spent working on the final exam of a course before turning it in). The measure of aspiration or risk preference was obtained on an earlier occasion in a simple

TABLE 1

NUMBER OF Ss STRONG (N = 47) AND WEAK (N = 45) IN ACHIEVEMENT MOTIVE WHO SOLVED COMPLEX PROBLEM AND WHO PERSISTED AT TASK UNTIL TIME LIMIT (34 MINUTES) WHETHER OR NOT THEY HAD SOLVED IT (AFTER FRENCH & THOMAS, 1958).[1]

Achievement motive	Performance level		Persistence	
	Solvers	Nonsolvers	Worked to limit	Stopped before limit
Strong	25	22	22	25
Weak	14	31	1	44

[1] With permission of the authors and publisher, American Psychological Association.

TABLE 2

THREE MEASURES OF ACHIEVEMENT-ORIENTED ACTIVITY OBTAINED
ON THE SAME GROUP OF MALE COLLEGE STUDENTS (AFTER ATKINSON
& LITWIN, 1960).[1]

n Achieve-ment	Test Anxiety	N	Prefer intermediate risk	High persistence on exam	High performance on exam
High	Low	13	77%	73%	67%
High	High	10	40	40	60
Low	Low	9	44	43	43
Low	High	13	31	25	25

Note: Ss classified in terms of median score on each variable.
[1] With permission of authors and publisher, American Psychological Association.

ring-toss game like the classic experiment of Hoppe (1930) with children and a more recent one by McClelland (1958b) which showed that even five-year-olds who are high in n Achievement prefer to shoot from an intermediate distance. The same result appears in this study with college men and using other tasks (see Atkinson & Feather, 1965). This study also provides a very clear demonstration that Test Anxiety and n Achievement have diametrically opposite effects on achievement-oriented behavior. Each of the dependent variables is positively related to n Achievement and negatively related to Test Anxiety, and the correlation between the two motives in the study is insignificant. The study also included the measure called n Achievement on the Edwards Personal Preference Scale. Unfortunately, there was no evidence to attest the construct validity of this objective test. Thus it cannot be recommended as an economical substitute for the thematic apperceptive measure. In fact, those who scored high on the PPS variable called n Achievement, which would appear to have face validity given the conventional wisdom about motivation, behaved more like those the theory describes as motivated to avoid failure. The challenging task of developing a valid objective test of n Achievement still lies ahead. I can think of no reason why renewed effort should not be successful now that we have some theory to guide the construction of items and the logic of what is paired with what in a preference test. Some initial steps have been taken by Patricia O'Connor and me to develop an achievement risk preference scale by sampling real-life instances of achievement-oriented activity (e.g., if you were a relief pitcher would you prefer to come into the game when the score is tied or when your team is behind 5 to 2?). Preliminary results (Atkinson & O'Connor, in press) show predicted correlations with TAT n Achievement and Test Anxiety scores, but this new test still lacks the predictive validity of the two other measures combined. We hope others trained in psychometrics will now be encouraged to undertake the task of developing *theoretically sound* objective tests of motivational dispositions. This will require greater interest in the conceptual and experimental analysis of the process of motivation than test makers have exhibited in the past.

n Achievement, Social Class, and Grades

Table 3 shows results obtained by Rosen (1956) in a study of scholastic performance of high-school boys differing in n Achievement and coming from different social class backgrounds. Other studies of n Achievement and grades with ability controlled have produced similar positive results (Lesser et al., 1963; Morgan, 1952; Riccuiti & Sadacca, 1955). Several, however, have produced little or no evidence of a positive relationship (Krumboltz, 1957). Whether the negative results are to

TABLE 3

Scholastic Achievement of High-School Boys in Relation to Strength of Achievement Motive and Social Class Background (After Rosen, 1956).[1]

	Middle class*		Working class†	
Achievement motive	High	Low	High	Low
Average grades:	(N = 38)	(N = 22)	(N = 16)	(N = 44)
"B" or above	66%	32%	75%	36%
"C" or below	34	68	25	64

* Hollingshead: Index I-II-III.
† IV-V.
[1] With permission of the author and of the publisher, the American Sociological Association.

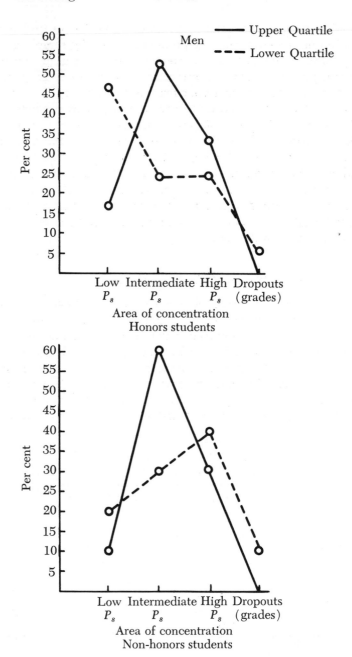

be attributed to some deficiency in methodology in administration or scoring of the TAT, to the overdetermined character of motivation for academic performance which masks or washes out differential effects of n Achievement (see Atkinson, 1958, Ch. 42), or to some other factor is unknown. My hunch is that the quality of motivation in different classrooms and schools differs greatly depending upon the social organization of the school and instructional methods employed and that the relationship between strength of any particular motive and level of achievement will vary markedly accordingly. We too often forget Lewin's guiding hypothesis, $B = f(P, E)$, which emphasizes interaction.

Rosen's results are particularly interesting in that they show that achievement motive is generally stronger in middle-class students, a finding replicated by a number of others, but that working-class boys who are strongly motivated to achieve do as well academically as their counterparts in the middle class. This fact fits well with Crockett's results concerning n Achievement and social mobility of men having working-class background to be considered later.

EDUCATIONAL AND VOCATIONAL CHOICE

Of considerable interest for education is a study by Isaacson (1964) which shows that strength of n Achievement relative to Test Anxiety is related to choice of major field by college students, as shown in Figure 7. From college records showing the grades given students of known scholastic aptitude in the various departments of natural science, the humanities, social science, etc., and from estimates by students which confirmed his inferences, Isaacson ordered different fields of study in terms of difficulty, i.e., perceived probability of success. He ordered students in terms of a combination of normalized n Achievement score minus normalized Test Anxiety score ($M_S - M_{AF}$). His

FIGURE 7. Percentage of male Michigan students high and low in resultant achievement motivation who chose to concentrate in areas considered low, intermediate, and high in P_s (after Isaacson, 1964, with permission of the author and of the publisher, American Psychological Association).

results show the extent to which the choice of major field is analogous to the choice of a task which represents a certain level of difficulty in a typical experiment on risk-taking or aspiration. Men highly motivated to achieve relative to their anxiety about failure decide to major in fields which are perceived as intermediate in difficulty. Their more anxiety-prone peers more frequently select the easy or very difficult fields as defined by local scuttlebutt and grading practices.

The same pattern of results occurs in an earlier study of vocational aspiration of college men by Mahone (1960). Mahone's data showed that occupations which are normally accorded high prestige are perceived as difficult to attain. When college men were asked "How many out of 100 students have the general ability needed to succeed in this occupation?" and were given a randomized list of occupations whose positions on the prestige hierarchy are well known from national survey data, it was found that the average estimate of probability of success correlated — .85 with the prestige rank of the occupation. This means that the critical assumption of the theory of achievement motivation, $I_s = 1 - P_s$, applies to the occupational hierarchy which so often defines what is meant by success in life by sociologists. Mahone obtained two indices of preference for intermediate risk in vocational aspiration for men classified according to strength of n Achievement relative to Test Anxiety. He asked three clinical psychologists to consider each student's ability, college performance, and stated vocational aspiration and to judge whether it represented a realistic aspiration, overaspiration, or underaspiration. The latter two categories are referred to as unrealistic. In addition, he measured the discrepancy between a student's own estimate of how many out of 100 students had enough ability to succeed at his chosen vocational aspiration and the student's own percentile rank on a measure of scholastic aptitude. This index, which corresponds to the goal discrepancy score of level of aspiration research, would be very high positive if the student aspired to an occupation which he thought demanded much more ability than he had, like shooting from 15 feet away from the target in a ring-toss game. It would be very low positive or even negative if the student aspired to an occupation which he thought demanded less ability than he had.

TABLE 4

Realistic (Intermediate) and Unrealistic Vocational Aspiration in College Men (N = 135) According to Strength of Achievement Motive (M_S) and Motive to Avoid Failure (M_{AF}) (After Mahone, 1960).[1]

n Achievement score	Test Anxiety score	N	Clinical judgments Realistic	Clinical judgments Unrealistic	Goal discrepancy Intermediate third	Goal discrepancy Extreme thirds
High	Low	36	75%	25%	50%	50%
High	High	31	48	52	30	70
Low	Low	40	68	32	38	62
Low	High	28	39	61	18	82

[1] With permission of the author and publisher, American Psychological Association.

Mahone divided the distribution of obtained discrepancy scores into thirds and found, as shown in Table 4, that the men in whom n Achievement is dominant more frequently have the realistic, moderately high aspirations; the men dominated by anxiety more frequently are unrealistic. They either set their vocational aspiration very low, or, what appears much more frequently, they appear to set their aspiration much too high for their ability. We have replicated these results of Mahone's in a group of high-school seniors who were above the median in intelligence and part of an accelerated program which emphasized achievement-orientation in about the same way it is emphasized in college (Atkinson & O'Connor, 1963) but not in less intelligent high-school students.

Table 5 shows one result obtained by Veroff et al. (1960) in a national survey employing a thematic apperceptive measure of n Achievement and other social motives. The major importance of this study was its analysis of the method itself when given a severe test in a nationwide survey study. Veroff found, for example, that it is inadequate for the least verbal 17 per cent of the population and that for the remainder of this very heterogeneous sample, the scores obtained from thematic apperceptive stories have to be adjusted to remove the effect of wide variations in length of protocol which correlated .20 with all motive scores obtained from the records. But we learned how to accom-

TABLE 5

STRENGTH OF ACHIEVEMENT MOTIVATION IN RELATION TO EDUCATION
OF RESPONDENT IN A REPRESENTATIVE SAMPLE OF ADULTS IN THE
UNITED STATES GIVEN A THEMATIC APPERCEPTION TEST IN A NA-
TIONAL SURVEY STUDY (AFTER VEROFF, ATKINSON, FELD, & GURIN,
1960).[1]

| Education | Above national median in n Achievement | | | |
| | Men | | Women | |
of respondent	N	%	N	%
Grade school	176	48%	222	44%
High school	271	49	422	49
College	146	62	127	52

[1] With permission of the authors and publisher, American Psychological
Association.

plish these adjustments and are satisfied with the general applicability and utility of the measuring instrument with a very
heterogeneous population. Among the substantive results of interest is one showing that n Achievement is stronger among more
highly educated groups. I think this means, in part at least, that
those who are most highly motivated to achieve are more persistent in the achievement-oriented activity we call getting an
education. They are, in other words, less frequently to be found
among the dropouts.

Crockett's (1962) analysis of social mobility in the same national survey data showed that men who are highly motivated
to achieve more frequently have attained occupations higher in
the status hierarchy than those of their father. Closer analysis
locates the relationship between n Achievement and upward
occupational mobility in men of working-class background, as
shown in Table 6. Why should this be? Crockett showed, in further analysis, that when the occupational status of the father is
upper-middle or high, about 50 per cent of the men have had
some college education, and there is no relationship between
getting a college education and n Achievement because, he
argued, there are so many other sources of inducement for persons of middle-class background to go on to college. It is the
expected thing to do, and the financial means are generally
available. (Crockett's data show, in fact, that n Affiliation, or

TABLE 6

STRENGTH OF ACHIEVEMENT MOTIVE AND OCCUPATIONAL MOBILITY
(AFTER CROCKETT, 1962).[1]

Occupational prestige category of father	Strength of n Achieve-ment	N	Occupational prestige category of respondent in relation to father		
			Below	Same	Above
High	High	20	55%	45%	0%
	Low	11	55	45	0
Upper-middle	High	50	42	32	26
	Low	43	42	35	23
Lower-middle	High	67	16	41	43
	Low	52	28	47	25
Low	High	60	0	33	67
	Low	65	0	54	46

[1] With permission of the authors and publisher, American Psychological Sociological Association.

perhaps what might more appropriately be called the need for social approval, is a more significant factor in upward social mobility in this upper-middle segment of the society.) Among men of working-class background, only about half as many manage to get some college education. And it is in this group, whose social values do not emphasize the central importance of education, and in which the financial means is so often lacking, that strength of need for achievement makes a difference in determining who gets a higher education. Crockett found that 27 per cent of men from lower-middle and low status backgrounds who are high in n Achievement get some college education. Only 17 per cent of the men in these social groups who are low in n Achievement had attended college. There is residual evidence of upward social mobility attributable to differences in strength of achievement motive among those who do not go on to college, particularly among lower status groups where one can move up in the occupational hierarchy without a college education, but it is quite clear that getting a college education, whatever the source of motivation for it, is almost always associated with upward movement for someone who has relatively low status background to begin with (see Crockett, 1964).

Crockett's results, then, show that strength of need for achievement is a factor in that form of persistence we call getting an education when there are not a lot of other inducements to do so and when the financial means are not easily available and that need for achievement is, in addition, a factor in upward mobility among those who do not get a college education.

These various studies of academic performance, choice of major field, vocational aspiration, and occupational mobility have produced results that are analogous to those obtained in studies of aspiration, performance, and persistence in controlled experiments. The same basic concepts—motive to achieve, motive to avoid failure, and expectancy of success—are useful in analysis of both sets of problems. A recent book by David McClelland, *The Achieving Society,* surveys other social studies of the kind I have touched upon and extends their logic to the analysis of motivational problems of whole societies, e.g., the problems of economic development and the rise and fall of whole civilizations.

EXPECTANCY OF SUCCESS AS A MOTIVATIONAL VARIABLE

Let us turn now to the dynamics of achievement-oriented tendencies, the changes that are brought about by success and failure. It is assumed that when an individual undertakes an activity and succeeds, the expectancy of success at that task and similar tasks is increased; that when he fails, the expectancy of success at that task and similar tasks is decreased. Since the incentive value of success is inversely related to expectancy of success, the cognitive change produced by success and failure also produces a change in the incentive values of future success and failure. There is, subsequent to success and failure, a change in the strength of the tendency to engage in the same and similar activities, a motivational change.

EFFECT OF SUCCESS AND FAILURE

Figure 8 shows the nature of this change, using a ring-toss game as our reference experiment, for an individual in whom the achievement motive is dominant. One of the curves shows the strength of the tendency to achieve at each of several tasks initially, as the subject approaches the task with only his past experience in similar situations influencing the strength of his expectancy of success at each level of difficulty. According to the theory, this individual will choose to undertake the task where P_s is .50. If he should do that and succeed, the change in expectancy of success and related change in the incentive value of success should produce the change in motivation shown in the curve labeled "after success."

Figure 9 shows the change in motivation predicted when the same individual fails in the curve labeled "after failure." His expectancy of success at the initially chosen task falls, this change generalizes to other similar activities, and so an initially

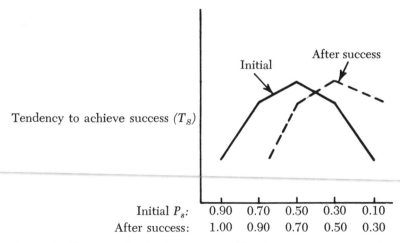

Initial P_s:	0.90	0.70	0.50	0.30	0.10
After success:	1.00	0.90	0.70	0.50	0.30

FIGURE 8. Change in level of aspiration following success when motive to achieve is dominant, i.e., $M_S > M_{AF}$. Success produces an increase in P_s at the same and similar tasks. Since $I_s = 1 - P_s$, the change in motivation following success favors a change in activity, viz., raising the level of aspiration.

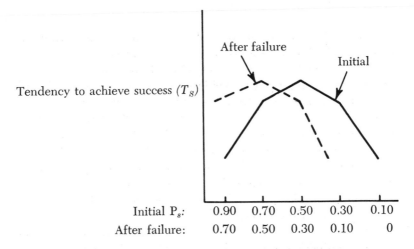

Tendency to achieve success (T_S)

Initial P_s:	0.90	0.70	0.50	0.30	0.10
After failure:	0.70	0.50	0.30	0.10	0

FIGURE 9. Change in level of aspiration following failure when motive to achieve is dominant, i.e., $M_S > M_{AF}$. Failure produces a decrease in P_s at the same and similar tasks. Since $I_s = 1 - P_s$, the change in motivation following failure favors lowering the level of aspiration.

easier task now appears the task of intermediate difficulty. You can see from the two figures how the theory of achievement motivation generates the hypothesis that among persons in whom the achievement motive dominates, the level of aspiration will generally tend to be raised after success and lowered after failure. Notice that the theory does *not* say that success will lead to a strengthening of the tendency to repeat the same action, which is what the empirical Law of Effect asserts.

TYPICAL AND ATYPICAL CHANGES IN EXPECTANCY

The results of all the earlier work on level of aspiration which did not include assessments of individual differences in personality (see Lewin et al., 1944) clearly show that the changes described here are the "typical," i.e., most frequent, results of success and failure on level of aspiration. We explain these "typical" results of earlier studies by referring to what is known from contemporary surveys about the strength of achievement motive in college-educated groups which have provided the subjects for the majority of studies of aspiration. The achievement motive is likely to be dominant in most persons who attend college.

The "atypical," i.e., less frequent, changes in level of aspiration—viz., lowering after success and raising after failure—are also explained by the current theory. Let us consider the individual who is dominated by the motive to avoid failure and refer back to Figures 5 and 6 for this discussion. His initial aspiration should be either a very easy task where failure is a rare event or a very difficult task where success is a rare event. If the most probable outcome occurs, success at the easy task and failure at the difficult task, there is no spur to change the level of aspiration. Success at an easy task raises the expectancy of success and reduces even more the tendency to avoid the task. Failure at the most difficult task lowers the probability of success and produces a similar motivational effect, a reduction in the strength of the tendency to avoid the task.

But note what should happen if the *improbable* outcome occurs. Suppose the anxiety-prone individual fails at the easy task. Then the probability of success is reduced from near certainty to some intermediate value closer to .50. As a result, the tendency to avoid failure at that task is greater on a subsequent trial. A few such failures and the task turns into the intermediate risk which this individual most wants to avoid. He should then do what might appear very irrational to the observer—shift from a very low to a very high level of aspiration. He should, in other words, choose the task for which the tendency to avoid failure is very weak. This happens to be the one where the P_s is very small at the other end of the continuum of difficulty.

What happens if this "anxious" individual has initially chosen a very difficult task and the unlikely thing happens, he succeeds? This atypical result should produce a very atypical change in his aspiration. Because he has succeeded at the task having a low P_s, the P_s is increased towards .50, and consequently the tendency to avoid this task is increased. He might be expected to shift his level of aspiration to a very easy task following success at a very difficult task.

These atypical changes in aspiration were present but infrequent in early studies of aspiration. Recently, Moulton (in press) has shown, as reported in Table 7, that they occur among persons who score high in Test Anxiety and low in n Achievement as the theory predicts. Moulton first ascertained each subject's initial preference among three tasks described to him as very easy, intermediate in difficulty, and very difficult, but without letting the subject perform the task he had chosen. Then, no matter which task was initially preferred, each subject performed the task of intermediate difficulty. Success and failure at this task were experimentally controlled. Following the experience of success or failure at the task of intermediate difficulty, the subject was then given the choice of working at either of the two remaining tasks—the easy one or the very difficult one. Moulton found that subjects in whom n Achievement was dominant, who normally preferred the task of intermediate difficulty, chose the very difficult task after success and the easy one after failure at that moderately difficult task. These are the typical changes in aspiration. But among the anxious subjects, those scoring low in n Achievement and high in Test Anxiety, he found the atypical shifts expected by the theory as shown in Table 7. The design was so arranged that half of the anxious subjects who had initially preferred the easy task as the one they wanted to perform were told they failed at the task of intermediate difficulty, and half of the anxious subjects who had initially preferred the very difficult task were told they had succeeded when they performed the task of intermediate difficulty. (A similar design was applied to the nonanxious subjects.) This meant that the P_s

TABLE 7

NUMBER OF SUBJECTS MAKING TYPICAL AND ATYPICAL SHIFTS IN LEVEL OF ASPIRATION IN RELATION TO n ACHIEVEMENT AND TEST ANXIETY (AFTER MOULTON, IN PRESS).[1]

n Achievement	Test Anxiety	Typical shift	Atypical shift
High	Low	30	1
Low	High	20	11

Note: "Typical" means raising following success and lowering following failure. "Atypical" means the opposite.

[1] With permission of the author.

would be reduced for all tasks for the person who initially had chosen what appeared to be the easy task, and the P_s would be higher for all tasks for the person who had initially preferred the task that appeared very difficult. These anxious subjects, in other words, were faced with the problem of choosing between a task that would now appear more like a .50 risk (the one they had initially chosen) or another task, one of very high P_s for some of them, one of very low P_s for others. Table 7 shows that the subjects in whom motive to avoid failure was dominant did react defensively with the atypical shift in aspiration about one-third of the time and significantly more often than their more positively motivated peers.

PERSISTENCE AFTER CONTINUAL FAILURE

The related problem of persistence following continual failure has been studied by Feather (1961, 1962). According to the theory, a person in whom n Achievement is dominant should be much more persistent following failure at a task which he believes initially to be easy than one he believes initially to be very difficult. Consider again Figure 4 to follow the argument. If the subject in whom n Achievement is dominant undertakes to solve a problem with P_s of .70 and repeatedly fails in successive trials, the P_s should at first drop toward .50 producing a heightening of interest and then drop toward zero causing gradual decrease in the tendency to achieve at the task until finally the tendency to do something else will be stronger and the subject will quit. If this same person began the task thinking the P_s was only .05, a very difficult task, it should take only a few failures to reduce the tendency sufficiently so that he would prefer to do something else.

We should predict something very different for a subject in whom motive to avoid failure is dominant. Consider again Figure 6 to follow the argument for him. If he perceives the task as relatively easy to begin with, having a P_s of .70, and then begins to fail in successive trials, the immediate result should be an increase in the tendency to avoid failure as the P_s drops towards .50. Consequently, there is a reduction in the total strength of the tendency to perform the task. He should quit the task very soon after his initial failures if it seemed easy to begin with. On the other hand, if he began the task thinking it was very difficult, let us say with P_s of .05, and then fails, the effect of failure is, paradoxically, to reduce the strength of his tendency to avoid failure. As a result, there is less dampening of extrinsic motivation to perform the task. The final strength of the tendency to undertake the task becomes stronger and stronger as the inhibition is reduced. The subject in whom the motive to avoid failure is dominant should, in other words, be very persistent in the face of failure at what initially appears to be a very difficult task. Feather's results, confirming these hypotheses, are shown in Table 8.

IMPLICATIONS

The Problem of Inadequate Motivation

These studies of change in aspiration and persistence following success and failure draw attention to the expectancy or subjective probability of success as a potent and manipulable motivational variable. When we consider the question of what is responsible for the inadequate motivation of particular individuals, we find that there are two possible answers. First, the deficiency in motivation may be the result of a deficiency in personality. The motive to avoid failure may be too strong and the motive to achieve too weak. This can produce a general resist-

TABLE 8

Persistence Among College Men (N = 35) in the Face of Continued Failure as a Function of Personality and Initial Difficulty of Task (After Feather, 1961).[1]

n Achievement	Test Anxiety	Per cent above median in persistence	
		Task seen initially as easy $(P_s = .70)$	Task seen initially as difficult $(P_s = .05)$
High	Low	75	22
Low	High	33	75

[1] With permission of the author and of the publisher, American Psychological Association.

ance to achievement-oriented activity that must be overcome by other extrinsic sources of motivation if there is to be any spur to achievement-oriented activity at all. Second, even when the personality is adequate, i.e., the achievement motive is relatively strong, there may be inadequate challenge. The task the individual faces may be too easy or too difficult *for him.*

Hopefully, we shall soon learn more than we now know about the antecedents of the personality dispositions called "motive to achieve" and "motive to avoid failure" so that practical steps can be taken to encourage change in basic personality structure in the schools. But until we know more than we now know it would appear that manipulation of the strength of expectancy of success is the most feasible means of bringing about changes in achievement-oriented motivation.

INDIVIDUAL DIFFERENCES IN EXPECTANCY OF SUCCESS

Once the theoretical importance of expectancy of success is appreciated, we begin to be concerned about a new set of questions for research. For example, is the expectancy of success (P_s) the same for all individuals in a classroom as they face a particular task, or do they differ in P_s because of their past experiences with similar material as much or more than they may differ in the strength of the two achievement-related motives? We gain some insight concerning this kind of question from some results reported by Spielberger (1962) shown in Figure 10. These results, viewed through the spectacles of the present theory, suggest that a measure of an individual's scholastic aptitude or intelligence may also be taken as an index of his subjective probability of success in academic work.

Spielberger used the Manifest Anxiety Scale to assess the influence of anxiety on the academic performance of college freshmen. He determined the average grade point average of students who scored high and low in anxiety at five different levels of ability as measured by a scholastic aptitude test. We can assume that the average strength of n Achievement, not measured in this experiment, is equal in the two anxiety groups. Thus the low anxiety group is the one in which the resultant tendency to achieve is strongest. Compare the results obtained

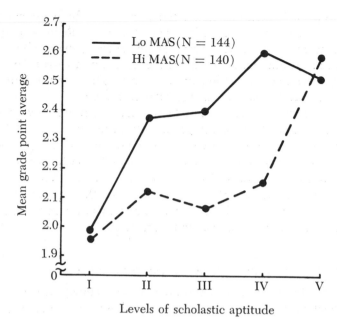

FIGURE 10. Mean grade point average of college students at five levels of scholastic aptitude according to their manifest anxiety score (*MAS*) (after Spielberger, 1962, with permission of the author and of the publisher, National Association of Mental Health, Inc.).

by Spielberger with what is expected according to the theory of achievement motivation if it is assumed that those who score very low in aptitude are persons who approach their college work with a very low expectancy of success and those who score high in aptitude are those who approach college work with a very high probability of success. The results fit the hypothesis that individual difference in disposition to anxiety will have very little effect on performance when the task is perceived as either very easy or very difficult but will have an effect when the task is one of intermediate difficulty, as it presumably is for those in the middle range on scholastic aptitude.

MOTIVATIONAL EFFECTS OF ABILITY GROUPING

The same basic idea provided the theoretical foundation for a study by Patricia O'Connor and me on the motivational effects of ability grouping. Our theoretical argument was quite simple. In the traditional heterogeneous class, where all levels of ability are represented, the chance of being a standout performer relative to peers must seem almost impossible for the student of low ability and is virtually assured for the student of very high ability. According to theory, when P_s is either very low or very high neither interest in achievement nor anxiety about failure will be aroused. Hence only the students of average ability are likely to be very motivated to achieve or anxious in the traditional heterogeneous class.

What happens when students of comparable ability are brought together in the same class? According to theory, the student of high ability now faces a more competitive situation. His P_s should drop from near certainty towards .50, an intermediate risk. Just the opposite should happen for the student of very low ability. Now, for the first time he is surrounded by peers of equal ability and so he has the opportunity for success relative to the others. His P_s is increased towards .50. In other words, homogenization in terms of ability should make the learning situation one of intermediate achievement risk for more students than the traditional heterogeneous class. Is this good? The theory asserts that ability grouping should enhance interest and performance when the achievement motive is strong and the motive to avoid failure is weak. But it should heighten the tendency to avoid failure when that motive is dominant in the person. The same treatment should, in other words, have *diametrically opposite motivational effects* depending upon the personality of the students.

Our study was conducted in sixth-grade classes of a midwestern city. The experimental classes were ability grouped for the first time in sixth grade. The control classes continued to be heterogeneous in ability in sixth grade. We measured amount of growth between fifth and sixth grade on achievement tests of reading and arithmetic. We measured amount of growth relative to average amount of growth among students comparable in intelligence. In addition, we assessed degree of interest and satisfaction in sixth-grade work as compared with fifth-grade work in one of our experimental schools by means of rating scales of various classroom activities. The results are shown in Tables 9 and 10. We expected and found that both boys and girls who

TABLE 9

STUDENTS SHOWING ABOVE MEDIAN GROWTH FOR THEIR LEVEL OF
INTELLIGENCE IN READING AND ARITHMETIC ON CALIFORNIA ACHIEVE-
MENT TEST (AFTER ATKINSON & O'CONNOR, 1963).[1]

	n Achievement — Test Anxiety	Ability groups N	%	Control classes N	%
(IQ 125+)	High	24*	71	37	46
	Low	10	50	27	37
(IQ 113-124)	High	11†	90	17	41
	Low	17	65	19	58
(IQ 112—)	High	8†	88	8	38
	Low	23	52	14	36

* Above median in both areas.
† Above median in one or both areas.
[1] With permission of the authors.

were strong in n Achievement relative to Test Anxiety show evidence of greater learning and stronger interest in ability grouped
classes than in control classes irrespective of the level of intelligence. We expected to find evidence of a decrement of interest
and performance among the students who scored low in n
Achievement relative to Test Anxiety when placed in ability
grouped classes. Our results show the predicted decrement in
reported interest and satisfaction but no significant change in
scholastic performance when the anxiety-prone subjects in the

TABLE 10

EFFECT OF ABILITY GROUPING ON REPORTED INTEREST IN SCHOOL-
WORK IN SIXTH AS COMPARED WITH FIFTH GRADE (AFTER ATKINSON
& O'CONNOR, 1963).[1]

n Achievement — Test Anxiety	Students above median Ability groups N	%	Control classes N	%
High	18	78	78	56
Moderate	22	41	82	43
Low	22	36	73	52

[1] With permission of the authors.

experimental and control classes are compared. Ability grouping did not weaken the performance of these students, though they may have maintained the same level of performance as comparable students in the control classes at a greater personal cost if we take the ratings of interest and satisfaction seriously. It would be nice to know, but we do not, if they spent longer hours at homework.

The results certainly suggest that ability grouping has important motivational implications and that what is so generally true of environmental manipulations in the domain of achievement-oriented activity is also true here: the same treatment may have diametrically opposite effects on different individuals. This, I believe, is one of the most important implications of contemporary research on human motivation—the challenge it poses for those who think there may be some *single* method of instruction or treatment which will produce optimal motivation for learning in all students irrespective of personality.

The Law of Effect—a Misleading Guide

Equally important is another general implication of the conceptual scheme which deserves some explicit comment. It is the argument that the Law of Effect is fundamentally inadequate as a guide to understanding in the domain of achievement-oriented activity. Success does not invariably produce a strengthening of the tendency to undertake the same activity on another occasion. Sometimes success weakens the subsequent tendency to engage in the same activity. The individual strongly motivated to achieve normally raises his level of aspiration following success: his behavior changes.

Gordon Allport (1943) noted this inadequacy of the Law of Effect more than twenty years ago, and now, at last, we have a reasonably clear explanation of why the traditional generalization does not hold. The law does not hold because in the domain of achievement-oriented activity an increase in the expectancy of success, which is the effect on the person of success, produces a change in the incentive value of success. Sometimes the effect of this change is an increase in the strength of the tendency to undertake the same activity. Sometimes it is just the reverse. It depends upon the personality of the subject—whether the motive to achieve or the motive to avoid failure is dominant in him— and it depends upon the initial strength of the expectancy of success at the task. The matter is complicated, certainly more complicated than the Law of Effect would ever lead us to imagine.

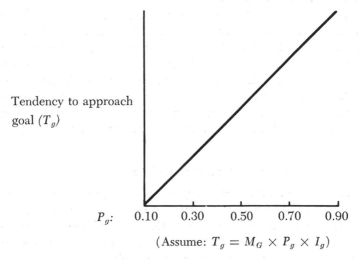

Tendency to approach goal (T_g)

P_g: 0.10   0.30   0.50   0.70   0.90

(Assume: $T_g = M_G \times P_g \times I_g$)

FIGURE 11. Theoretical effect of increasing the strength of expectancy of attaining a goal (P_g) when the incentive value of the goal (I_g) is constant and not affected by a change in P_g (derivation of the Law of Effect).

From the viewpoint of an Expectancy $\times$ Value theory of motivation, one which asserts that the tendency to undertake an activity is determined by the strength of the expectancy that the activity will produce certain consequences and the value of those consequences, the Law of Effect summarizes what is observed when there is no relationship between the value of the consequence of an action and the expectancy of attaining it. This is shown schematically in Figure 11. Holding the strength of motive and the incentive value of the consequence constant, we see that the strength of tendency to undertake an activity should increase as the strength of expectancy of attaining that consequence increases. This is what happens in a series of "reinforced" trials.

The Law of Effect should also provide an adequate summary of what happens when the value of the consequence of an action increases as the expectancy of attaining it increases. But the Law of Effect simply does not hold under the conditions of achievement-oriented activity when the incentive value of the consequence of activity (success) is inversely related to the strength of expectancy of producing it.

How good is the evidence that the incentive value of success is inversely related to the expectancy of success: $I_s = 1 - P_s$? There are three sources of evidence. First, reported expectancies of success are found to be inversely related to estimates of the prize that ought to be awarded for success at a task and to reports of degree of satisfaction immediately after success at a task. Second, there are the results of all the studies of aspiration, change in aspiration, and persistence as a function of initial level of difficulty that are predicted and integrated when it is assumed that $I_s = 1 - P_s$. Finally, there is one more bit of indirect evidence which is previously unpublished. We have attempted to construct a simple money model of achievement-oriented activity. The subject is confronted with a set of containers each holding 100 beads. In each container there are a certain number of distinctively colored "lucky" beads. The subject cannot see the beads, but he can see a sign on top of each container which tells him how many lucky beads—10, 20, 30, 40, 50, 60, 70, 80, or 90—are in the container and how much money he will be given if he should pick a lucky bead from the container. Thus, for example, the subject must decide whether to put his hand into a container having a sign which says "10 lucky beads—lucky bead worth 9¢" or another container having a sign which says, "50 lucky beads—lucky bead worth 5¢." The value of the monetary incentive was arranged to fit the rule $I_w = 1 - P_w$. Thus the subject could win 9¢ if he picked a lucky bead when the probability was .10; 5¢ when the probability was .50; 1¢ when the probability was .90; etc. It was obvious to all the subjects that no skill or competence was involved in the task, yet, as the bell-shaped curve in Figure 12 shows, there was a very strong preference for intermediate risk in this lottery—comparable to the often observed preference for intermediate risk in achievement activity where the rule $I_s = 1 - P_s$ is assumed to hold. Every probability was paired with every other for each subject. The curve represents the percentage of times a given alternative was chosen in preference to all others.

The other curve in Figure 12, that relatively straight line having its peak where the probability of winning a lucky bead is .90, shows the results obtained *when the incentive value of the lucky bead was held constant at 1¢ no matter what the probability of winning.* When this condition exists in a state of nature —that is, when the incentive value of the consequence of an activity is constant—the effect of repeated reward should be a strengthening of expectancy of reward, and the Law of Effect is then a useful summary of what is likely to happen.

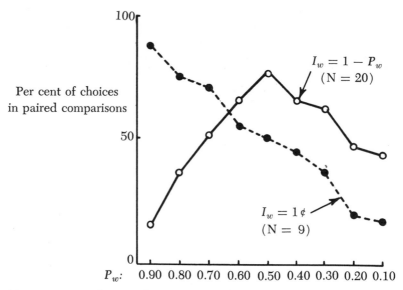

FIGURE 12. Preference for various probabilities of winning (P_w) in a choice between lotteries when the monetary incentive was constant $(I_w = 1¢)$ and when the monetary incentive (1¢ to 9¢) was inversely related to probability of winning $(I_w = 1 - P_w)$.

CONCLUDING COMMENT

If this essay had been prepared ten years ago, I am sure the title would have been "The *mainspring* of achievement-oriented activity." It would have been concerned only with the achievement motive. You can look at a book published in 1953 under that title, *The Achievement Motive* (McClelland, et al.), to see what would have been included.

Today's version, marking some progress in a decade of work, is called the *mainsprings* because our research has finally caught up with the relatedness of "anxiety" and need for achievement as determinants of activities when performance is evaluated. The present conceptual scheme gives equal emphasis to each of these motives and to the expectancy of success as the manipulable determinant of achievement-oriented motivation. You will find the beginnings of discussion along this line in *Motives in Fantasy, Action, and Society* (Atkinson, 1958) and *The Achieving Society* (McClelland, 1961) and more thorough treatment in more recent publications, *An Introduction to Motivation* (Atkinson, 1964) and *A Theory of Achievement Motivation* (Atkinson & Feather, scheduled for 1966).

Ten years from now, when we have sharpened and extended our conceptual analysis to embrace those other motivational factors that now are merely lumped in the category "extrinsic motivation," particularly the tendency to gain social approval in achievement activities which has already gained the special status of most neglected variable in research on achievement-oriented activity, a similar essay may have to be titled *the springs* of achievement-oriented activity. Some may feel that would have been a more appropriate title and topic even for the present effort. I do not believe the current state of empirical knowledge supports that view. But if the reader feels that some extra justification is needed for the title and the special emphasis of tendency to achieve success and tendency to avoid failure as mainsprings of achievement-oriented activity, let the justification lie in the fact that they are wound up differently from the others, in a way that we would never have discovered if we had let our thought be constrained by that traditional notion, the Law of Effect, which has so long—too long—dominated thought about matters of learning and motivation in education.

REFERENCES

Allport, G. The ego in contemporary psychology. *Psychol. Rev.*, 1943, 50, 451–478.

Alpert, R., & Huber, R. N. Anxiety in academic achievement situations. *J. abnorm. soc. Psychol.*, 1960, 61, 207–215.

Atkinson, J. W. (Ed.) *Motives in fantasy, action, and society.* Princeton, N.J.: Van Nostrand, 1958.

Atkinson, J. W. *An introduction to motivation.* Princeton, N.J.: Van Nostrand, 1964.

Atkinson, J. W., & Feather, N. T. (Eds.) *A theory of achievement motivation.* New York: Wiley, scheduled for 1966.

Atkinson, J. W., & Litwin, G. H. Achievement motive and test anxiety conceived as motive to approach success and motive to avoid failure. *J. abnorm. soc. Psychol.*, 1960, 60, 52–63.

Atkinson, J. W., & O'Connor, Patricia. Effects of ability grouping in schools related to individual differences in achievement-related motivation: Final report. Office of Education Cooperative Research Project 1238, 1963. (Available in microfilm⁻ [$2.25] or photocopy from Photoduplication Center, Library of Congress, Washington, D.C.)

Atkinson, J. W., & O'Connor, Patricia. Neglected variables in studies of achievement-oriented performances: Social approval as incentive and performance decrement. In J. W. Atkinson & N. T. Feather (Eds.), *A theory of achievement motivation.* New York: Wiley, scheduled for 1966.

Brown, M. Factors determining expectancy of success and reactions to success and failure. Unpublished manuscript, Univer. of Michigan, 1963.

Crockett, H. J., Jr. The achievement motive and differential occupational mobility in the United States. *Amer. sociol. Rev.*, 1962, 27, 191–204.

Crockett, H. J., Jr. Social class, education, and motive to achieve in differential occupational mobility. *Sociol. Quart.*, 1964, 5, 231–242.

Cronbach, L. J. The two disciplines of scientific psychology. *Amer. Psychol.*, 1957, 12, 671–684.

Edwards, W. The theory of decision making. *Psychol. Bull.*, 1954, 51, 380–417.

Feather, N. T. The relationship of persistence at a task to expectation of success and achievement-related motives. *J. abnorm. soc. Psychol.*, 1961, 63, 552–561.

Feather, N. T. The study of persistence. *Psychol. Bull.*, 1962, 59, 94–115.

French, Elizabeth G., & Thomas, F. H. The relation of achievement motivation to problem solving effectiveness. *J. abnorm. soc. Psychol.*, 1958, **56**, 46–48.

Hoppe, F. Untersuchungen zur Handlungs- und Affekt-Psychologie: IX. Erfolg und Misserfolg. [Investigations in the psychology of action and emotion. IX. Success and failure.] *Psychol. Forsch.*, 1930, **14**, 1–63.

Isaacson, R. L. Relation between achievement, test anxiety, and curricular choices. *J. abnorm. soc. Psychol.*, 1964, **68**, 447–452.

Krumboltz, J. D. Measuring achievement motivation. A review. *J. counsel. Psychol.*, 1957, **4**, 191–198.

Lesser, G. S., Krawitz, Rhoda N., & Packard, Rita. Experimental arousal of achievement motivation in adolescent girls. *J. abnorm. soc. Psychol.*, 1963, **66**, 59–66.

Lewin, K. *Conceptual representation and measurement of psychological forces.* Durham, N. C.: Duke Univer. Press, 1938.

Lewin, K., Dembo, Tamara, Festinger, L., & Sears, Pauline S. Level of aspiration. In J. McV. Hunt (Ed.), *Personality and the behavior disorders.* Vol. 1. New York: Ronald Press, 1944. Pp. 333–378.

Litwin, G. H. Motives and expectancies as determinants of preference for degrees of risk. Unpublished honors dissertation, Univer. of Michigan, 1958.

Mahone, C. H. Fear of failure and unrealistic vocational aspiration. *J. abnorm. soc. Psychol.*, 1960, **60**, 253–261.

Mandler, G., & Sarason, S. B. A study of anxiety and learning. *J. abnorm. soc. Psychol.*, 1952, **47**, 166–173.

McClelland, D. C. *Personality.* New York: Wm. Sloane, 1951.

McClelland, D. C. Methods of measuring human motivation. Ch. 1 in J. W. Atkinson (Ed.), *Motives in fantasy, action, and society.* Princeton, N.J.: Van Nostrand, 1958. (a)

McClelland, D. C. Risk taking in children with high and low need for achievement. Ch. 21 in J. W. Atkinson (Ed.), *Motives in fantasy, action, and society.* Princeton, N.J.: Van Nostrand, 1958. (b)

McClelland, D. C. *The achieving society.* Princeton, N.J.: Van Nostrand, 1961.

McClelland, D. C., Atkinson, J. W., Clark, R. A., & Lowell, E. L. *The achievement motive.* New York: Appleton-Century-Crofts, 1953.

Morgan, H. H. A psychometric comparison of achieving and non-achieving college students of high ability. *J. consult. Psychol.*, 1952, **16**, 279–298.

Moulton, R. W. Effects of success and failure on level of aspiration as related to achievement motives. *J. person. soc. Psychol.*, 1965, **1**, 399–406.

Murray, H. A. *Explorations in personality.* New York: Oxford Univer. Press, 1938.

Riccuiti, H. N., & Sadacca, R. The prediction of academic grades with a projective test of achievement motivation. II. Cross validation at the high school level. Princeton, N.J.: Educational Testing Service, 1955.

Rotter, J. B. *Social learning and clinical psychology.* Englewood Cliffs, N.J.: Prentice-Hall, 1954.

Rosen, B. The achievement syndrome. *Amer. sociol. Rev.*, 1956, **21**, 203–211.

Sarason, S. B., Davidson, K. S., Lighthall, F. F., & Ruebush, B. K. *Anxiety in elementary school children.* New York: Wiley, 1960.

Spence, K. A theory of emotionally based drive (D) and its relation to performance in simple learning situations. *Amer. Psychol.*, 1958, **13**, 131–141.

Spielberger, C. D. The effects of manifest anxiety on the academic achievement of college students. *Ment. Hyg.*, 1962, **46**, 420–426.

Taylor, Janet A. Drive theory and manifest anxiety. *Psychol. Bull.*, 1956, **53**, 303–320.

Tolman, E. C. Principles of performance. *Psychol. Rev.*, 1955, **62**, 315–326.

Veroff, J., Atkinson, J. W., Feld, Shiela, & Gurin, G. The use of thematic apperception to assess motivation in a nationwide interview study. *Psychol. Monogr.*, 1960, **74**, No. 12 (Whole No. 499).

Chapter 3

CURIOSITY AND EDUCATION

D. E. BERLYNE, *University of Toronto*

The history of the psychology of learning has taken the form of a turbulent, on-and-off, ambivalent liaison with the laws of association. The two principal laws of association, association by contiguity and association by similarity, can be traced back— a little tenuously perhaps—to the writings of Plato and Aristotle.

Have we really made very much progress or added much since, in Plato's *Phaedo*, Socrates asked: "May you not also from seeing the picture of a horse or a lyre remember a man? And from the picture of Simmias you may be led to remember Cebes? . . . or you may also be led to the recollection of Simmias himself?" Like Simmias in the dialogue, we feel bound to say: "True!" in answer to these rhetorical questions, and we have to admit that this view reflects in large measure how learning works.

Yet for centuries, there have been arguments and tussles, an inability to abandon the laws of association and yet a conviction that they are far from being enough. There have been disputes over the kinds of elements that participate in the associative relation. Are "ideas" associated with one another, or are

The preparation of this paper was facilitated by Research Grant MH-06324 from the National Institute of Mental Health of the United States Public Health Service.

"stimuli" associated with "responses"? Can two "stimuli" or internal correlates of stimuli ("images") be associated with each other? Can two motor acts?

There has also been a feeling that the fruits of learning must consist of more than simply a collection of associations. Surely, we often acquire not merely an association between two or more specific elements but something of more general applicability that we could properly call a "rule" or a "strategy" or a "principle." Further, it seems fairly obvious that the associations acquired through learning are organized in elaborate structures and that a great deal of their value depends on the fact that they do not exist in isolation but interact and collaborate with one another.

ASSOCIATION AND MOTIVATION

From our present point of view, the most glaring inadequacies of the laws of association seem, however, to lie in their neglect of motivational factors. It seems indisputable that, if something (whether it be a stimulus or a response or a central process such as an idea or image) is to participate in a learning process, it must have occurred together with something else or it must resemble something that has occurred together with something else. Nevertheless, we experience many simultaneous pairs of events in the course of a day, and we perform many responses in the presence of particular stimulus patterns in the course of a day, but most of these contiguities produce no learning at all. And of those that produce learning, some produce much more effective learning than others. So whether or not learning will occur and, if so, how effective it will be depend not merely on conjunctions of events but also on the psychophysiological state of the learner, and especially on what we call his "motivational condition."

In the more primitive forms of learning, it makes a great difference whether or not the subject is hungry or in pain or afraid. In the more intellectual kinds of learning that are of interest to the schoolteacher, we say that it matters how "interested" the learner is. There must apparently be a sufficient level of mobilization or alertness, of openness to incoming information, of "arousal" (to use a term that is enjoying a current vogue among both psychologists and neurophysiologists). Secondly, it helps if there is some correspondence between the motivational condition of the learner (what he wants at the moment) and what he is being given an opportunity to learn. A rat will be more likely to recall a means of obtaining food if it was discovered while he was hungry, and a school child will presumably remember material that belongs to a topic in which he "is interested," that contains something that he would like to know.

Moreover, it seems that, in at least some, if not all, forms of learning, it is not enough for the elements that are to be associated to occur together. There must be some additional event, which we call a source of *reinforcement*. In classical or Pavlovian conditioning, the reinforcing event is the *unconditioned stimulus*, the biologically important stimulus (such as the appearance of food or the application of an electric shock) that elicited the response in the first place. In instrumental conditioning, exemplified by the acquisition of manual or social skills, the reinforcing agent is a *reward* that closely follows the performance of the act to be learned (although some writers would also speak of a punishing consequence that weakens the response as a "negative reinforcer").

As far as human remembering and intellectual learning generally are concerned, it is still not clear how far they conform to the classical-conditioning pattern and how far to the instrumental-conditioning pattern, just as the relations between these two kinds of conditioning have not yet been fully worked out. But since some combinations of experienced events lead to remembering and some do not, it seems clear that reinforcing conditions of some kind must be playing a part. We can recognize that intellectual activities—patterns of thought—are frequently employed as means of achieving specific ends, whether practical or theoretical, and that how successful they are determines whether they will recur or whether they will be abandoned in favor of others. So there is reason to suppose that their occurrence, like that of instrumentally conditioned motor response, is governed by rewarding consequences, although the forms of reward to which they are most susceptible may well be different.

EXTRINSIC AND INTRINSIC MOTIVATION

Psychologists began to take motivational questions seriously at the time when, under the influence of evolutionary theory, they were learning to view psychological problems in a biological perspective. They had come to see that the behavior of lower animals and of human beings consists of devices contributing to the aims of survival and health and reproduction. So it seemed reasonable to assume that the motivational conditions or drive states that impelled organisms to seek new forms of adaptive behavior and to retain them, once they had been found, would be ones in which some prerequisite of biological well-being is needed and lacking. Reinforcing conditions would, it appeared, consist of external agents that have biologically crucial effects on bodily tissues. So we find the earliest experimenters on motivation in the 1920s, the neo-behaviorists of the 1930s who were beginning to elaborate the concept of "drive," and also theorists working away from the beaten track of psychology, like Freud and McDougall, concentrating on external irritants, like pain or excessive heat, or on internal physiological disturbances, like those due to deprivation of food or to sexual arousal, as sources of motivating discomfort or "drive." At the same time, they saw anything that relieved these distresses, or, in other words, reduced drive, as a source of satisfaction or reward.

The limitations of this view became manifest as soon as motivation theorists ceased to confine their attention to standard animal learning situations and began to consider a wider range of real-life human behavior. They broadened their view of motivation enormously by invoking the laws of association in a new motivational guise. They postulated that biologically neutral or indifferent stimuli that have regularly accompanied pain or other forms of distress will become aversive in their own right and induce "secondary drive." Indifferent stimuli that happen to coincide with biological gratification or relief will, they postulated, come to function as "secondary rewards" or "secondary reinforcers." Essentially the same hypotheses underlay Freud's assertion that objects and thoughts without beneficial or harmful effects in themselves would come to occasion profound anxiety or would alternatively come to be eagerly sought after, if resemblances or contiguities between them and events of biological importance had given them the power to symbolize the latter or caused them to be "cathected."

Although there have been debates over details and wording, these hypotheses have in essence stood the tests of time and of intensive experimentation, at least in relation to the simpler kinds of human and animal learning. In recent years, however, a feeling has grown that still further additions and extensions to our motivational concepts are needed if many psychological phenomena, including activities classed as "recreational," "aesthetic," and "intellectual," are to be adequately explained. So the latest phase in the development of motivation theory has seen mounting attention paid to what are coming to be called *intrinsic* motivational conditions and *intrinsic* rewards.

The term "intrinsic motivation," which educationists have been using for some time in a kindred sense, is invoked to account for activities that are apparently performed, as we say, "for their own sake," that are "satisfying in themselves" or, as the Russians have sometimes put it, that are "self-reinforcing." These kinds of behavior have, of course, important consequences of a rewarding nature. They may well bring about changes in the perceptible external environment, and they invariably affect the subject's psychophysiological state. If these consequences fail to satisfy, the activities will cease or their form will be altered. The peculiarity of intrinsically motivated activities lies, however, in the fact that they depend for their reward-value on events in the central nervous system rather than, as in the case of food-seeking or pain-escaping behavior, on events in other tissues.

ORIGINS OF CONCEPTIONS OF INTRINSIC MOTIVATION

The best way to acquire some notion of what these newly recognized motivational factors amount to and, above all, of how

72 *Learning and the Educational Process*

multifaceted they are is to review briefly some of the varied lines
of research that have drawn attention to them.

1. EXPLORATORY BEHAVIOR

During the last fifteen years, a great deal of experimentation
has been devoted to the exploratory behavior of animals and
human beings (Berlyne, 1960; Berlyne, 1963). Exploratory behavior is behavior aimed at receipt or intensification of stimulation with no manifest biological significance. Higher animals
characteristically spend a high proportion of their time exploring
their environments. This is especially so when no emergency is
making overriding demands on their behavior, although curiosity
will at times even take priority for a while over hunger or fear.
While some exploratory behavior is aimed at stimuli bearing
vital information, e.g., stimuli indicative of the whereabouts of
food or of a path of escape, and can thus be termed *extrinsic*
exploration, much of the exploratory behavior found in higher
animals brings the organism into contact with stimuli that it
subsequently does little about.

This *intrinsic* exploration presents some serious challenges
to motivation theory. The strength and direction of intrinsic exploration can be affected by many factors, internal and external,
but, as far as we can see, it is primarily evoked by, and aimed
at, stimulus patterns that are novel, surprising, complex, incongruous, or ambiguous. The common thread tying together all
these "collative" stimulus properties, as we call them, seems to
be that they all mean the evocation of discrepant reactions in the
nervous system when components of the pattern in question are
compared with one another or with elements experienced in similar contexts in the past. They involve, in other words, *conflict*.
When exploratory behavior has done its work and exposed the
subject's sense organs to appropriate stimulation, a rewarding
state of affairs is brought about and can evidently provide reinforcement for new learning. This can happen, apparently, either
because additional stimulation brings with it additional information that resolves conflict associated with uncertainty or because
the disturbance—the rise in drive or arousal—is relieved once the

initial impact of the stimulus has been sustained and the nervous system recovers its equilibrium.

2. AFFECTIVE CONSEQUENCES OF DEVIATIONS FROM EXPECTATIONS

Amsel (1958) in North America and Anokhin (1955) and Sokolov (1963) in the U.S.S.R. have asserted, on the basis of experimental evidence, that, when an animal has regularly experienced a sequence of events, especially one culminating in a reward, an internal anticipatory process occurs representing what can be expected to come next. If ever the reward, or whatever else was due to ensue, fails to materialize, various signs of disturbance may appear, including manifestations of emotional upset, extinction of learned responses, exploratory behavior, refusal to eat an unexpected but otherwise acceptable food, and replacement of old by new forms of learned behavior. Bühler et al. (1928) and Hebb (1946) have observed how effectively a human infant or an ape can be scared by a stimulus pattern that deviates slightly from a familiar one—e.g., a well-known person speaking in a strange falsetto voice in the case of the baby and a model of a chimpanzee's head in the case of the ape. McClelland et al. (1953) and Fiske and Maddi (1961) have offered evidence that stimulation differing moderately from what a subject is set to receive will be judged pleasurable whereas more marked deviations will be judged adversely.

3. PERSONALITY THEORY

Students of personality have, in recent years, been discussing dimensions like "intolerance of ambiguity" (Frenkel-Brunswik, 1949). They have devised tests whose results show that individuals differ in the extent to which they are troubled when brought face to face with something that is difficult to classify or to understand, some individuals being quite deeply discomfited. Individuals also differ in the means that they characteristically use to cope with ambiguous situations, some tending to withdraw attention from anomalous features and others to devote excessive attention to niggling details.

4. ATTITUDE CHANGE

Social psychologists have been giving more and more emphasis to "incongruity" (Osgood & Tannenbaum, 1955), "imbalance" (Abelson & Rosenberg, 1958) and "dissonance" (Festinger, 1957) as factors promoting attitude change. The attitudes that a person has built up to guide his behavior and judgment with respect to social objects are apt to interact with one another, and their interactions will sometimes be less than harmonious. Incompatibilities among attitudes may well lie dormant for quite a long time and lead to inconsistencies of behavior that fail to worry the subject or even escape his notice. There will, however, be times when he is made sensitive to points on which his attitudes are at variance with one another. The resulting discomfort can give a powerful impetus to revaluations and changes in belief, as can confrontation with unusual external conditions, e.g., those that are prevalent at times of social crisis when external reality jars painfully with what existing evaluations and beliefs lead one to expect.

5. CHILD DEVELOPMENT

Coming somewhat nearer to the topic of immediate interest to us, we find Piaget (1957), after spending decades assiduously investigating the development of perceptual and intellectual processes in the child, voicing a rather radical conclusion. He holds that psychological development is kept moving not only by maturation and learning, as is usually believed, but also by a third and distinct factor making for change, which he calls "equilibration." This is a tendency for the child to abandon structures characterized by relative disequilibrium, which means inconsistency of judgment, uncertainty, or even, in certain conditions, inability to make a judgment at all, in favor of structures possessed of better equilibrium. According to Piaget, equilibration is the main force that conducts the child from his early complete reliance on unorganized perception, with its inherent susceptibility to illusion, to the systems of intellectual operations that make logical, mathematical, and scientific thinking possible. Although Piaget is at pains to distinguish equilibration from "learning," his conception of learning can be adjudged excessively narrow and outmoded. Equilibration fits the contemporary learning theorists' conception of learning, although it has some peculiarities which may be explained, in part at least, by its dependence on intrinsic motivation and reinforcement (Berlyne, 1965).

6. EDUCATION

Finally, recognition of the importance of intrinsic motivation and reward has come out of examination of the problems of education, the principal pioneer in this regard being—and this may surprise some readers—Dewey. On reading Dewey's writings, one comes across passages where he sounds very much like a spokesman of the contemporary curriculum-reform movement, which is sometimes thought of as a reaction against Dewey. He has certainly been maligned and misrepresented at times. In fact, it is hard to know whether he has suffered more wrongs at the hands of his detractors or of his followers. In the book *How We Think* (1910), he describes how thinking begins with a "felt difficulty," which commonly takes the form of a conflict "between conditions at hand and the desired or intended result, between an end and the means of reaching it." In his pedagogical writings, particularly in *Democracy and Education* (1916), he singles out the stimulation of thinking as one of the prime functions of education. The aims of education can, he claims, be achieved most effectively through "experience," which he defines as "trying to do something and having the thing perceptibly do something to one in return." Experience is particularly instructive when the child's efforts fail to have the outcome that he was anticipating or fail to achieve their goals.

The period during which North American education was dominated by Dewey's influence was one marked generally by a fear of hastening the educational process and of overstraining the child's intellectual capacities. Recent psychological research concurs with the experience of educators in other parts of the world in suggesting that the rate at which the average child, let alone the gifted child, can advance has been grossly underestimated, with unfortunate consequences. Jones and Carterette

(1963) have found the reading-matter that children borrow from libraries for home reading to be distinctly more difficult, as judged by information-theoretic measures of redundancy, than the readers to which they are exposed in school. Admiral Rickover (1963) has deplored the neglect of book learning in favor of field trips and manual activities. Above all, there was a grave underestimation of the extent to which the ordinary child can find intellectual substance appetizing and intellectual effort satisfying, provided they are introduced at the right time and in the right way.

Those who have tended in these directions will find scant comfort in Dewey's writings. He made it clear that the "doing" that constituted the basis of experience could take the form of brain-work and that the "problems" to which schoolwork needs to be related may very well be theoretical problems, provided that the child experiences them as such. He condemned the misunderstanding that makes "interest" mean "merely the effect of an object upon personal advantage or disadvantage, success or failure." He denied that "to attach importance to interest means to attach some feature of seductiveness to material otherwise indifferent; to secure attention and effort by offering a bribe of pleasure." "This procedure," he writes, "is properly stigmatized as 'soft pedagogy,' as a 'soup kitchen' theory of education."

CONFLICT AND CURIOSITY

The upshot of all these currents of thought, converging from vastly different starting-points, is that motivating disturbances (i.e., rises in drive or arousal that impel action and, where no effective recourse is readily available, new learning) can come not only from visceral upheavals and external irritations but also from discrepant or disharmonious relations among processes going on in the subject's nervous system or, to use the term in its most comprehensive sense, from conflict.

Conflict can be generated, by stimulus patterns possessing novelty, surprisingness, incongruity, or complexity. These, it will be recalled, are the "collative" properties that exert a preponderant influence over exploratory behavior. Every environmental feature that excites a person's sense-organs is compared with other features that accompany it, with others that might have occurred instead, with others that have been encountered in the past. More accurately, reactions called forth by the feature in question have to interact with reactions corresponding to accompanying features or previously encountered features or features whose occurrence was anticipated but did not materialize. The interacting processes may be mutually supportive and complementary, but there may alternatively be some degree of incompatibility, and therefore of mutual interference and competition, among them (i.e., conflict).

A state of conflict may be of such a kind that additional information, e.g., specification of some hidden attribute of an object or identification of some impending event, will relieve it. If this is so, the subject is beset by what both common language and the technical language of information theory call "uncertainty." It is likely that prior learning will make him resort to exploratory activity to gain access to the information whose lack is being felt. If so, the subject will be in the kind of state of heightened drive or arousal that we call "perceptual curiosity."

When a child is in a classroom, the activities, covert or overt, that are induced in him, or that we hope will be induced in him, are to a great extent aimed at the acquisition of knowledge. Knowledge is information not merely taken in through sense-organs but stored for future use in the form of systems of associations which, when appropriate circumstances are encountered in the future, will make available internal symbolic responses (thoughts) to guide behavior in conjunction with the external environment of the moment. Activities whose function is to build up knowledge constitute *epistemic* behavior, which can include thinking, rehearsing to oneself symbolic responses copied from teachers, asking questions, and observing. Epistemic curiosity, the motivational condition making for epistemic behavior, apparently results from *conceptual conflict*, which means conflict due to discrepant thoughts or beliefs or attitudes (Berlyne, 1954a; Berlyne, 1960; Berlyne, 1963; Berlyne, 1965). Epistemic behavior will be intrinsically reinforced, and the knowledge derived from it retained, when it resolves conceptual conflict or, to use Dewey's expression, "introduces a congruity" and thus relieves epistemic curiosity.

CONCEPTUAL CONFLICT AND DISCOVERY METHODS

In recent educational practice, intrinsic motives and rewards have been used most conspicuously and deliberately in connection with so-called discovery methods. These are methods in which the child is encouraged to take steps to find the information required for the solution of a particular problem by his own efforts rather than passively registering information supplied by the teacher. Different forms of conceptual conflict are readily applicable to different educational subject matters, and it is noteworthy that those who have experimented with discovery methods have resorted to quite a wide assortment of them. So we may find it worthwhile to examine in turn some of the different ways in which epistemic curiosity can be induced through conceptual conflict and subsequently relieved to provide reinforcement for school learning.

1. SURPRISE

In several subject-matters, but especially in the natural sciences, it is possible to present the student with a phenomenon that violates expectations derived from his existing beliefs, a phenomenon that his prior training and experience have led him to regard as improbable or impossible. The motivational potentialities of surprise are commonly utilized in lessons using demonstrations of physical, chemical, or biological phenomena. The skills of the experimenter and the stage magician have, in fact, been fruitfully combined on many such occasions. Among recently introduced methods, Suchman's (1959) "Inquiry Training" systematically exploits the pedagogical value of surprise. The student is first shown a film sequence depicting a train of events that is unprecedented within his experience and inexplicable to him, e.g., a brass ball that is just small enough to slip through a ring sits on the ring after being heated. The student is then invited to seek an explanation by putting questions to the teacher that can be answered "yes" or "no," being encouraged especially to formulate questions that relate to the outcome of possible experiments. The conflict due to surprise is eliminated as the reality of the surprising phenomenon is established and explained.

2. DOUBT

In subject matters like mathematics, surprise is difficult to engineer because the student will generally have insufficient previous knowledge to make firm expectations likely and, in any case, it is hard (but perhaps not always impossible) to devise a concrete situation or verbal statement to convince him of a mathematical truth that seems initially unlikely. Doubt, i.e., conflict between tendencies to believe and disbelieve, is put to good use in some of the new mathematics curricula. I once had the privilege of witnessing a sample lesson given by Dr. David L. Page under the auspices of the University of Illinois Arithmetic Project, in which third-grade children were being introduced to the fact that the difference between the squares of two adjacent integers [i.e., $(n + 1)^2 - n^2$] is always an odd number. On another occasion, I heard a lecture by Professor G. Polya, describing how, using essentially the same method as Dr. Page, he would teach Euler's theorem (that $R - E + V = 2$, where R, E, and V are, respectively, the numbers of faces, edges, and vertices of a polyhedron).

Both lessons began by showing the principle to hold true for one specific case after another. As it was confirmed with each example, the question of whether it would work for the next example was raised and the corresponding curiosity induced. Once enough examples had been given to make the universal validity of the principle seem credible, a different sort of conflict was introduced by asking whether the principle must always hold true and why. In this way, the pupils were motivationally prepared for the equivalent of a proof.

3. PERPLEXITY

When students are faced with a problem and can specify a number of possible solutions but have no way of knowing which is the correct one, they are in the kind of conflict that can be called perplexity, a special case of the kind of situation to which both everyday language and information theory apply the term "uncertainty." For example, Bruner (1960) refers to an experimental geography lesson in which high-school students were shown a map of the United States with only natural features such as rivers and mountains displayed on it and were required to deduce where cities would have grown up. Conflict will have stemmed from competition among tendencies to select various alternative locations, and then, once a guess has been recorded, there will have been additional conflict due to doubt—wondering whether or not the guess was correct—which was relieved when the student was allowed to compare what he had deduced with a fuller map showing what was actually the case.

4. BAFFLEMENT

Conflict can occur when a student is confronted with a situation in which a number of apparently irreconcilable demands are made of him. Until he has found a course of action that will satisfy all of them, any response that is called to the fore by one of the requirements is inhibited, either because it seems to have consequences that violate other requirements or because, in the light of some feature of the situation, it seems to be impracticable. This state of affairs may be realized when a practical task is imposed on the student but, as studies by Morozova (1955) in Russia have illustrated, it is often enough to present the problem in verbal form. For example, a student is asked to consider how he would find out where he is—what the longitude and latitude of his location are—in the middle of the desert. Younger children are told a story about a fictitious hero, with whom they can identify, who finds himself faced with this problem, but, for older children, it is enough to present the problem in an abstract form.

5. CONTRADICTION

In another experiment of Morozova's (personal communication), children are first told how plants use chlorophyll to carry out the photochemical reactions on which their existence depends, and they are later told that there are plants (fungi) that lack chlorophyll and can live without sunlight. The conflict due to the apparent contradiction brings into focus the inadequacies of their picture of plant life, reinforcing the lesson that the way of life of the green plants is not the only one possible in the plant kingdom and making the children particularly attentive to the significant characteristics of vital functions in fungi. Students of mathematics can likewise be motivated to acquire new symbolic structures by their initial encounters with paradoxical inferences, such as that the number of even integers is the same as the number of odd and even integers or that the number of points in a one-inch line segment is the same as the number of points in a one-mile cube.

PROGRAMED INSTRUCTION

Techniques of programed instruction are not counted as part of the discovery-method movement, but they, likewise, make use of intrinsic motivation and reward. The early teaching machines of Pressey (1926) presented the students with multiple-choice questions and required them to press a button indicating which they took to be correct. Here, perplexity conflict is presumably at work and is relieved when the machine moves on to the next question, showing the correctness of the last choice. An experiment of mine performed some years ago (Berlyne, 1954b) showed, in fact, that retention of facts was improved by first exposing subjects to multiple-choice questions which the facts to be remembered answered. The kind of teaching machine favored by Skinner (1954) requires the student to construct and supply the answer, whereupon he is given an opportunity to compare what he has supplied with the correct answer. In this case, motivation is likely to come from doubt and reinforcement from relief of doubt as the validity of the answer given is established.

There have long been disputes over whether knowledge of results, such as teaching machines provide, acts as a reinforcing agent or simply as a source of information (e.g., Annet, 1964;

Postman, 1947). If it reinforces, is this the kind of reward that can be attributed to drive reduction? Since information about the rightness or wrongness of the response causes an association to be strengthened more than it would be by contiguity alone, the information must be counted as a reinforcing agent. Although there are exceptional cases when unsought items of information are rewarding (as when one catches sight of a "Believe-it-or-not" cartoon in a newspaper), information is usually reinforcing only when the subject is in a state in which he feels the lack of it, i.e., a state of uncertainty that is also a state of raised drive or a motivational condition. Does information reduce drive? This is equivalent to asking whether the subject ceases to be in a state in which the item of information is welcome, and therefore rewarding, once the information has been received. It certainly seems that the provision of the same item of information a second or a third time will not be so powerfully rewarding as the first presentation, except when it has been forgotten between presentations. There are therefore grounds for answering this question affirmatively.

EVALUATION OF DISCOVERY METHODS

Ausubel (1961) has published a cautionary article, pointing out how shaky much of the evidence in favor of discovery methods is and suggesting that, in at least some circumstances, they may not be superior to more conventional methods at all. McConnell (1934), in one of the earliest relevant studies, found a discovery method of teaching arithmetical operations to produce less accuracy and speed than a drill method, although it facilitated transfer to different problems.

Anybody who has had contact with school children knows how much enthusiasm and alertness will be elicited by any departure from routine, a phenomenon well known to industrial psychologists as the "Hawthorne effect." He will be justifiably leery when he hears of zestful university professors, who have not had time to become jaded by the daily classroom grind, playing to responsive audiences for one-hour stands. But even if their novelty value were the sole reason for such success as they have, it should be remembered that novelty is one of the prime sources of intrinsic motivation and that ways of enlisting and putting it to work can surely be found by any imaginative teacher.

Another thought that readily occurs to one when witnessing exponents of discovery methods in action is that, apart from content, what they are doing is not very different from what able and zealous teachers have always done of their own accord. There must be a good deal of truth in this, but one of the aims of scientific research is surely to lay bare the workings of devices that creative individuals have arrived at through independent trial-and-error or through example and thus make them available to anyone.

The present state of knowledge calls incontrovertibly for caution in judging the potentialities of discovery methods and, above all, for intensive research on the psychological processes that they bring into play. Nevertheless, much about them is in tune with recent experimental and theoretical work on motivational problems, and it is highly significant that interest in them has sprung up simultaneously both in North America and in the Soviet Union (cf. Simon & Simon, 1963). Initial experience suggests that these new methods of instruction can substantially facilitate (1) retention of new material, (2) degree of understanding of new material, as shown by appropriate transfer and adaptation to new situations, (3) the eagerness and skill with which information is sought, (4) efficiency at solving problems by directed thinking, and (5) recognition of solutions to problems once they have been attained.

There are, in fact, indications that discovery methods can produce a qualitatively different kind of learning from traditional methods relying on rote memory and on passive absorption of facts, precepts, and habits, a kind of learning that works through "understanding," that interrelates items and builds up integrated structures of knowledge. This distinction recalls Wertheimer's (1945) distinction between "structurally sensible" learning, productive of "structural insight," and "structurally blind" learning, which works by "drill, by external associations, by external conditioning, by memorizing, by blind trial and error." It is also reminiscent of the contrast drawn by Piaget (1959), and further developed by Smedslund (1961a; 1961b), between the young child who is taught a logical mathematical or scientific truth before he is capable of understanding it and the older child who has mastered it in the normal course of development. The latter knows when to apply the principle to new situations and when not to, he defends it by appeal to deduction rather than to empirical observations that illustrate it, and he is resistant to giving it up when appearances are against it.

Discovery methods have two distinctive features. First, there is insistence that the student find solutions to problems through his own thinking or research. Secondly, there is systematic exploitation of intrinsic motivation and reward with a clearer-than-usual differentiation between an earlier phase in which the motivating conflict is induced and a later phase in which conflict is relieved by means of the response patterns that are to be acquired. These two features are, however, by no means inseparable. Independent discovery can be aimed at extrinsic or even highly mercenary goals, as in the traditional treasure hunt or in the case of the student who steals the answers to forthcoming examination questions. On the other hand, intrinsic motives can be skillfully aroused and assuaged by a writer or lecturer who wants his message to be trustfully accepted and assimilated.

The feeling that it is best for a student to search for answers by himself has derived support from at least two sources. One is the maxim, widely current among learning theorists, that, if a response is to be learned, it must be performed so that it can be followed by reinforcement. But there are by now plenty of indications that learning can occur in the absence of an overt muscular response. An internal response—a thought, a perception, an unuttered verbal statement—may be all that is elicited by a stimulus situation and retained to regulate motor activity on future occasions. Even a rat, a cat, or a dog will apparently learn its way round a maze or a room if it is carried from one point to another in a wheeled cage (see Berlyne, 1964). Human beings are evidently capable of a much wider range of "observational" or "vicarious" learning (see Bandura & Walters, 1963). Secondly, learning theory was for a long time dominated by animal experiments in which the response to be reinforced was first performed after a protracted period of trial and error. Until recently, little attention was paid to the various ways of abbreviating the search for the correct response and minimizing or eliminating random groping that are open to higher animals, especially human beings. These methods would include passive movement (e.g., guiding the hand of a child who is learning to write), imitation, verbal instruction, and reasoning. Mowrer (1950) once offered a definition of teaching (suggested by one of his students) as "the process whereby one individual enables another to learn something (solve a problem) more quickly than he would on the basis of his own trial and error behavior." It will be noted that the intervention of another individual—a teacher—is required by all of these shortcuts except the last—reasoning—and that contact with a teacher can immeasurably facilitate this one.

So while independent search may facilitate the exploitation of intrinsic motivation by bringing the subject sharply up against the latent incompatibilities within his knowledge systems and by adding the motivating contribution of frustration and surprise, it may not be essential, and it may even waste time unnecessarily. As Admiral Rickover· has pointed out, it may be possible to "grasp the principle of primitive looms in half an hour from a book" instead of spending "endless hours *reinventing* such things as how to make cotton, flax, and wool cloth, how to card wool, and so on." The element of enduring value in new teaching techniques, including discovery methods and programed instruction, the secret of whatever success can be claimed for them, the real germ of a pedagogical revolution, may well turn out to lie not in independent discovery but in the attempt to pinpoint and harness the sources of epistemic curiosity.

In 1835, Herbart stressed the desirability of presenting new material in such a form that it will be easy to relate to past experience and cause the reproduction of an "apperceptive mass of ideas" as a prerequisite for attention and interest. It is a truism, amply corroborated by experiments on verbal learning, that items with "high associative value" are relatively easy to retain and to preserve from confusion with others. Herbart (1824, 1825) realized that the tendency to perceive new events in terms of old ones must make us particularly sensitive to deviation from what is expected. "How a solecism grates in the ear of the purist!" he points out, "How a false note offends the musician or a breach of etiquette the man of the world!" Perhaps a prior, motivating phase, in which the new is made to clash with the old in this way, needs to precede the phase of assimilation. The pupil is thus made sensitive to the vulnerable points in his existing knowledge structures and receptive to new information that can remedy them. In other words, a question begins to gnaw at him. Every new item of knowledge is the answer to a question and is, we may assume, most readily ingested when the question is astir within the learner.

It seems likely that the peculiarities of the intelligent kinds of learning and thinking described by Wertheimer and by Piaget are largely due to their special dependence on intrinsic motivation. Wertheimer speaks metaphorically of "stresses and strains" within thought structures as factors inducing reorganization. Some recent experiments by Smedslund (1961c; 1961d) encourage the speculation that the child is led to abandon immature ways of thinking by having their inconsistencies brought home to him and that this is what moves him on to more advanced intellectual operations that are capable of relieving the conflict. From this point of view, we can see how learning motivated primarily by conceptual conflict should be especially conducive to interrelation and integration of items of knowledge, since conceptual conflict is relieved, with consequent reinforcement, only when discrepant combinations of responses are replaced by concordant ones (Berlyne, 1965). Furthermore, the connection between the response and the reinforcement is not arbitrary, like the connection between, say, bar-pressing and the receipt of a food pellet, but inherent. Only response patterns that relieve the motivating conflict, that, in other words, solve the motivating problem and thus further understanding and integration, are amenable to reinforcement by reduction of conceptual conflict.

The experimental analysis of attention and curiosity and interest is just beginning. As Dewey (1916) put it, "No one has ever explained why children are so full of questions outside of the school (so that they pester grown-up persons if they get any encouragement), and the conspicuous absence of display of curiosity about the subject matter of school lessons." [Sic.] When research has proceeded farther, this remark of Dewey's will be out of date, and the zest for action, including intellectual action, of the normal child that so often obstructs the teacher's efforts can be pressed into service as a potent ally.

REFERENCES

Abelson, R. P., and Rosenberg, M. J. Symbolic psychologic: A model of attitudinal cognition. *Behav. Sci.*, 1958, 3, 1–13.

Amsel, A. The role of frustrative nonreward in noncontinuous reward situations. *Psychol. Bull.*, 1958, 55, 102–119.

Annet, J. The role of knowledge of results in learning: A survey. In J. P. DeCecco (Ed.), *Educational Technology*. New York: Holt, Rinehart & Winston, 1964.

Anokhin, P. K. [Peculiarities of the afferent apparatus of the conditioned reflex and its significance in psychology.] *Vop. Psikhol.*, 1955, 1, 16–38.

Ausubel, D. P. Learning by discovery: Rationale and mystique. *Bull. nat. Ass. sec. sch. Princ.*, 1961, 45, 18–58.

Bandura, A., & Walters, R. H. *Social learning and personality development*. New York: Holt, Rinehart & Winston, 1963.

Berlyne, D. E. A theory of human curiosity. *Brit. J. Psychol.*, 1954, 45, 180–191. (a)

Berlyne, D. E. An experimental study of human curiosity. *Brit. J. Psychol.*, 1954, 45, 256–265. (b)

Berlyne, D. E. *Conflict, arousal and curiosity*. New York: McGraw-Hill, 1960.

Berlyne, D. E. Exploratory and epistemic behavior. In S. Koch (Ed.), *Psychology. A study of a science*. Vol. 5. New York: McGraw-Hill, 1963.

Berlyne, D. E. Emotional aspects of learning. *Annu. Rev. Psychol.*, 1964, 15, 115–142.

Berlyne, D. E. *Structure and direction in thinking*. New York: Wiley, 1965.

Bruner, J. S. *The process of education*. Cambridge, Mass.: Harvard Univer. Press, 1960.

Bühler, C., Hetzer, H., & Mabel, F. Die Affektwirksamkeit von Fremdheitseindrücken im ersten Lebensjahr. *Z. Psychol.*, 1928, 107, (Abt. 1), 30–49.

Dewey, J. *How we think*. Boston: Heath, 1910.

Dewey, J. *Democracy and education*. New York: Macmillan, 1916.

Festinger, L. *A theory of cognitive dissonance*. Palo Alto, Calif.: Stanford University Press, 1957.

Fiske, D. W., & Maddi, S. R. *Functions of varied experience*. Homewood, Ill.: Dorsey Press, 1961.

88   Learning and the Educational Process

Frenkel-Brunswik, E. Intolerance of ambiguity as an emotional and perceptual personality variable. *J. Pers.*, 1949, **18**, 108–143.
Hebb, D. O. On the nature of fear. *Psychol. Rev.*, 1946, **53**, 259–276.
Herbart, J. F. *Psychologie als Wissenschaft, neu gegründet auf Erfahrung, Metaphysik und Mathematik.* Königsberg: Unzer, Vol. 1, 1824; Vol. 2, 1825.
Herbart, J. K. *Umriss pädagogischer Vorlesungen.* Göttingen: Dieterich, 1835.
Jones, M. H., & Carterette, E. C. Redundancy in children's free-reading choices. *J. verb. Learn. verb. Behav.*, 1963, **2**, 489–493.
McClelland, D. C., Atkinson, J. W., Clark, R. A., & Lowell, E. L. *The achievement motive.* New York: Appleton-Century-Crofts, 1953.
McConnell, T. R. Discovery vs. authoritative identification in the learning of children. *Univer. of Iowa Stud. Educ.*, 9, No. 5, 1934.
Morozova, N. G. [The psychological conditions for the arousal and modification of interest in children in the process of reading popular scientific literature.] *Izvestiia Akad. Pedag. Nauk. R.S.F.S.R.*, 1955, **73**, 100–149.
Mowrer, O. H. *Learning theory and personality dynamics.* New York: Ronald, 1950.
Osgood, C. E., & Tannenbaum, P. H. The principle of congruity in the prediction of attitude change. *Psychol. Rev.*, 1955, **62**, 42–55.
Piaget, J. Logique et équilibre dans les comportements du sujet. In L. Apostel, B. Mandelbrot, & J. Piaget, *Logique et équilibre (Etudes d'epistém génét., II)*. Paris: Presses Universitaires de France, 1957.
Piaget, J. Apprentissage et connaissance. First part in P. Gréco & J. Piaget, *Apprentissage et connaissance (Etudes d'epistém génét., VII)*; Second part in M. Goustard, P. Gréco, B. Matalon, & J. Piaget, *Apprentissage et connaissance (Etudes d'epistém. génét., X)*. Paris: Presses Universitaires de France, 1959.
Postman, L. The history and present status of the law of effect. *Psychol. Bull.*, 1947, **44**, 489–503.
Pressey, S. B. A simple apparatus which gives tests and scores—and teaches. *Sch. & Soc.*, 1926, **23**, 373–376.
Rickover, H. G. *American education—a national failure.* New York: Dutton, 1963.
Simon, B., & Simon, J. *Educational psychology in the USSR.* Palo Alto, Calif.: Stanford University Press, 1963.
Skinner, B. F. The science of learning and the art of teaching. *Harvard educ. Rev.*, 1954, **24**, 86–97.
Smedslund, J. The acquisition of conservation of substance and weight in children: II. External reinforcement of conservation of weight and of the operations of addition and subtraction. *Scand. J. Psychol.*, 1961, **2**, 71–84. (a)
Smedslund, J. The acquisition of conservation of substance and weight in children: III. Extinction of conservation of weight acquired

'normally' and by means of empirical controls on a balance. *Scand. J. Psychol.*, 1961, **2**, 85–87. (b)

Smedslund, J. The acquisition of conservation of substance and weight in children: V. Practice in conflict situations without external reinforcement. *Scand. J. Psychol.*, 1961, **2**, 156–160. (c)

Smedslund, J. The acquisition of conservation of substance and weight in children: VI. Practice on continuous vs. discontinuous material in problem situations without external reinforcement. *Scand. J. Psychol.*, 1961, **2**, 203–210.

Sokolov, E. N. [The modeling process in the central nervous system of animals and man.] *Gagra Symposia*, 1963, **4**, 183–194.

Suchman, J. R. Training children in scientific inquiry. Paper read to the Society for Research in Child Development, Bethesda, Md., 1959.

Wertheimer, M. *Productive thinking.* New York & London: Harper, 1945.

Chapter 4

THE HIDDEN CURRICULUM IN THE MIDDLE-CLASS HOME

FRED L. STRODTBECK, *University of Chicago*

One alarming social problem in America today concerns those families who, despite our present efforts to help them, are still unable to rear their children in a way that will make them self-sufficient as adults. *Time* magazine expresses it this way:

> The tragedy of Harlem is that yet another generation of such men is being bred because they cannot break out of the vicious cycle of the ghetto: poor schooling, leading to a low-paying job or no job at all, leading to housing in a rundown neighborhood, leading anew to poor schooling for the children (*Time*, July 31, 1964, p. 16).

A generation ago, the comparable popular explanation would have started the cycle with reference to poverty; today it is started with a reference to poor schooling. It is no longer believed that the central problem is poverty because, in its grosser economic aspects, poverty alone could be remedied. Morgan (1962) has pointed out that for about ten billion dollars a year,

Prepared under Grant No. HEW-WA '24 (C1)-4-184 Research from The Social Security Administration. Reprinted from *Urban Education and Cultural Deprivation*, C. D. Hunnicutt (ed.), Syracuse, N.Y.: Syracuse University Press, 1964, with permission of editor and publisher.

the income of every family in the nation now below the subsistence level could be raised to it. Morgan views the problem of poverty as having become the dilemma of giving aid without creating continuing dependency upon governmental support.

At this moment, perhaps for the first time in the history of our nation, one can look objectively at the economic cost of maintaining the poor and know that we can afford this expenditure—*if* there is no long-range alternative. Most would be willing, however, to spend even more than that amount in efforts to discover an alternative which would reduce the magnitude of the long-range problem. As the *Time* quotation indicates, in Harlem and elsewhere in the great cities, it is to education that America is turning for a solution.

In such matters, one must find for himself the balance of optimism or pessimism which is best matched to his own involvement, but judging from past efforts, the chances of failure are great. Our most recent well-intentioned and single-minded effort to solve such problems has involved housing. As a prelude to the discussion of education, let me comment upon a recent study of the effects of public housing. I draw upon a "before and after" study of a carefully chosen sample of 600 persons who were moved from crowded tenements to public housing. The investigators, Wilner and others, regretfully concluded in their 1962 report that:

> In general . . . it is not clear . . . that the change from bad to good housing has brought . . . distinguishable alteration in relations among persons within the family (p. 159).

There was no greater freedom from illness, no difference in the rate of pregnancies, no improvement in the children's mean arithmetic and reading test scores. There was no change in concern for the larger community, no improvement in self-concept, and very little heightening of aspiration for the husband's job or the children's education. This study does report that the rehoused group liked the space they occupied better and their neighbors more—findings which, though positive, certainly fall below the community's expectations for what might be accomplished by improving housing at great public expense.

The mushrooming Aid to Dependent Children Program

(hereafter called ADC) is assumed to function like improved housing—it is supposed to provide partial rehabilitation by meeting short-run needs so that the families involved can later assume responsibility for their own welfare. Burgess and Price (1963), in a study of a national sample of 5,398 ADC cases closed in the first three months of 1961, reach very pessimistic conclusions as to the effectiveness of the rehabilitation. At the time their cases were closed, 68 per cent of all families in the sample earned less than 60 dollars per month. Forty-seven per cent of ADC children were either educationally retarded or out of school between the ages of 14 and 17. By 18 years of age, only 25 per cent had completed high school. Long-term evidence for failure of rehabilitation was provided by the large number of cases in which relief was a family tradition. Forty per cent of the recipients had grown up in homes which had received public assistance. Here again, one can only conclude that the combined efforts of public relief and the schools fall below reasonable expectations.

It is my fear that despite the limited success of housing and public assistance programs, there is still a disposition to see the problems of the dependent poor as if they were self-evident. Given the multiple handicaps of being fatherless, poor, and Negro, it scarcely seems necessary to call in a social scientist to see precisely why dependency results. Yet direct attacks on housing and supplementation of low income have not improved the situation. The schools have admittedly done poorly with the population in question, so why is it believed that they will be able to launch a more fundamental attack upon their problem? The current answer is that the schools are expected to modify their traditional methods. But is it self-evident that we know what modifications to make?

If one reasons that the curriculum of the school supplements the curriculum of the home, then the compensatory preparation of students from culturally deprived families may require an analysis of what is learned in the middle-class home.

THE ZACHARIAS REPORT

Despite the considerable sophistication of current approaches, the "hidden curriculum" I have in mind is often overlooked. To illustrate, I shall comment upon the recommendations for the education of the deprived and segregated made by the Panel on Educational Research and Development of the President's Science Advisory Committee (1964) often known as the Zacharias Committee. The population the Committee had in mind is the "difficult thirty per cent," a population larger than the children of the dependent poor, but inclusive of them. The suggestions of the Committee tended to be focused upon amelioration of the language deficit and included the following:

1. Special programs are needed for helping deprived children learn to read. One approach may be to concentrate first on spoken English, encouraging children to talk in school rather than constantly admonishing them to listen, and then encourage them in reading when they take it up (p. 32).

One might guess that the Committee wishes to encourage spoken-aural techniques for transforming direct, perhaps non-syntactic and dialectical speech into standard English before taking up the problems of a written language.

The Committee suggests that unreal situations be avoided, presumably in order to make the conditions of performance less discriminatory against lower-class children. This is elaborated as follows:

2. The culturally-deprived child may become frustrated when he reads about middle-class privileges (such as a boy's having his own room in the house). The answer may be to let the child develop his own story materials, thus giving children the freedom to shape the manner of his [sic] learning (p. 32).

In repeating these recommendations, I do not mean to infer that they are all especially good. Concerning this one, I must say that, having been frustrated when I read the *Just So Stories* (for not only did I not own a mongoose, I had never seen one) I am ill prepared to think about life protected from the knowledge of such relative deprivations. Carried to an extreme, being restricted to current reality could in itself be very unreal.

3. The deprived child should be taught arithmetic and science in intuitive, nonbookish ways (p. 32).

The Committee wishes science and arithmetic to be taught

in ways that will increase readiness to read, rather than making these subjects dependent upon reading skill.

4. Curriculum units can be designed which are self-contained and self-demonstrative; that is, units should be structured in a way which enables deprived children to discover things for themselves (p. 32).

This suggestion possibly grows out of the conviction that children, engaged in building the highest possible tower out of Plasticene, can see the results of their efforts immediately. The teacher can then present the theory of Calder's "stabiles" or some other exciting engineering perspectives. The Committee believes that such approaches will keep student interest high primarily because of the intrinsic stimulation of the materials and secondarily by avoidance of the ill effects of passive listening. Both curricular objectives may well increase the school adjustment of the deprived child without affecting his position relative to nondeprived children for, if these work as most reforms do, they will elicit even better response from the middle-class child.

5. The teacher should aim at developing "self-scrutiny, honesty, and careful observation" through social studies to the deprived. What the child needs is a growing knowledge of who he is and what kind of a world he is living in; much effort in this area is now destroyed by irrelevance, hypocrisy, and misplaced emphasis (p. 33).

The Zacharias Committee apparently assumed that they would need to work largely with persons who were not professional educators in order to gain support for this simple, uncamouflaged indictment of the current social studies curriculum. The Committe may well have identified an area in which the schools have needlessly lagged behind what the community would accept. It cannot be denied that there are "hot" topics relating to stratification which all children could better understand. But without greater specification, their brief statement is not too helpful in anticipating what the effects might be on the culturally deprived.

6. Deprived children should be encouraged to develop entrepreneurial skills and industry, such as those related to commerce. It is not enough just to understand the

world in which they live; they should also be taught the
need for inventiveness in developing new enterprises
(p. 33).

This suggestion I view as a kind of Bank Street Ben Frank-
linism. The economic part of the message does not seem sensitive
to the contribution which civil service or similar bureaucratic
employment makes to Negro adjustment. Opportunities which
provide an organizational structure and require little capital on
the part of the new recruit are of increasing importance to our
economy.

The Committee apparently believes that deprived children
need more unconditional demonstrations of affection from the
teacher, perhaps to compensate for a harsh home life. However,
if the suggestion that the teacher relate to deprived children
warmly is interpreted to encourage relating as a parental sur-
rogate, this may be inappropriate preparation for later non-
familial roles. More generally, throughout the Zacharias report,
there is little emphasis upon personality theory, the facilitation
of learning through identification, or the social psychology relevant to development.

The Committee, perhaps wisely, gives more emphasis to
the feasibility of institutional innovations such as keeping the
school open on what amounts to a settlement house schedule,
schools—not custodial nurseries—for the three- to six-year-old
children of the culturally deprived, expanding facilities into
buildings not designed as schools, and zoning schools with sufficient flexibility so that changes in residence will not inevitably
result in changes in enrollment. They further suggest using enthusiastic amateurs in voluntary programs, promotion according
to need in a nongraded elementary system, and teaching in
teams to increase specialization of teachers. The schools should
have music and art centers, the teachers more resource and conference rooms, and the students a $10 yearly book allowance to
be used for paperbacks in whatever subject the student may be
engaged. The Committee suggests that preservice teacher training internships of six months could be alternated with six-month
study periods which, on occasion, could be used for special
preparation related to curricular innovations.

The Committee is convinced that a school system is the

"natural unit" for reform. Hence subsystems comprising about 20,000 pupils and 30 principals would be the model size unit within a big city. The audacity of this suggestion, which might lead to a great university taking over such a segment, probably justifies the existence of the Committee. We will all be interested to see how well this one works out.

The Committee takes a somewhat radical but currently popular position on testing. The Committee is convinced that "whatever the shortcoming of tests as a means of grouping children in the more fortunate segments of the population, they are slight as compared with the tests for grouping the deprived and segregated" (p. 37). The Committee here alludes to their belief that abilities and achievement are more complex and subtle than any qualities the tests have been able to measure. There is very little research, they believe, on the nature of complex educational attainments, on acquisition of political ideals, style in writing, mechanical comprehension, etc. Given this state of affairs, the use of tests for guidance, college entrance, and job selection may unduly (perhaps "unfairly") fix the classification of a student. As a remedy, the Committee suggest that testing be made a matter of "local option," not an item to be required by the Superintendent. At the same time, they believe it would be good to devise tests which distinguish quickly between mental retardation and what for slum children can be regarded as pseudoretardation.

This treatment of testing is to my mind an intellectually inferior answer to the question, "Are Intelligence Tests Unfair to Culturally Deprived Children?" (Ausubel, 1963). Let us hope that America can be taught that tests measure achieved functional capacity. The earlier belief that they measure *innate* potentiality should be changed. The lower-class child's failure to develop test-taking skills, responsiveness to speed requirements, and familiarity with the specific vocabulary required should not be discounted as a matter of error in testing. These lacks are realities which affect the child's classroom performance, his future job performance, and his test score. The Committee, and all persons fundamentally concerned with the education of the culturally deprived, face a dilemma which grows from this reality. Should the school environment be engineered so as to filter away the importance of verbal intelligence, or should the school environment be modified so as to cultivate verbal intelligence more effectively?

In fairness to the Committee, they have probably reasoned that deprived persons can, with proper instruction, learn reading skills later and have concluded that it is a shame to impede the growth of mechanical and related competence by relying so heavily upon reading as a tool in the lower grades. Even so interpreted, it still seems to me that the Committee may inadvertently aggravate the problem it seeks to correct. They do not have any explicit premises about the different styles of language or the social organizational context which facilitates the development of particular verbal skills. In their emphasis upon the cognitive aspects of learning, they place little importance upon the role of verbal skills in maintaining interpersonal relations and motivation.

Not only are verbal skills of importance in the complex functioning of relatively established groups, they are also important in increasing one's vulnerability to involvement in group activities and, through this, to the shaping of motivation which group activity contributes. I believe that there are general linkages between organizational structures and verbal skill and that the understanding of such linkages, if they exist, is essential to the theory of compensatory education. More particularly, it is my guess that the conditions which facilitate the development of verbal ability in children relate much less to curricular stimulus material than to power differentials and organizational considerations.

THE CONCEPT OF PUBLIC AND FORMAL LANGUAGE

I am most particularly indebted to Basil Bernstein who, in his analysis of the difference between working-class and middle-class speech in England, elaborated the difference between so-called public and formal language. In our country, the gradients of usage may not be so sharply defined. For this reason, Bernstein's formulation is to be viewed as no more than a provocative hypothesis for the lower classes as a whole, but is probably much more descriptive of the difference between the language of the dependent poor and the middle classes. Thus public language is characterized by short, grammatically simple sentences which have poor syntax and are often unfinished. There is a repetitive use of conjunctions ("then," "and," "because"), and the verb is in the active mood. There are many short commands and questions, a rigid and limited use of adjectives and adverbs, and an avoidance of impersonal pronouns (such as "one" and "it") as subjects of sentences (Bernstein, 1959).

In a public language, Bernstein suggests, idiomatic phrases operate on a low level of causal generality in which descriptive, visual, and tactile symbols are frequently employed more to carry emotive impact than to develop meaning logically. In contrast, a formal language has accurate grammatical order and syntax. Logical modifications and stress are mediated through a grammatically complex sentence structure, especially through use of a range of conjunctions and relative clauses. Impersonal pronouns are frequently used as subjects of sentences. Logical relationships and temporal and spatial contiguity are carefully indicated by the frequent use of the appropriate prepositions. A wide range of adjectives and adverbs is used, and sequences of sentences are organized so that there are qualifications *between* as well as *within* them. (More evidence on these differences is presented by Walter Loban in Chapter 5.)

The difference between saying "Shut up" to a child in contrast to "Johnny dear, mother would prefer that you not make that noise just now" is the essential element of the style difference under consideration. The second version makes it clear to the speaker of formal language that the mother regarded Johnny as a good person, that she wanted him to stop but recognized that he might not if making noise were really important to him, and that making loud noises might be allowable at some other time than the present. The admonition to "Shut up" might not necessarily lead the child to conclude that he wasn't loved. The child might reason that the mother was feeling bad. However, he could hardly conclude that there might be some situation in which he could legitimately make noise. He would more than likely conclude that there were some persons with whom he might get away with it. Thus, while one can't identify how many of the contingencies are left open for interpretation after the first message, there are probably fewer after the second. Imbedded in the broader information set of formal language are premises about interpersonal relations which are different from those included in the public language in that they motivate further verbal exploration.

Bernstein assumes that public language is more appropriate for some purposes—all formal language speakers use public language on occasions. But not all public language speakers master formal speech. Some people do not have the skill to categorize by multiple criteria and indicate subtle gradations of relationships. Without this ability, reliance on public speech is absolute. There seems to be a disposition for the speaker restricted to public language to interpret or "translate" formal language communication into less precise public terms. A public language speaker may respond to a formal clarification simply by stating, "That's what I said," being unwilling to admit the importance of an alternate phrasing, which, when translated in his mind, is in fact no more precise. It is also possible for many lower-class persons to read for pleasure without modifying their spoken vocabulary, in part because they do not catch the subtleties of what they read, in part because they have so few opportunities to play roles in which they can comfortably respond in formal language. Expressed in terms of life styles, lower classes ask their visitor to take off his jacket and speak public language, the middle classes put on formal language when jackets are required, and the elite classes tend to talk formally at play and at work— and frequently even when drunk.

If one asks whether it is true that lower-class persons are more frequently limited to public speech, the answer would again seem to be yes. It is the next question that contains the catch: Why is this distinction maintained? Is it enough to say that lower-class children speak public language because their parents do, or because they, and their parents, have less education? Both are true, but do we make an error in assuming that because higher education and formal speech capacity are so often associated, it is education, particularly the bookish kind, which creates it? If we take the middle-class mother's elaborated suggestion that her child be quiet as simply an instance in which she is socializing her child to participate in a polite middle-class interaction, we may be correct. But we need a more analytic explanation if we are to identify fully the conditions which promote maximum refinement of verbal skills.

COMMUNICATION AND POWER RELATIONS

Consider for a moment two functions of the group, sociability and work. In sociability groups like cocktail parties, the importance of expressive gratification is high. The smaller the group, the greater the participation of each person; for this reason, people tend to break into groups of two or three. The conversation tends to be linked together only to the extent that it is necessary to build upon, or relate in a slight degree to, the remarks of the other. The conversation is thus continuously divergent (Riesman, Potter, & Watson, 1960). The topics frequently have the function of establishing the identity of the participant, or establishing the solidarity and value consensus of those present—frequently by judicious gossip about the behavior of persons who are mutually known. Such sociable interaction illustrates conditions under which participants are motivated to talk, and their remarks are under very mild review as to their relevance or accuracy.

Sociability groups may be compared with work groups in which problems of a routine nature are' reiteratively present. When such problems are handled by something like a family unit, the respective duties soon fall into patterned allocation and the resources for conversation are produced by the unfolding events of daily life. In such groups, if there is a democratic atmosphere, a consensus will grow about agreed-upon premises or norms. These serve as a kind of shorthand reference to previous conversations and conserve the time of the participants as they face daily decisions. The patent familiarity of this process sometimes hides from recognition the very complicated social behavior which is involved.

For example, the presence of both a father and a mother who are relatively equal in power provides a child with a motivation to attend closely to the state of normative integration. If he knows that the value emphasis of one parent is slightly different from that of the other, he is provided an incentive to act so as to win advantages from this insight. The task is made more complicated and challenging when there are great warmth and consensus between the parents. A child not only has to make his move at the right time with a strong case, he must also be sure that the ensuing action does not exceed the threshold of protest of the other parent, who might then, through the parental solidarity relation, object as a point of privilege. The existence of two persons of power with small value differences, yet parallel commitment to a core of common values, creates a situation in which careful use of language and recognition of subtle difference are required to attain personal goals.

More generally, secure membership in a relatively stable group creates motivation to attain collective goals which require further communication. The middle-class family needs a car which is clean, appropriate, and not too expensive, and a home in a neighborhood with good schools and similar people. Yet the new home must not entail an imprudent sale of the old house or the disruption of the adolescent children's high-school associations. The children must have many dates but not become too intimate. Commitments to bowling as opposed to work on the church newsletter must be balanced. These and things like them all proceed under the discipline of two economic processes. First, there is the economic allocation of money; second, there is the economic allocation of time.

So long as coparticipants have slightly different utilities to be achieved from expenditures of resources, the requirements for carefully monitored discussion are present. A premium is set upon accuracy in the description of the external world, consistency in argument, and, most importantly, awareness of the degree to which a given action impinges upon others.

In this somewhat ideal-typic description of the middle-class home, we do not imply that because of the surface appearance of equalitarian functioning, one cannot recognize the greater essential power of the parents. Parental pressure exceeds the resistance most children can mobilize but, importantly, only in those rare circumstances which require full mobilization of power. Role inductions in operating social systems can take place under conditions in which the full mobilization of power is only rarely required.

One important meaning of there being a correspondence between the norms of a family and the norms of the larger community relates to the absolute power of each member of the family. With the increase of integration into the larger community, there is an expansion of the gradations of inducement and resistance the participants can use as they argue the relevance of various norms for the action in question. The time required to review these considerations is democratizing because during the longer period required to reach a full showdown, extraneous events often produce some other challenge to the system of relationships. Such challenges may distract attention from the controversy by requiring a collective response which, if successful, adds to the solidarity of the system. A long-standing argument between a boy and his father over the boy's choice of a university may be more easily resolved after the two of them have worked together to paint the garage.

The importance of the duration of the period of assumed equality before a show of power may be illustrated by the example of a system in which the low-power person has little strength in the larger community and is convinced that his life opportunities depend upon his relationship with the stronger. When the tensions of the relation mount, the typical response of the low-power person is to escape by disengagement. To state the point in still another way, a low-power person will talk longest and most inventively in resistance to another's inducement when both are near middle rank in a system with normative consensus and when compliance with the other's inducement would reduce the actor's rank.

In family interaction studies (Strodtbeck, 1951; Strodtbeck, 1954) it is our observation that the ultimate disposition of the revealed difference is recognized by the three family members after about one-third of the conversation. The remaining two-thirds of the discussion is devoted to explaining how the original difference did not arise from a difference in values but rather from the different interpretations of the particular example. The family appears to act as if having the ultimate decision follow from previously agreed-upon norms produces a solution in which there is no loss of rank (in this instance the term "face" is also appropriate) as a result of the concession of one member to achieve consensus. The family's disposition to play and replay the game of verbal flourishes in the defense of rank is the source of the urge to talk well.

From this point of view one would avoid overestimating the importance of the sheer mass of printed and visual stimulus material which is found in a middle-class home. There are histories of isolated children having read themselves into a degree of specialization that formed the basis of their later career. This, obviously, could not have taken place if the materials were not present. But to a degree that few have recognized, good readership is motivated by the anticipation of the relevance that such information will have to later interaction. The problem encountered in the home and solved by reference to the encyclopedia both effects a change in information state which permits all participants to know what was decided and at the same time reassures the child that what he learns can be relevant to what he does. The relevance of an external and validated source of knowledge to the increase of an individual's absolute power is dependent upon the consensus in the group that validated knowledge can be the basis of action. This is particularly true for knowledge which has relevance for gratifications of the family at some time in the future. If a family's wherewithal to respond to expectations lags no more than might be made up by careful attention to detail, then it is possible to argue about and select the validated plans of actions which are believed to best meet family needs. Whenever it is clear that no matter how hard a family tries they cannot at the same time replace the car, have dental work done, rent extra space, etc., then an important tension goes out of the system. The motivation for verbal flourishes is lost. The delay to consider all factors is purposeless.

THE SITUATION OF THE DEPENDENT POOR

The stable lower class, who still meet necessary demands of a somewhat more limited spectrum of institutional expectations, tend to do so at the cost of expending their reserve. Their security system then becomes a set of social relationships in which the common themes communicated by public language prevail. Muir and Weinstein (1962) describe the attempt of the lower-class person

> to evolve a way of life that will reduce his insecurity and enhance his power in ways that do not depend on achievement in the universalistic sector and on command of a rich and sophisticated variety of perspectives. He can do this by forging a network of relationships, with people similarly circumstanced, that is in some ways like a mutual insurance scheme. People linked by such a network provide one another with a sense of status and worth, and also with aid and support in time of need . . . . Such a network differs from a conventional insurance scheme in that the kinds of benefits to which one is entitled are not specified in advance . . . but consist broadly of "help in time of trouble" . . . and of "doing whatever he can" when another is in need.
>
> If one has a sufficiently extensive network of such obligations, and he has honored his obligations in the past, there is probably some one he can turn to if ever he should need help . . . until he is "back on his feet." Title to these benefits is not tied to incumbency of specific roles, approaches through prescribed channels, or conformity to legalistic requirements. On the contrary the relationships are valued precisely because they are not hedged about by such conditions . . . they are diffuse, reciprocal, durable and particularistic (p. 538).

In contrast with lower-class persons, the dependent poor in the great cities suffer the even greater deprivation of being reduced to fearfulness of their neighbors. Let me illustrate this concretely with comments elicited from Negro mothers who are receiving Aid to Dependent Children. The comments were elicited by having the mothers listen to recordings of other Negro women's spontaneous comments upon what it means to be on ADC, how hard it is for a Negro man to get a job, why one doesn't want a man in the house if there are daughters, why it's foolish to think of marriage or divorce, etc. The mothers

talked from five to seven minutes after each stimulus recording
—their interviewer rarely spoke. She just nodded with interest
as the remarks were recorded.

This is a free response of one mother talking about the
threat of rape. The sentence structure has been slightly clarified
and the dialect eliminated, but otherwise the respondent is
quoted in the public language she used on the threat of rape as
she experienced it:

> We had that two times since I've been in the build-
> ing, but that's in the back apartment where you can see
> the husband, or whatever man is sleeping in, leave. The
> first time the man came on the first floor. He came
> through her kitchen window and he had a knife against
> her child and told her if she said anything he was going
> to kill her and so he tried to do it to the mama and she
> screamed and he went to get the child and that's when
> she got to the door. When she got to the door she left
> him in there with her child and that's the part I wouldn't
> have done. He'd just have had to kill me. She got the
> girl across the hall's husband to go down there and get
> that man out of her house. So when they got down
> there, he was gone.

The meaning of the triple locks Chicago Negroes place on
their doors may be inferred from the following comments on
transiency and fear of disasters.

> As soon as someone moves out, someone else moves in.
> Before you can get acquainted with them, they're moved
> out. They don't be there long enough for you to know
> their names. But all the old tenants from when I moves
> in there are gone.

And another mother commented:

> Because so much fires breaking out, I don't want to
> leave the children. It's hard to get somebody to keep
> them, it's dangerous to leave them by themselves. So
> that means I don't hardly get a chance to go nowhere.
> I'm scared to leave them at the house by themselves
> because so much fire breaking out. I just sit at the house
> all day long with the children. I just never go nowhere.
> I suspect that when I get around people I get nauseated,
> just nauseated. I just can't stand a crowd of people. I
> would like to go back to school, but my nerves are too

bad. I don't think I could take it. If I was there, my mind would be right back at home with my girl, she's a young lady now, and I'd be afraid to leave her in the house by herself.

To support the thesis that the isolated Negro mother's socialization strategy is designed to cope with violence from hostile neighbors, consider this mother's comment upon her style of child-rearing.

When I go to the store I tell the children, don't open that door for Jesus. And they won't, 'cause I know my worker came and he wouldn't let her in and she said but I'm Mrs. X and he said I'm sorry, but you can wait outside, and she'll be back and sure enough, I came in before she left the building and she said he wouldn't let her in and I said if he lets you in he might let someone else in. I told him don't open that door for Jesus. You know what that means. He's a spirit and that's the only thing that can go through. Anybody can say I'm the case worker.

The uneasy strategy that emerges is one of not getting too involved. One ADC mother stated it very reflectively: "I just visit a few people. If the group gets too big there's confusion. I have coffee every couple mornings with just two now. I used to be guilty of visiting around out of loneliness and lack of self-control. You need people around to do favors and fight loneliness." If you are too close to people, you can become overwhelmed by demands they might make in times of great need. A child can be taken care of while a friend comes in for a "nap," but more complicated actions relating to guard rails, letter boxes, or signal systems at the door, seem bafflingly difficult to arrange.

The way in which distrust of others prevents the growth of institutions which capitalize on cooperation was illustrated by the mothers' reactions to a hypothetical cooperative housing project. This project would have involved private apartments for the mothers and their small children, and dormitories for the older children. A common kitchen would have reduced the labor of food preparation. The negative reactions given revealed the mothers' lack of trust. They were concerned about the stealing of food and the possibility that some people would fail to carry their share of the responsibilities. Seven of the nine also rejected having their older children sleep away from them on the grounds that they would learn bad practices from others, it would lead to fights between the parents, and it would require excessive supervision. One mother felt that it might not be sanitary. Only one mother thought the children might not like it.

The rudimentary simplicity of the systems of relations of the ADC family starts of course with the absence of a continuously visible and effective father. Dealing with sexually differentiated adults who are in some degree in league with one another provides experience which helps one with a self-definition and also probably provides a sensible preparation for talking one's way through the complex bureaucracies of adult life. Just as the absence of membership in larger collectivities deprives the mother of external support, it also deprives a child of his family-based introduction to the complexity of role relations. Since mother's brothers are not important, the deprivation which attends the absence of a father is not compensated for. It is my guess that in the absence of such experiences with organizational complexity, an individual does not learn to see the actions of others as arising from organizational role expectations. Negro corner boys report no clear notion of who was boss on jobs from which they have withdrawn after having been placed by an employment counselor (Short & Strodtbeck, 1965). Persons who knock at a door are reacted to as if they loomed up out of a cloud; there is no premise about the organization which sponsored the visitors (Wilson, 1960). There is a disposition to assume that relations can continue so long as they are closely balanced as to the satisfactions provided. This implies that if either person chooses, the relation may be terminated and thereby cease to exist. There is no thought that a relationship bond will sustain an exchange which is seriously imbalanced over a protracted period. This is the crucial mechanism by which the reduction of absolute power undercuts the motivation for protracted verbal exploration of action possibilities.

One rarely goes into an ADC home without encountering another adult there. Yet in the interviews, many of the respondents insist that there is no one fo whom they can turn if they are in trouble. There is widespread evidence of an uneasy tension between the need to affiliate and fear of involvement. There is a code of cooperation against the threat of collectors and investigative agents, but the rapid shift in residence erodes the sense of security. If you have made friends once, you don't want to try again, at least not every six months.

The most profound insight we have won into the recurrence of the syndrome of poverty and low-educability is through the linkage of Negro mothers' sense of threat and their actions to socialize their children. In some practices they appear to set up in their children certain expectations which are sharply frustrated. They wean children later, but more abruptly; they feed on demand and report few feeding problems; and they start bowel training later but take less time than the Sears, Maccoby, and Levin (1957) middle- and lower-class mothers. Their children are more frequently eneuretic and continue to be so at later ages. Negro ADC mothers are less responsive to crying and less punitive toward dependency. They exert strong pressure against masturbation and sex play and are strict in modesty training. They are not permissive of aggression toward parents and siblings, and they place more restrictions upon physical mobility. Although they expect less of the children in terms of performance of household tasks, they are more strict about obedience.

The ADC mothers' training techniques include more physical punishment and little use of praise, positive models, and reasoning. Isolation and withdrawal of privileges are rare. They reward and punish their children immediately and their children are rarely required to delay gratification. The failure to discipline in terms of language symbols as well as the related dependence upon physical means of punishment reduces the necessity for cognitive mediation in impulse control. The child gets much less assistance in discovering the relationship between his behavior and the responses it is likely to elicit.

A middle-class mother would be surprised by the amount of the Negro ADC mother's energies which go into admonishing the child to "be good" instead of rewarding and punishing for acts freely entered into. In the context of an overcrowded living space, "being good" means being physically inactive, verbally nonparticipative, and nonobservant. It is not that the achievements of the child are negatively viewed; rather, it is the "trouble" that achievement activity may lead to that is so consistently avoided. The mothers are extremely vulnerable to threat which is serious and unpredictable, and their children—above all else—are taught to be generally fearful rather than selectively cautious.

IMPLICATIONS FOR INTERVENTION

The conclusion to be drawn from this analysis is that in the degree the Negro ADC mothers and Negro gang boys studied in Chicago are representative of culturally deprived persons, the educational intervention must reduce fear and motivate verbal participation by increasing the absolute power of the child in the school setting. Middle-class educational objectives cannot be seriously undertaken in the absence of some equivalent of stable lower-class security systems.

Beyond this, the children must be given the opportunity to make decisions and then be permitted to suffer the consequences of their decisions. If they have book stamps which may be spent for classroom materials, each student must have some say as to how his stamp is used. If every child chooses to buy the same book, the class must be given the opportunity to see how much better another class has done in obtaining a variety of books. If the class chooses to decorate their room in a garish way, they must live in it also. If factions grow concerning the allocation of resources, they should be encouraged to test alternatives which do not lead to the immediate amalgamation of the factions.

There should be student organizations broader than a given classroom. Through these organizations, the students must be given the opportunity to make suggestions for administrative consideration which are not cleared by their teachers. Each child should have a friendly contact with an adult in the school who is as powerful as the child's teacher, but who has no authority over the child. Older children should be given the motivation of reducing the length of their school day by getting their work done early. They should be permitted to organize so as to participate in the determination of what is a fair day's work.

These suggestions may never be tried, or, if they are tried, they may be defective in detail, but the underlying principle should be clear. The broader a range of problems an individual approaches as a member of a group, and the larger the number of working groups participated in, the greater his experience in explaining the external situation and in taking the role of the other in order to increase the relevance of his attempt to get the group to follow a given course of action. Though the implications of this process are profound, the preparation for it occurs almost unconsciously in primary groups whose members have different skills, work to do, and a concern about consensus, that is, in groups like the middle-class family. It is this hidden curriculum, which is absent from both the schools and the culturally deprived family, which must be added to accomplish the objectives of compensatory education.

REFERENCES

Ausubel, D. P. The influence of experience on the development of intelligence. Paper read at a conference on Productive Thinking in Education, Washington, D.C., 1963.

Bernstein, B. A public language: Some sociological implications of a linguistic form. *Brit. J. Sociol.*, 1959, **10**, 311–326.

Burgess, M. Elaine, & Price, D. O. *An American dependency challenge.* Chicago: American Public Welfare Association, 1963.

Henry, J. Spontaneity, initiative, and creativity in suburban classrooms. In G. D. Spindler (Ed.), *Education and culture.* New York: Holt, Rinehart & Winston, 1963. Pp. 215–233.

Morgan, J. N., et al. *Income and welfare in the United States.* New York: McGraw-Hill, 1962.

Muir, D. E., & Weinstein, E. A. The social debt: An investigation of lower class and middle class norms of social obligation. *Amer. sociol. Rev.*, 1962, **27**, 532–539.

Panel on Educational Research and Development of the President's Science Advisory Committee. *Innovation and experiment in education.* Washington, D.C.: U.S. Government Printing Office, 1964.

Riesman, D., Potter, R. J., & Watson, Jeanne. Sociability, permissiveness, and equality: A preliminary formulation. *Psychiatry*, 1960, **23**, 323–340.

Sears, R., Maccoby, Eleanor, & Levin, H. *Patterns of child rearing.* Glencoe, Ill.: Row, Peterson, 1957.

Short, J. F., & Strodtbeck, F. L. *Group process and gang delinquency.* Chicago: Univer. of Chicago Press, 1965.

Strodtbeck, F. L. Husband-wife interaction over revealed differences. *Amer. sociol. Rev.*, 1951, **16**, 468-474.

Strodtbeck, F. L. The family as a three-person group. *Amer. sociol. Rev.*, 1954, **19**, 23–29.

Wilner, D. M. *The housing environment and family life.* Baltimore: Johns Hopkins Press, 1962.

Wilson, J. Q. *Negro politics: The search for leadership.* Glencoe, Ill.: The Free Press, 1960.

Chapter 5

LANGUAGE PROFICIENCY AND SCHOOL LEARNING

WALTER LOBAN, *University of California at Berkeley*

Regardless of any philosophical differences men may have about education they agree in assigning great importance to thinking and reasoning. To develop the powers of reasoning becomes a central purpose of education (National Education Association, 1961). Most thinking and reasoning depend upon ability with language. Man's control over nature depends upon his skill with language, his ability to use words as symbols. Without language human thought is severely limited. A fundamental difference between the animal and human worlds is linguistic: animals can use and understand *signs;* they cannot cope with *symbols.* A growl, a call, even a green traffic light—signs like these, directly tied to concrete situations—can take on meaning for animals as well as for human beings. Symbols, however, are instruments of complicated thought. Unlike signs they are not necessarily tied to the immediate situation. By means of symbols human beings can allude to objects or concepts even in the absence of those objects or concepts. The language human beings use for discourse is therefore a system of arbitrary symbols used to designate concepts, relationships, and things, thus making complex thought and reason possible.

This language system can be enlarged to name new concepts, such as *camouflage* in 1918 or *jet plane* in 1960. Response to a linguistic symbol in the system is contingent upon the symbols with which it is combined. For instance, in English-speaking communities, response to the symbol *crop* differs in the following three sets of utterances because of the accompanying symbols:

The stone stuck in the bird's crop.
She carried a riding crop in her hand.
The shepherd watched his sheep crop the grass.

The next two utterances elicit strikingly different responses because of a single symbol, *not*.

Go away!
Do not go away!

Thus in any human language, a system with arbitrary symbols in contingencies of relationship makes possible advanced thought.

Without symbolic language, there would be among men no civilization, no passing on of cultures. The signs used by animals never become language for discourse because animals are incapable of separating the signs from the particular concrete situations in which the signs are embedded. No evidence of animals having made the leap from signs to symbolic language, to words freed from concrete situations and arranged in systems and contingencies, has ever been verified.[1] Until the day she learned *w-a-t-e-r* as a symbol and thereby *disassociated it from any particular wetness*, Helen Keller lived the life of a gifted animal using signs. On that day, in a spectacular leap, she extended her potential limits to the mental horizon of the human family. Human beings use signs, of course, but they also use symbols. Without symbolic language there would be no formation of concepts, no dominance of abstract knowledge over concrete knowledge.

Growth in this use of symbolic language involves a complex of factors. Presumably the development of an individual's proficiency with language depends upon the relation between the

---

[1] A discussion of animals' use of signs and sounds may be found in Chapter V of *Words and Things* by Roger Brown (1958). The ideas in this paragraph are indebted to the discussion by Langer (1942).

individual and his environment. The child who is acquiring linguistic skill should have vitality and health; he should also have an environment fostering exploration, an active approach to experience, and a confident attitude toward trying and using language. Thus language development appears to be affected by numerous factors, all varying simultaneously and in complex interrelationships. In the interests of establishing a guiding theory for the research reported in this paper, some of these factors have been identified tentatively. An attempt has been made to list here, in the order of their presumed importance, those biological and environmental factors contributing most prominently to language development:

Environmental Factors	*Biological Factors*
security in relations with parents (or parent surrogates) and other authority symbols	glandular balance and total biological homeostasis
degree of facility in family use of language (usually, but not always, this factor will vary in the same direction as socioeconomic status)	energy (rate and balance of metabolism and whatever else contributes to energy)
amount, variety, and quality of language heard and used in the family (conversation, stories, table talk, etc.)	physical facility in speech production; motor controls of speech organs
variety of experience including much nonthreatening, self-enhancing interaction with other people and opportunity to verbalize this experience	visual acuity and spatial perception
encouragement and opportunity for self-expression, not only in language but in other ways also	hearing acuity

adequate balanced diet (over a period of time)	tactile acuity
sufficient rest (over a period of time)	immunity to disease

instruction that focuses attention on the principles of effectiveness in language (such instruction would occur as much as possible in problem situations involving the child's interests and drives)

It is possible, also, that nervous systems vary biologically in adequacy and in capacity to integrate electrophysical nerve impulses into those patterns by which perceptions become transformed into symbols. Whether or not such variations at the deepest physical and chemical levels do or do not exist in human beings of varying verbal skill is not known, but it is certainly interesting in this matter to know that maze-bright and maze-dull animals differ in brain chemistry (Rosenzweig, Krech, & Bennett, in press). Certainly, one can agree that *regardless* of biological endowment, positive changes in the *environmental* factors listed above should contribute to improved language skill. Children with the most fortunate combination of both biological and environmental factors should develop controls over symbolic language earlier and more effectively than children with less fortunate combinations of these factors.

All living is a process of adjustment, and language is one means by which individuals satisfy needs and accommodate frustrations. Obviously language cannot dispel hunger or subzero weather, but since Cro-Magnon man the race has had sufficient control over the physical environment to make possible a shift from biological to cultural evolution. With the advent of language, social evolution became possible, an evolution much more rapid than biological evolution.

In cultural matters, therefore, where symbols occupy a central position, language is a common means of adjustment, so much so that a child who is either deprived as Strodtbeck described in Chapter 4, isolated, or overly protected may acquire only the lowest levels of language skill. Language develops best in situations where individuals feel a need to express themselves and seek to be understood and where individuals have a deep interest in receiving communication, either through listening or through reading. This would mean that children who are, for whatever reason, much alone or who play with only one other child, such as a twin, will develop less skill in language than those who have genuine language interaction with other children and adults. This language interaction, often called reciprocal reinforcement of language, is an important form of learning symbols as a means of adjustment to the social environment.

Language proficiency develops through a sequence, a series of developing controls of meaningful forms—for instance, the ability to handle pronouns according to convention; the use of subordination instead of coordination to show relationships more adequately; the accurate and consistent use of verb tense; the exact use of relational words such as *until, although, however.* All these and more develop earlier in some children than in others. The rapidity with which these attainments occur and the order in which they occur among individuals will probably vary, but a general picture of the situation deserves to be revealed empirically. Through research, base lines may be charted for more effective instruction, and for individual children the relative stages of growth can be determined.

Which of such identifiable language attainments will appear early and which ones late? Their order, presumably, will be conditioned by the requirements of language situations as well as by the successful combinations the speaker has already mastered. Regressions will occur in situations of social threat, and previous accomplishments will require relearning in the setting of new, more complicated expressions. Very likely, the order and duration of these stages of growth will vary with individuals. Although no precise formula can be imposed on this development of language power, an accurate description should reveal order and pattern rather than obscure accident.

These stages of language growth are related to socioeconomic status and to home environment. In an increasing number of research studies, socioeconomic status shows a positive relation to language proficiency, and the extent to which a child utilizes his linguistic abilities and potential is influenced by his home environment. It is not at all impossible that by finding out more concerning language and how children use language in thinking and learning we can increase the educational potential of large numbers of children, especially those from the least favored socioeconomic groups of society.

A STUDY OF LANGUAGE DEVELOPMENT

The study reported here concerns the verbal learning of children from the time they were in kindergarten until the present when most of them are in the last year of high school.

SAMPLE

The subjects were in 1952 a representative group of 338 kindergarten children. At regular intervals over a period of 12 years, comparable samples of their language have been collected, and 214 subjects are still in the study. The samples of language—speech, writing, and reading—have been drawn once a year from controlled situations identical for all subjects. Listening tests have been given since Grade 8.

In addition to the larger representative group of subjects, two special subgroups have been selected from the total sample. These two subgroups consist of subjects representing extreme deviations from the mean of the total sample. In the first special subgroup are those ranking extremely high in language proficiency; in the second subgroup are those extremely low in language ability. For these two special subgroups more extensive data have been gathered and analyzed.[2]

---

[2] The basis of selection was the average of ten years of teachers' ratings of the subjects' language ability. This criterion was used in lieu of any better or established standards of general language proficiency. By means of this criterion as a temporary way of selecting subgroups, the experimenter proposes to locate empirically more refined evidence of language proficiency.

After 12 years, the number remaining of the original 338 is 214, a remarkably high retention figure. The aim is to retain as many as possible, with the expectation that 200 of the original 338 subjects will still be available for study at the twelfth grade level. Further details on this study are available in two reports (Loban, 1963; Loban, 1964).

The subjects used were chosen to represent a stratified sample of a larger universe of children. Eleven kindergarten classes were matched with family backgrounds typical of the city of Oakland, California. Thus subjects included a range of family status from definitely poor economic circumstances in the industrial areas down by the Bay through the middle-class areas up to the more favored socioeconomic circumstances of the hilltop districts. The evidence on socioeconomic status for the subjects in this research places the median at middle class.[3]

However, stratification was not tied to one particular variable such as socioeconomic status. The choice of subjects also included representativeness on the bases of sex, racial background, and spread of intellectual ability. Care was taken to avoid any unique or unusual factor of selection. In other words, these four general stratification variables were used, together with proportional allocation. The characteristics used for defining the strata were chosen because other studies of children's language have identified socioeconomic status, sex, and intelligence as factors related to language proficiency.

Of the 338 subjects initially in this study, 156 were male and 182 were female in the age range of 5.0 to 5.9 years. The percentage of Caucasian (62.4%), Negro (32.0%), and Oriental (5.6%) approximates very closely the current percentages of these racial groups in Oakland (a city of about 385,000). Measures of intelligence (Kuhlman-Anderson) for this same group (administered in second grade) reveal a mean of 102.5 and a standard deviation of 9.18. The sample provides clear evidence of representing the school population of Oakland. Oakland, in turn, is assumed to be typical of the urban center in twentieth-

---

[3] For these subjects the median score is IV, which is also the median of the *Minnesota Scale for Parental Occupations*.

century America: a population varying in religion, ethnic and national backgrounds, and socioeconomic conditions.

DATA COLLECTION

Each subject was interviewed individually and his spoken responses recorded annually on either a tape or a similar recording device (the Audograph). Each interview followed a standardized form, and, when an extra question was asked, the purpose was solely to encourage a flow of language already on its way. At the beginning of the interview, the examiner encouraged the subject to become talkative by asking him questions about playmates, games, television, illness, and wishes. Next the subject was shown, for the remainder of the interview, a series of six pictures, the same pictures being used for all subjects. The pictures were chosen for their interest, their success in preliminary trials, or their value in previous research. The subjects were asked to talk about what they saw in each picture and what each picture made them think about. The recorded interviews were then transcribed into typewritten form according to a careful set of directions.

Additional data include measures of the subjects' intelligence and evidence of achievement in vocabulary, use of relational words (such as *however, consequently*), and achievement in reading, writing, and listening. In addition, for each school year, the teachers rated the subjects on selected language factors and kept accurate records of school attendance. Background information on homes, parental occupations, health, siblings, and date of birth completes the data.

SEGMENTING THE SUBJECTS' ORAL LANGUAGE

In this research, devising an objective method for segmenting the flow of oral language was a critical problem. Certain familiar systems of dividing language into segments proved to be inadequate. Words alone, for instance, offered a crude basis for numerical count and showed nothing about relations among words. The traditional grammatical division, the sentence defined as the expression of a complete thought, blurred important distinctions and often did not correspond to the actuality of oral language where utterances may be only phrases or single words. The system of segmentation finally chosen was one which combined several approaches. First the subject's speech was segmented by oral intonation signals and then, within such intonation segments, syntactic units (each independent predication) were identified.

1. The first of these methods of segmenting language—intonation—is dependent upon the patterns of sound made by the human voice; it is judged by the contours of pitch, stress, and pause in the subjects' voices. Because the segmentation is made in accordance with the sound-system of English, this first and more comprehensive segment will be called a *phonological unit.*

2. The second unit, always a subdivision of the larger phonological unit, will be called a *communication unit* because it can be identified by the semantic meaning being communicated.

3. Beyond these two kinds of segmentation, a third element still remained to be accounted for, an exceptionally interesting and frequent occurrence, best described as a tangle of language not making semantic sense and impossible to classify phonologically or semantically. These language tangles have, therefore, been segmented separately and have been labeled *mazes.*

The third kind of segmentation, the *mazes,* are a series of words or initial parts of words which do not 'add up, either to meaningful communication or to structural units of communication as defined in this research. They are unattached fragments or a series of unattached fragments which do not constitute a communication unit and are not necessary to the communication unit.

Sometimes the mazes are very long, consisting of from ten to twenty or more fragments of words. Sometimes the subjects persevere with the ideas they are trying to formulate and, at the end of the maze, do achieve a unit of communication. Other times the subjects abandon the ideas they are trying to express, perhaps finding the problem too difficult or too tiring to express, or not worth the effort. It is entirely possible that in another situation, where the motivation was much greater, the same thoughts represented by the maze might find their way to a clear expression of meaning. The energy level or the health of the subject may also be decisive factors in the child's success or failure in converting an idea into a genuine unit of communication.

SOME FINDINGS

The findings of the research just described are briefly summarized here. For more detailed presentation of the study, the reader may wish to turn to the original publications (Loban, 1963; Loban, 1964).

Fluency with Language

1. During the first ten years of schooling, the subjects speak more words in each succeeding year of measurement; the same is true of the number of communication units, although after Grade 6 the rate of increase on this measure slows considerably as a result of the subjects' using more complexity (reflected by a higher *average* words *per* communication unit). The measurement of average words per communication unit is of particular interest. For all groups there is a steady increase indicating more complexity of expression, but the high group always maintains a *sizable lead* on this measure. Thus the high group uses more words, more units, and greater complexity than does the low group and maintains its initial superiority over those low in language ability. The fact that members of the high group use more communication units than do members of the low group is of particular significance because they are also, through greater subordination, reducing the number of units they need for expression. Even so, they produce *more* units than the low group.

2. During the first four years of schooling, the subjects as a whole decrease the number of mazes and words in mazes, but the average number of words in mazes increases for the low group. After Grade 3, both groups *increase* the amount of mazes and words in mazes while *reducing* their average words *per* maze. In the later years (Grades 4 through 9) it becomes increasingly apparent that one must look not at raw figures alone but at percentage relationships. When this is studied it becomes

obvious that the high group has *far lower a proportion* of mazes and words in mazes than does the low group. Thus subjects rated as skillful in language are reducing their *proportion* of mazes and words in mazes *as well as* reducing their average words per maze. In other words, the low group says less than the high group and some of them have more difficulty in saying it.

3. At the kindergarten level, subjects proficient in language have a median score of 67 on a vocabulary test of 100 items and the subjects low in language ability have a median score of 35. Vocabulary and proficiency in language appear to be related at the kindergarten level.

4. A type-token analysis comparing the number of *new* words used in each 100-word segment of language indicates that the high group uses more types (new words) per number of tokens on a segment-by-segment, year-by-year basis. Thus the high group shows greater diversity of vocabulary.

5. An analysis of *height* of vocabulary using the Thorndike-Lorge word counts on frequency of word occurrence indicates a definite superiority on the part of the high group. *New* words appearing in each succeeding segment of 100 words were rated, and it was found that the high group uses not only more new words but also more words in every Thorndike-Lorge category. Thus the high group shows greater diversity of vocabulary *and* greater height of vocabulary.

6. As measured by spoken style of language, the high group is significantly more fluent than a random group selected from the total sample, but their readiness of response does not differ from the random sample. Readiness of response was measured by timing the silence between presentation of pictures or questions and the subjects' first word of response. The low group is less fluent than the random group, and there is evidence that they may be somewhat slower to respond orally. The possible implications of this result for the impulsive-reflective dimension described by Kagan in Chapter 6 may bear further study.

Effectiveness and Control
   Structural patterns.
   1. The low group uses many more partial expressions—sentence patterns that are incomplete—than does the high group.

2. The high group employs the linking verb sentence pattern to a greater extent than does the low group. This is accounted for by the fact that more Negroes who use dialect (and thus avoid the verb *to be*) are in the low group. The presence and absence of linking verb sentence pattern are exemplified in such sentences as "He is a good dog" versus "He a good dog."

3. Except for the linking verb pattern and the use of partials, the *median* differences in structural patterns used by the two groups are negligible. This similarity in the use of patterns in oral language is considered to be an important finding of this study, especially when considered in relation to the findings which immediately follow.

Elements within the structural patterns.

4. Although differences in structural patterns are not notable—with the exception of partials and linking verbs—very important differences do show up in the dexterity with which subjects use elements *within these structures.* For instance, in the English language, a *nominal* such as the subject of a sentence may be a single noun, a gerund phrase, an infinitive, a dependent clause, or several other arrangements of words. The nominals, whether in subject or object position, and the movable elements show marked differences when low and high groups are compared. The high group always has a larger repertoire. This holds true consistently for any syntactical nominal structure. This finding on the elements of structural patterns is considered to be one of the important findings of this study and should be considered in relation to the findings (above) on the similarity of structural patterns. *Not pattern but what is done to achieve flexibility within the pattern* proves to be a measure of effectiveness and control of language.

5. In the movable elements of the patterns (such as adverbs, many phrases and clauses) the high group consistently shows a greater repertoire of clauses and multiples (movables within movables).

6. For subject nominals, the low group depends almost exclusively on nouns and pronouns. The high group can use noun clauses, infinitives, and verbals, a larger repertoire for achieving flexibility of structure and nuances of meaning.

7. For nominals used as complements, both groups use nouns and pronouns with the same frequency, but the high group invariably exceeds the low group in the use of infinitives and clauses, another example of flexible structure to achieve shades of meaning.

8. Boys in the low group are clearly more limited in their repertoire of syntax than girls in the low group. On the other hand, boys in the high group tend to excel the girls in the high group.

Tentative thinking through the use of provisional and conditional statements.

9. Those subjects most proficient with language are the ones who most frequently use language to express tentativeness. Supposition, hypothesis, and conditional or concession statements occur much less frequently in the spoken language of those lacking skill in language.

Figurative language and generalizations.

10. Very few examples of figurative language or of analogies or generalizations occur in the oral transcripts of the subjects' language, high or low.

Reading and writing.

11. Those high in oral language ability are also high in reading ability. Those who are low in oral language ability (the low group in this study) are also low in reading ability. In addition, the gap between the high and the low groups is apparently widening from year to year.

12. Reading ability is related to socioeconomic position. As one goes down the socioeconomic scale, reading ability steadily decreases.

13. Those who are high in oral language ability (the high group) are also high in writing ability. Those low in oral language ability (the low group) are also low in writing ability.

14. Writing ability is related to socioeconomic position. As a subject places lower on the socioeconomic scale, his writing ability decreases.

Coherence through the use of subordination.

15. All subjects show an increasing use of subordination as chronological age increases. They achieve coherence and empha-

sis in a sentence by subordinating some ideas to others, using dependent clauses, participial and infinitive phrases, gerunds, and appositives.

16. The boys in the low group use consistently less subordination than do the girls in the low group. On the other hand, the boys in the high group exceed the girls in four out of the first seven years of their schooling.

17. An analysis of subordination on written language indicates that the high group is superior on this measure to both the low group and the total group for all years except Grade 9. In Grade 9 the total group actually exceeds the high group, and this development is being followed in order to determine if it is a new trend or merely a quirk in the data.

18. Complexity of grammatical structure is associated not only with chronological age but also with proficiency in language and with socioeconomic status.

Coherence through the use of subordinating connectives.

19. The use of subordinating connectives increases with chronological age, mental ability, language ability, and socioeconomic status.

Summary of Mastery of Conventional Usage

A preliminary study of the data indicated that some deviations are ethnic in origin and as a result three special subgroups were selected. These were designated High Caucasian, Low Caucasian, and Low Negro, in terms of language proficiency.

1. At the kindergarten level, on the agreement of subject and verb in the third person singular (excluding all forms of the verb *to be*), the Low Negro group (which uses a dialect rather than standard English) has 12 times as much difficulty as the Low Caucasian group and over 100 times as much difficulty as the High Caucasian group. By Grade 9 the Low Negro group has improved considerably on this agreement but still has substantially more difficulty than either Caucasian group.

2. At the kindergarten level, on the omission of auxiliary verbs, the Low Negro group has 5 times as much difficulty as the Low Caucasian group and 16 times as much difficulty as the High Caucasian group. Again, the Low Negro group improves considerably by Grade 9.

3. On the use of nonstandard verb forms, the Low Negro group has twice as much difficulty as the Low Caucasian group and four times as much difficulty as the High Caucasian group. Again the Low Negro group shows improvement by Grade 9.

4. On total deviations from standard speech there is an abrupt increase at Grade 5 for both low groups and a slight increase for the High Caucasian group. This indicates that as complexity increases (demonstrated by an increased average words per unit), there is a *more than proportional increase in deviations from accepted English usage.*

Interrelations Among the Language Arts

At all grades, those who read well also write well, have the highest oral language ratings, and perform best on listening tests. The medians, interquartile ranges, and scatters (on those data presented on scattergrams) indicate clear and positive relationships when any language art is compared to any other. There is overlapping to some degree as indicated by the total ranges on various measures and the dispersion on scattergrams, but for the most part these are individual exceptions.

Language and Social Class

Because the socioeconomic rank of the high group exceeds that of the low group, it appears that coherence through subordination is also related to social class. The importance of social class in relation to language appears not only on this matter of subordination but also on the measures of writing, mazes, subordinating connectives, reading, and conventional language. Bernstein (1960), on the basis of research with British working-class youth, found language proficiency grossly depressed in relation to scores on a nonverbal intelligence test. He believes the level of linguistic skill may be independent of potential intelligence and that different environments affect language structure. The linguistic differences he finds between working-class youth and middle-class youth do not, in his view, reflect differences in potential capacity. Rather they represent entirely different forms of the English language, forms which systematically orient children to differing relationships with people and the world about them. The middle class, for instance, uses forms of speech "in which the arrangement of syntax varies greatly from one individual to another and in which the formal possibilities of sentence organization are used to clarify meaning and make it more explicit" (p. 273). The lower working classes show a "rigidity of syntax, a limited and restricted use of the structural possibilities for sentence organization, a form of relatively condensed speech in which certain meanings are restricted and the possibility of their elaboration . . . reduced . . ." (p. 274).

Nothing in the present research with subjects on the West Coast of the United States controverts Bernstein's findings or conclusions. It also seems entirely possible that subjects from the least favored socioeconomic categories can find themselves at a disadvantage in schools where the verbal linguistic skills of the middle class prevail. Such subjects may find themselves increasingly ill at ease and self-conscious to the point of avoiding oral performance. Such avoidance could, in turn, progressively affect performance in the related activities of reading and writing and in the present study could quite logically account for the larger number of mazes among the children in the low subgroup.

LANGUAGE AND LEARNING

"Give me the right word and the right accent, and I will move the world." Thus Joseph Conrad paid tribute to the power of language to influence the thought, feeling, and action of others. But language is also the means by which an individual exercises some degree of control over his own thinking and receives the culture. His language does not stand apart from experience but interpenetrates with it. Nor is language merely a vehicle for thought; rather both are interdependent. If children from the least favored classes do not have the development of language which makes possible more exact or more insightful thought, they will be handicapped in their learning and in their ability to cope with life's problems, as Strodtbeck has pointed out in Chapter 4. This may, of course, be true of any child, wealthy or poor, whose experiences in language are not favorable to his learning. Milner's study (1951) shows that differences in readiness to read are related to verbal attainment. A richer verbal environment in the home, more books, being read to by adults, meals with parents, and talking with parents characterize the backgrounds of children advanced enough in language to read. They do not characterize the backgrounds of comparable children whose development is not sufficient for starting reading.

Gagné in Chapter 1 has pointed out how one behavior category is built upon another. Just as a hierarchy of prerequisite learning is necessary in mathematics, so too does it seem sensible to look for hierarchical sequences of verbal learning in language. If there are deficiencies at the lower levels of the hierarchy of tasks, there will be failures and difficulties at the later levels. It is entirely possible that many children of the least favored economic levels are not as dull or slow or incapable of learning as their school marks and IQ scores indicate. More likely they are in a situation of not knowing how to learn their present tasks because they have not had assistance in learning prerequisite verbal tasks.

FURTHER RESEARCH

As research turns more and more to the study of man himself and particularly to his language, some of the following kinds of research will most certainly be needed:

1. The use of syntactical mediation in paired-associate learning needs study. Jensen and Rohwer (1963) indicate that much can be learned about the different parts of speech and different degrees of complexity through which learners imbed pairs of items in meaningful syntactical structures in order to learn the pairs. Differences between children of various social class backgrounds should prove illuminating.

2. Learning nonsense syllables that correspond to the syntactical structures of the English language should show a difference between children who have incorporated the syntactical structure of the language and those who have not.

3. In research of the kind described in the present chapter, one of the most important directions must be that of establishing empirical evidences of language proficiency. Separate skills such as avoidance of vague reference and clarity of antecedents

must be studied and related to careful judgings of verbal proficiency. The same kind of empirical approach must be used to
study consistency of tense in verbs; the use of subordinating
connectors like *although, because, in spite of,* and other words
of condition and concession; the use of the pluperfect tenses in
verbs; the vitality and vividness of colorful verbs as contrasted
with such colorless verbs as *went, did, were;* the use of infinitives; the flexibility of moving about in a sentence those words
and phrases which can be moved; the ratio of verbs to the rest
of the words in a sentence. As studies of such elements are completed, their combination should provide an objective method
of determining proficiency in language and replace the present
methods of using panels of judges.

4. The transformational method of analyzing language, devised by Chomsky (1957), should be applied to the oral and
written language of subjects judged strong and weak in language. The results should show whether or not another empirical
method of determining proficiency in language has been made
available to language research.

5. The use of analogy and metaphor is extremely significant
in human language. Studies of analogical thinking as expressed
in language are of great importance to further knowledge.

6. The whole subject of mazes in oral language is fascinat-
ing and promises to be a valuable topic for research. Those who
work with this feature should consider Vygotsky's (1962) theory
that in mastering external speech, the child starts with one word,
then connects two or three words, advancing through simple sentences to complicated ones. Yet in terms of inner meaning, the
child starts from the whole, from a meaningful complex. "The
external and the semantic elements of speech develop in opposite
directions—one from the particular to the whole, from word to
sentence, and the other from the whole to the particular, from
sentence to word" (p. 126). Fitting together these two processes
might account for mazes in the present study.

7. The interrelations between speaking, listening, reading,
and writing need to be more carefully explored. In the present
study, the relations are positive, but in other research they are
not. Eventually research will establish the truth on this matter.

8. The findings both of Bernstein (1960) and of the present

research in reference to the relation of socioeconomic status to language proficiency need to be replicated and extended.

Investigation of problems like these may lead us to a better understanding of the nature of proficient language ability and the ways in which language and thought relate to each other.

REFERENCES

Bernstein, B. Language and social class. *Brit. J. Sociol.*, 1960, 11, 271–276.

Brown, R. *Words and things.* Glencoe, Ill.: Free Press, 1958.

Chomsky, N. *Syntactic structures.* The Hague, The Netherlands: Mouton & Co., 1957.

Jensen, A. R., & Rohwer, W. D. Verbal mediation in paired-associate and serial learning. *J. verb. Learn. verb. Behav.*, 1963, 1, 346–352.

Langer, Susanne K. *Philosophy in a new key.* New York: Mentor Books, The New American Library, 1942.

Loban, W. *The language of elementary school children.* Champaign, Ill.: National Council of Teachers of English, 1963.

Loban, W. *Language ability: Grades seven, eight, and nine.* Washington, D.C.: Cooperative Research Program of the Office of Education, United States Department of Health, Education, and Welfare, 1964.

Milner, Esther. A study of the relationship between reading readiness in grade one school children and patterns of parent-child interaction. *Child Develpm.*, 1951, 22, 95–112.

Minnesota Scale for Parental Occupations. Minneapolis: University of Minnesota Press.

National Education Association, Educational Policies Commission. *The central purpose of education.* Washington, D.C.: National Education Association, 1961.

Rosenzweig, M. R., Krech, D., & Bennett, E. L. Modifying brain chemistry and anatomy by enrichment or impoverishment of experience. In G. Newton (Ed.), *Early experience and behavior.* Springfield, Ill.: C. C. Thomas, in press.

Vygotsky, L. S. *Thought and language*, Eugenia Hanfmann and Gertrude Vakar (Trans.-Eds.). Cambridge, Mass.: Massachusetts Institute of Technology, 1962.

Chapter 6

IMPULSIVE AND REFLECTIVE CHILDREN: SIGNIFICANCE OF CONCEPTUAL TEMPO

JEROME KAGAN, *Harvard University*

The aims of most educational enterprises are four in number: to create conditions that will facilitate the child's acquisition of new knowledge, to promote a continuing desire for intellectual mastery, to minimize the doubts and fears that derive from chronic anticipation of failure, and to inculcate standards of quality in cognitive products.

The routes by which these goals are reached are beclouded, and the most dramatic changes in curriculum reform during the last decade have concentrated on the incentive value of the classroom materials presented to the child. This strategy assumes that creative management of learning materials will maximize the likelihood of success during the learning process and, by so doing, create a self-generating motivation for continued involvement in new learning.

There are, however, many interacting dispositions within

This research was supported, in part, by research grant M-4464, M-8792 and GM-10146 from the National Institutes of Health, United States Public Health Service.

the child that ultimately affect the delicate balance between motivational zeal and apathy through their influence on the quality of the child's intellectual products. One such disposition describes the child's tendency to reflect upon the quality of a cognitive product, in contrast to an impulsive and unconsidered response. The child who is prone to respond impulsively in difficult problem situations (i.e., to initiate a reasoning sequence suggested by the first hypothesis that occurs to him and/or report an answer without sufficient reflection on its possible validity) is more likely to produce an incorrect response than the child whose natural inclinations prompt him to reflect over the differential adequacy of several solution hypotheses and to consider the quality of an "about to be reported answer."

Research at the Fels Institute during the past half-decade has been directed at this "decision time" variable, which has been called "reflection-impulsivity." Succinctly stated, the reflection-impulsivity dimension describes the child's consistent tendency to display slow or fast response times in problem situations with high response uncertainty. The results are persuasive in suggesting that a tendency for reflection increases with age, is stable over periods as long as 20 months, manifests pervasive generality across varied task situations, and is linked to some fundamental aspects of the child's personality organization. The sections that follow document the empirical basis for the conclusions stated above.

THE TESTS

MATCHING FAMILIAR FIGURES (MFF)

In this task the child was shown a picture (the standard) and six strikingly similar stimuli, only one of which was identical to the standard. The task of the S was to select the one stimulus that was identical to the standard. Both the standard and variations were always available to the subject. The major variables scored were number of errors and average response time to first selection. Figure 1 illustrates two sample items from the 12-item test.

FIGURE 1. Two sample items from Matching Familiar Figures (MFF) Test.

HAPTIC VISUAL MATCHING (HVM)

In this task, the child first explored with his fingers a wooden form (approximately 3 inches square) to which he had no visual access. He was allowed an unlimited time to explore the form and, when he withdrew his hands, he was presented with a visual array of five stimuli, one of which illustrated the form he had explored haptically. The child had to select the visual stimulus that corresponded to the form he had explored. The 20-item test contained geometric forms as well as familiar objects and yielded three variables: errors, response time, and palpation time (i.e., time the child devoted to tactual exploration of the wooden form). Figure 2 illustrates two sample items.

These two tests have been administered to children in Grades 1–3 in a variety of schools by both male and female examiners. Table 1 presents the mean error and response time scores for the sexes separately across the three grades. The two third grades are from different communities. Sample D tends to have parents with slightly more education than Sample C.

The results indicate a clear trend for decreasing errors and increasing response latencies with age. The difference in response time to MFF or HVM between Grade 1 and the average of the two third grades was highly significant ($p < .01$). But there was no difference in Wechsler Intelligence Scale for Children (WISC) verbal IQ among the different age groups.

Many developmental studies of quality of perceptual discrimination also find increasing accuracy with age, and the investigators typically attribute the superior performance of the older child to the possession of more mature cognitive structures, rather than to his disposition to reflect longer over the validity of his answer. As will be seen later, there is always a high negative correlation between response time and errors on MFF or HVM. The children who respond quickly make many errors. Since response times become longer as the child matures, it is likely that the more accurate recognition scores of the older children are a partial result of these longer decision times. An experiment in which decision time was manipulated experimentally validated this statement (Kagan et al., 1964).

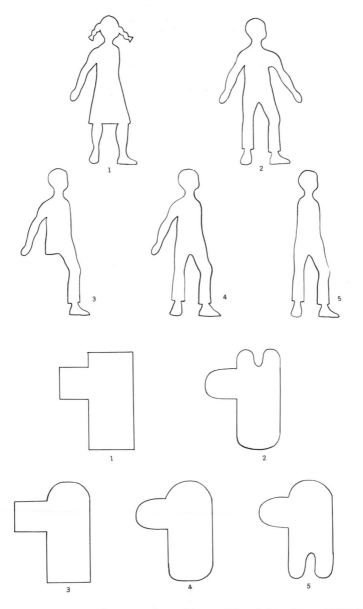

FIGURE 2. Two sample items from Haptic Visual Matching (HVM) Test.

TABLE 1

Developmental Changes in Errors, Response Time, Palpation Time, and Verbal Skills

Variable	Sample A Grade 1		Sample B Grade 2		Sample C Grade 3		Sample D Grade 3	
	M (N=65)	F (N=65)	M (N=46)	F (N=46)	M (N=84)	F (N=62)	M (N=52)	F (N=45)
MFF: errors	15.1	15.0	14.1	10.9	12.4	11.8	12.2	9.7
HVM: errors	31.9	28.4	30.7	30.2	25.2	27.0	22.8	22.1
MFF: response time	11.7	11.0	11.2	13.0	16.9	16.4	20.3	22.6
HVM: response time	5.9	6.2	6.5	6.9	7.2	6.9	8.3	9.8
HVM: palpation time	10.6	11.5	10.7	9.9	13.1	10.9	15.0	20.0
WISC: verbal scaled scores	11.2	10.6	10.7	9.6	11.9	10.8	11.5	11.3

There are other instances in which differential quality of performance on a relatively difficult task is attributed to central organization variables rather than to response systems involving evaluative decisions about the validity of cognitive products. For example, it is common practice for school psychologists to give a Bender-Gestalt to ten-year-old children who are having difficulty learning to read. These psychologists are prone to conclude that a poor Bender score warrants a diagnosis of "perceptual motor deficit resulting from minimal brain damage" and to use this diagnosis as an explanation for the academic retardation. However, an impulsive approach to problems is correlated with recognition errors in reading as well as poor performance on the Bender test. The former association will be documented in detail later. The latter association was discovered in a study of 29 first-grade children for whom the correlation between response time to MFF and good Bender-Gestalt score was in the .70's. Moreover, many children who could not reproduce a Bender-Gestalt design could easily discriminate that design from an array of similar ones. Thus, their poor graphic reproductions of the designs could not be ascribed to visual deficit, but seemed to be a consequent, in part, of an impulsive approach to execution of this problem.

STABILITY OF THE REFLECTION-IMPULSIVITY DIMENSION

At present, the stability of the reflection-impulsivity disposition has been tested on two independent samples of children using MFF response time as the index of reflection. In the first study, 104 boys and girls were individually administered the MFF when they were in Grades 3 or 4. One year later each S was administered a slightly different version of the MFF. The correlations between response time on the first and second administrations were high for both boys and girls in both grades; the average coefficient was .62.

A second study of stability involved a group of 102 children who were given the MFF in the spring of their first year in

140   *Learning and the Educational Process*

school and one year later were given the same test (i.e., in the spring of the second grade). The correlations for response time between the two administrations were .48 for boys and .52 for girls. Thus, the tendency to display fast or slow decision times to problems with high response uncertainty was relatively stable when restricted to the same test.

GENERALITY ACROSS TASKS

More impressive evidence for the stability of a reflective or impulsive disposition comes from the generality of this attitude across varied tasks. The correlation between response time on MFF and response time on HVM is consistently high across all samples. Table 2 presents the intercorrelations among MFF response time, HVM response time, HVM palpation time, and verbal skills (the vocabulary and information scales of the WISC) for the four samples involved in Table 1.

The high degree of generality across MFF and HVM is evidenced by the coefficients that range from .61 to .87, with a median coefficient of .64 for the four samples and two sexes.

It is also of interest to note that the time the child took to explore the wooden form in HVM (palpation time) was positively related to response time on HVM (r ranged from .36 to .72, with a median r of .61).

Moreover, there was generally a low and typically nonsignificant relation between verbal skills and the reflection-impulsivity dimension. The correlation between response time on HVM and verbal skills ranged from $-.05$ to .34, with a median coefficient of .17, and none of the coefficients was significant at $p < .01$. The relationship between response time on MFF and verbal ability was slightly higher (r ranged from $-.16$ to .46 with a median r of .19), and three of the eight coefficients were significant at $p < .01$.

In summary, the tendency to show the fast or slow decision times was not highly related to verbal ability. However, the direction of the relationship goes counter to the common stereotypic belief that "bright children think quickly in problem situations."

TABLE 2
INTERCORRELATIONS AMONG DECISION TIMES AND VERBAL SKILLS
(FOR EACH SAMPLE, CORRELATIONS FOR BOYS ARE TO THE RIGHT OF
THE DIAGONAL, GIRLS TO THE LEFT)

Sample A: Grade 1; 65 boys, 65 girls $(p<.01$ when $r>.32)$

	1	2	3	4
1. MFF: response time	—	.73	.51	.27
2. HVM: response time	.63	—	.53	.26
3. HVM: palpation time	.46	.56	—	.19
4. WISC: verbal skills	.35	.30	.34	—

Sample B: Grade 2; 46 boys, 46 girls $(p<.01$ when $r>.37)$

	1	2	3	4
1. MFF: response time	—	.87	.29	.00
2. HVM: response time	.64	—	.36	.09
3. HVM: palpation time	.68	.72	—	.23
4. WISC: verbal skills	.46	.34	.43	—

Sample C: Grade 3; 84 boys $(p<.01$ when $r>.28)$,
62 girls $(p<.01$ when $r\geq.32)$

	1	2	3	4
1. MFF: response time	—	.70	.61	.36
2. HVM: response time	.64	—	.71	.18
3. HVM: palpation time	.53	.61	—	.34
4. WISC: verbal skills	.19	.17	.18	—

Sample D: Grade 3; 52 boys $(p<.01$ when $r>.35)$,
45 girls $(p<.01$ when $r>.38)$

	1	2	3	4
1. MFF: response time	—	.64	.52	.12
2. HVM: response time	.61	—	.72	.11
3. HVM: palpation time	.56	.71	—	.12
4. WISC: verbal skills	—.16	—.05	.16	—

FURTHER EVIDENCE OF GENERALITY

The tendency to reflect over alternative hypotheses generalizes not only across tasks where all the response alternatives are given (as in MFF and HVM) but also shows generality on tasks where the child must generate his own alternatives. This result was demonstrated in a study in which ink-line drawings of incongruous scenes were presented tachistoscopically to a group of young children in the second and third grades. The pictures were shown at increasing exposures for a minimum of 18 trials. Each child made a minimum of 108 descriptions across all six scenes, and the response latency from exposure of picture to first significant verbalization was recorded.

Response time on the tachistoscopic recognition task was positively related to response time on MFF ($r = .40$; $p < .01$ for 60 boys, and $r = .40$; $p < .01$ for 53 girls) for Ss who took the tachistoscopic test when they were in the second and third grades and the MFF task about six months later. The HVM was administered about one year after the tachistoscopic session, and the correlations between response time on HVM and response time to the tachistoscopic exposures were .30 ($p < .05$) for boys and .32 ($p < .05$) for girls. There was, therefore, both temporal stability and intertask generality from a test with a fixed number of alternatives to one where the child had to generate his own solution hypotheses.

This tachistoscopic task also provided further evidence for the assumption that a reflective disposition is more characteristic of older children. A group of eighth-grade children was administered the same tachistoscopic recognition task given to the second- and third-graders. Despite the fact that the older children were verbally more facile, less frightened, and more sophisticated in problem-solving techniques than the younger second- and third-grade subjects, the former group had significantly longer response latencies, suggesting that the disposition to reflect over alternative response possibilities increases with age.

Further evidence for the generality of decision time is furnished by a study of temporal delay in answering questions in an interview situation. Briefly, 56 boys and 52 girls in Grades 4 and 5, each of whom had been administered the MFF and HVM a year earlier, were interviewed by a female adult about their hobbies, best and poorest subjects in school, favorite pastimes, etc. Sample questions were as follows: "What games do you like best to do? What are you best at? What are you poorest at? After school, what do you spend the most time doing? Do you think school is important? What subject do you like best in school?" Most of the questions had some degree of response uncertainty. That is, to the question, "What is your favorite subject in school?" we assume that several alternatives came to mind simultaneously and the child either paused to consider each alternative or impulsively selected the first one that occurred to him. This interview was tape recorded and the interviewer was instructed not to speak after the termination of a question until the child had spoken. The taped interviews were scored for the temporal delay between termination of the question and the beginning of the child's reply for a series of twenty questions in the interview. The average delay score across the twenty questions was computed for each child and this score was correlated with the measures of reflection-impulsivity gathered earlier. The correlations with response time on MFF were .30 for boys ($p < .05$) and .38 for girls ($p < .01$). The correlation between delay in the interview and response time to the tachistoscopic exposures was even higher ($r = .42$, $p < .01$ for boys; $r = .45$, $p < .01$ for girls). Finally, the correlations with response time on HVM were .27 for boys ($p < .05$) and .40 for girls ($p < .01$).

In sum, the tendency to show long or short decision times generalized across problems with fixed response alternatives, recognition problems where S had to generate his own solution hypotheses, and an informal interview situation. It is to be noted that the generality of a fast or slow decision tempo occurred primarily for problems where response uncertainty was present. There is no generalized tendency for reflective children to have long response times in situations with minimal uncertainty. There is no relationship, for example, between response time on MFF and the latency to begin the drawing of a face under conditions where the examiner says, "Here is a pencil and paper, please draw a face." The correlations hover near zero. Similarly, there is no correlation between response time on MFF and the time taken to complete the face. The phrase *conceptual tempo*, as used in this essay, refers only to problems with some degree of response uncertainty (i.e., several response alternatives are available simultaneously or contiguously in time and one must be selected).

RELATIONSHIP BETWEEN DECISION
TIME AND ERRORS

As noted earlier, there was always a high negative correlation between response time and errors on tasks like HVM and MFF. This association holds because the tasks are sufficiently difficult to insure that children who respond quickly will be inaccurate. Table 3 presents the correlations between response time and error scores on MFF and HVM for the four samples.

Negative relationships between errors and response time for both tests appeared for all eight groups (the 16 coefficients ranged from $-.27$ to $-.75$ with a median coefficient of $-.48$). More impressive is the fact that response times on HVM are as highly correlated with errors on MFF as MFF response time. For example, the association between response time and errors on MFF is $-.65$ for Grade 2 boys and girls; the correlations between response time on HVM and errors on MFF are $-.63$ and $-.50$. This cross-task consistency between response time on one task and errors on a second is persuasive evidence for the existence of a stable conceptual tempo disposition.

Although response time on MFF or HVM is typically independent of verbal skills, recognition errors usually display a low negative relationship with verbal ability (r in the .30 to .40 range). The coefficients between WISC verbal skills and errors on MFF ranged from $-.02$ to $-.38$, with a median coefficient of $-.28$. For HVM the range was $-.06$ to $-.51$ with a median coefficient of $-.43$. Thus, HVM errors were more highly related to verbal skills than were MFF errors. The moderate relation between recognition errors and verbal skills suggests that the basic cognitive processes implied by the phrase "high verbal ability" (e.g., richer verbal resources, greater self-confidence, greater problem-solving skills, stronger motivation to perform with competence) have some relevance for accuracy in perceptual recognition tasks among school-age children, although there is no clear and obvious reason why verbal ability should facilitate performance on MFF. Multiple correlation coefficients with recognition errors as the criterion and verbal ability and response time as the two predictors have yielded coefficients in the high .70's. Finally, there was good consistency of recognition error scores across the

TABLE 3

CORRELATIONS OF ERRORS WITH RESPONSE TIME AND VERBAL SKILLS

Y variable	X variable	Sample A Grade 1		Sample B Grade 2		Sample C Grade 3		Sample D Grade 3	
		M	F	M	F	M	F	M	F
MFF: response time	MFF: errors	—.50	—.61	—.65	—.65	—.75	—.47	—.46	—.62
HVM: response time	HVM: errors	—.37	—.38	—.27	—.48	—.41	—.46	—.42	—.49
MFF: response time	HVM: errors	—.44	—.42	—.21	—.44	—.55	—.26	—.46	—.24
HVM: response time	MFF: errors	—.35	—.49	—.63	—.50	—.51	—.47	—.42	—.65
WISC: verbal skills	MFF: errors	—.26	—.32	—.25	—.20	—.36	—.30	—.38	—.02
WISC: verbal skills	HVM: errors	—.43	—.45	—.20	—.51	—.50	—.42	—.30	—.06

two tasks (coefficients ranged from .27 to .47 with a median coefficient of .39).

RELATION OF REFLECTION
TO ERRORS OF COMMISSION

The evidence presented so far argues convincingly for the importance and generality of a reflective versus impulsive orientation in intellectual tasks. This section describes two attempts to demonstrate the effect of an impulsive attitude on errors of commission in two academically related tasks: (a) reporting words in a serial learning task that were not initially presented and (b) reading recognition errors in both textual and non-textual contexts.

REFLECTION AND ERRORS OF COMMISSION IN SERIAL LEARNING

A group of 60 boys and 53 girls were given the MFF and HVM when they were in Grades 3 and 4 in separate sessions separated by about six months. In addition, each was administered a serial learning task between these two sessions. The variable of primary interest was the occurrence of errors of commission (i.e., reporting words not present on the list). The expectation was that impulsive children would be more likely than reflectives to offer errors of commission, hereafter called intrusion errors, throughout the serial learning procedure.

Procedure

Each child was asked to learn four different lists of familiar words, each list containing 12 items. He was given two trials with each list, the words presented in reverse order on the second trial. The lists were read by a male voice delivered by a tape recorder. The words on Lists 1 and 4 were presented at the rate of one per second; the words on Lists 2 and 3 were read at a rate of one item every four seconds. The major experimental variable was a threatening communication, administered after the two trials of the second list, informing the child that his performance was inadequate. The examiner said, "You are not remembering enough words. You should be remembering more, most children can remember more than you. If you can't do better you will not get the prize I showed you earlier. I will give you another chance to win the prize. Try and do better."

Lists 3 and 4 were then presented. The variable of primary concern was number of intrusion errors (i.e., reporting words not present on the list).

Relation Between Intrusion Errors and Conceptual Variables

The distribution of intrusion errors on each of the four lists was skewed toward low scores. Each distribution was divided at the median for each group separately, and phi coefficients assessed the consistency of intrusion errors across all four lists. There was moderate interlist consistency and intrusion errors were generally independent of verbal ability. Since the relationships between intrusion errors and other conceptual variables were similar for each of the four lists, the mean number of intrusion errors across *all four lists* was computed, and this "pooled" variable yielded better relationships with the reflection-impulsivity dimension.

There was only a suggestive relationship between response time and intrusion errors. The best response time correlate of intrusion errors was MFF response time ($r = -.22$ for boys, $p < .10$; $-.21$ for girls). Recognition errors on MFF, which is a quality of performance variable, were moderately correlated with intrusion errors for boys ($r = .44$, $p < .001$) but not for girls. HVM errors were related to intrusion errors for both sexes ($r = .23$ for boys, $p < .10$; .39 for girls, $p < .01$).

Moreover, there was a suggestive relation between the increase in intrusion errors following the "threat" and impulsivity. In this analysis the number of intrusion errors on the first trial of List 2 was subtracted from the number of errors on the first trial of List 3, so that high scores meant an increase in intrusion errors following threat. The correlation between MFF errors and amount of increase in intrusion errors was .38 for boys ($p < .01$), but only .08 for girls. The correlations with HVM errors were .19 for boys and .24 for girls ($p < .10$).

In sum, boys who made many errors on MFF made more intrusion errors prior to threat and showed larger increases in the number of intrusion errors after threat. It should be noted that there was no relation between errors on MFF or HVM and the number of words recalled, either pre- or postthreat. Thus, the impulsive children were as competent as the reflective ones with respect to the task as it was defined to them. However, their preferred strategy was to offer a great many inaccurate responses along with their correct recalls. The reflective children apparently censored incorrect responses.

A REPLICATION

Although the above results were in the expected direction, the magnitude of the relation was not strong. It was decided, therefore, to replicate this study with more elegant controls in order to assess again the validity of the hypothesis that errors of commission would be characteristic of impulsive children.

Method

A large group of third-grade children in two different schools (136 boys and 107 girls) was given the MFF, HVM, and vocabulary and information subscales from the Wechsler Scale for Children in individual testing sessions. From this large subject pool Ss were placed into one of three groups: threat, dissonance, or control. The Ss in the three groups were matched on verbal ability, and there were an equal number of reflective and impulsive children in each of the experimental groups. The index of reflection was determined in the following way. The distribution for MFF errors for all boys (or all girls) was split at the median into high and low groups. Similarly, the distribution of MFF response time was split at the median into fast and slow groups. The child who was both above the median on errors and below the median on response time (fast response times) was classified as impulsive. The child below the median on errors and above the median on response time (slow response time) was classified as reflective. There were a minimum of 13 subjects in each of the 12 groups in this 2 × 2 × 3 design—boys vs. girls, reflective vs. impulsive, and three experimental groups (threat, rejection, and control) with mean verbal ability equal across the three experimental groups.

The serial learning lists contained 12 familiar words. The lists were recorded on tape and played to the child at a rate of one word every four seconds. Each S was given two trials with each list, the second list read in reverse order. The E recorded the number of words recalled and the number and type of intrusion errors. After the first two lists, which were administered under similar conditions to all children, the three different experimental instructions were introduced. The Ss in the threat group were told that the lists that were coming next were very difficult and only children with high intelligence could master them. The exact instruction was, "O.K., that is fine. These two lists we just finished were really practice lists to give you an idea what this kind of test is like. The next two lists really count. You will have to do very well on these next two lists. They are hard and children that don't have good memories usually don't do very well. So try and concentrate."

The experimental instructions to the "rejection" group were intended to make the child feel he had not performed adequately on the list he had just completed. The exact instruction was, "That was poor. You are not remembering enough words. You should do better than that. You should have remembered more words than you did."

The control group was merely told, "O.K., let's take a little break and then do some more lists." Then two new lists were administered to all children with two trials on each list.

Results

The impulsive children had significantly more intrusion errors both pre- and postthreat, although the difference was greater for the prethreat lists. The mean number of intrusion errors for reflective and impulsive children for the pre- and post-threat lists are presented in Table 4.

The impulsive children produced more intrusion errors than the reflectives for the two lists prior to the experimental intervention ($p < .01$), and this result held for both boys and girls. The "threatening" and "rejection" instructions after List 2 attenuated this difference, for both interventions produced an increase in intrusion errors with the "threat" instruction having the greatest effect. The increase in intrusion errors following

TABLE 4
AVERAGE NUMBER OF INTRUSION ERRORS FOR REFLECTIVE
AND IMPULSIVE CHILDREN ON SERIAL LEARNING TASK

	Threat		Rejection		Control	
	M	F	M	F	M	F
Prethreat						
Reflective	1.2	1.0	1.1	1.2	1.4	1.5
Impulsive	1.7	1.5	2.0	2.1	2.9	2.0
Postthreat						
Reflective	5.8	3.2	3.2	2.3	3.1	1.6
Impulsive	4.3	3.6	3.9	3.3	5.2	3.1

"threat" was larger than the increase displayed by the control group. The "threat" children showed a mean increase of close to three errors in contrast to an increase of approximately one error for the control group.

REFLECTION AND READING ERRORS

A second cognitive performance variable with clear academic implications is reading skill. The six- or seven-year-old child who is learning to read is confronted with a discrimination task with high response uncertainty. The word "kitten" or "wagon" typically elicits several solution possibilities, and the child must consider their differential validity before responding. It seemed reasonable to expect that children who were characteristically reflective would commit fewer word recognition errors than impulsive children and make fewer incorrect substitution errors in reading textual material.

Subjects

The subjects were 65 boys and 65 girls in the first grade in three public schools. The Ss were primarily middle class, and all three schools were in the same city which had a population under 100,000.

Test Procedures

Each S was initially seen for two test sessions separated by one week. In the first test session, S was administred the HVM,

MFF, and the vocabulary and information scales of the WISC. In the second test session S was tested for ability to recognize the letters of the alphabet and word recognition.

Tests for Letter Recognition

Each S was shown each of the 26 letters of the alphabet printed in lower case on individual 3 × 5 inch cards in random order. The E presented the card to the child and asked him to say aloud the letter illustrated.

Test for Word Recognition

The S was given a card on which five words were printed in lower-case letters. The E said, "I will say a word and then I will show you a card with five words on it. I want you to point to the word that I said. Look carefully and point to the word I say."

The E then read aloud one word from each of the cards. The major variable scored was the total number of errors. If the child was initially incorrect, the E told him he was wrong and asked him to try again. Some sample items from the 15-item test included the following: sap, cat, rat, ran, tap with "rat" as the word read by the E; pit, tat, tap, tip, pin with "pit" read by the E; bay, dad, yap, pay, day with "day" read by the E.

Results

Product-moment correlations were computed between the reading test scores and the error and response time scores to HVM and MFF. The error and latency scores were first converted to McCall T-scores. These correlations were run for the sexes separately and for children high or low on WISC verbal ability. The verbal ability dichotomy was based on a median split for the average scaled score for the vocabulary and information subtests. This split yielded 30 low-verbal boys and 35 high-verbal boys, 32 low-verbal girls and 33 high-verbal girls. The range on the WISC verbal skills for the low-verbal group was between 6 and 10; the range for the high-verbal children was between 11 and 18.

Word recognition errors were related to recognition errors on MFF and HVM for both sexes (r's ranged from .31 to .55, all significant at $p < .05$). Moreover, long response times on MFF also predicted low word error scores ($r = -.36$, $p < .01$ for boys; $r = -.41$, $p < .001$ for girls). The longer the child delayed before offering a solution hypothesis on MFF, the more accurate his initial recognition of the word spoken by the examiner. Among the girls, long exploration times and long response times on HVM also predicted low word error scores. Although verbal ability predicted reading performance, the relation of a reflective orientation to reading errors remained significant after the influence of verbal skills was partialled out (partial $r = .28$ for boys and .28 for girls, $p < .05$, for the relationship between MFF response time and word recognition errors). The multiple correlation, using word errors as the criterion and verbal skills and MFF response time as separate predictors, was .51 for boys and .59 for girls.

When the correlations were computed for children high or low on verbal skills, the results were most dramatic for high-verbal children. For example, among high-verbal children the correlations between response time on MFF and reading word errors were $-.40$ for boys and $-.44$ for girls. Corresponding correlations for low-verbal children were $-.14$ for boys and $-.21$ for girls. Thus, for Ss of below average verbal ability reflection had only a slight relationship with accuracy of word recognition. Possibly the low-verbal boys had acquired minimal reading skills, and lack of basic ability, rather than a preferred conceptual strategy, was a primary determinant of word recognition. This suggestion is supported by the fact that the low-verbal boys made more than three times as many errors as the high-verbal ones (median of 0.7 versus 0.2 reading errors). Response uncertainty was minimal for low-verbal boys, for it is likely that many solution hypotheses did not occur among this group. Errors were not a function of impulsive decisions.

There was no significant relationship between errors or response time on MFF and letter recognition errors for all girls and high-verbal boys. Among the low-verbal boys, however, there was a negative relationship between MFF response time and number of letter errors. This finding is consonant with the earlier statement that the influence of reflective delay is maximal when the subject has already learned the rudiments of the skill necessary to perform a task but has not overlearned the skill. The correlation of $-.52$ between response time on MFF and letter recognition errors for low-verbal boys indicates that a preference for delay was associated with accurate letter recognition.

RELATIONSHIP OF REFLECTION TO READING PERFORMANCE: A FOLLOW-UP

Of the 65 boys and 65 girls seen in the spring of their first year in school, 46 boys and 56 girls were retested exactly one year later (the remaining 28 children had moved from the area). Each of these 102 children was seen individually by two new adult females, none of whom knew the child's position on the reflection-impulsivity continuum at the time of testing. Each child was administered the same MFF given a year earlier and a formal reading test.

The Reading Test

Each S was administered four paragraphs to read aloud to the examiner. The paragraphs contained approximately 75 words. The E gave S the following instructions: "I want you to read some short stories to me. Here is the first one. If you think you know the word, take a guess. If you don't know the word, then skip it." The E neither corrected the child nor told him any word he did not know. The E recorded the total time to read the story and the nature of each error and omission made by S. The types of errors were grouped *a priori* into ten independent categories.

Results

The most frequent error was one in which the child articulated a word that had some graphemic similarity to the correct word (e.g., nose for noise, truck for trunk, eight for eat). It is intuitively reasonable that this kind of error should be characteristic of impulsive children. The separate correlations between response time on the current administration of the MFF and the frequency of occurrence of these errors for children high and low on verbal ability were negative for boys and girls of both verbal skill groups (average $r = -.12$ for boys; $r = -.30$, $p < .05$ for girls).

The average correlations with error scores on MFF were also in the predicted direction. The relationship with MFF errors in Grade 1 were .39 ($p < .01$) for boys and .34 ($p < .01$) for girls. The average correlations between this class of reading errors and MFF errors in Grade 2 were .12 for boys and .40 ($p < .01$) for girls. There were three additional categories of reading errors that one might expect to be characteristic of impulsive children. These were *meaningful substitutions* (Tuesday for Wednesday), *nonmeaningful substitutions* (bat for orange), and *suffix errors* (hope for hoping). The sum of these three types of errors was computed, and the correlations between this pooled score and MFF errors was positive for both administrations of the MFF (average $r = .39$, $p < .01$ and .28, $p < .05$ for girls; .15 and .15 for boys).

Some error categories were not related to reflection. For example, the correlation between response time on MFF and the *addition of words not present* was $-.14$ for boys and $-.11$ for girls. One error category—called "self-correction"—was positively associated with reflection for high-verbal boys ($r = .51$; $p < .01$), but unrelated to reflection for the low-verbal boys ($r = .00$) or girls ($r = -.07$).

In sum, the data support the predicted negative relationship between a reflective disposition (as measured by MFF) and errors of recognition in reading, the results being more striking for girls than for boys.

PERSONALITY CORRELATES OF THE REFLECTION-IMPULSIVITY DIMENSION

The links between the reflection-impulsivity disposition and the diverse motives and sources of anxiety of the child have been a central and continuing concern in this work. At present it is believed that a major determinant of the child's position on this dimension involves the differential value placed upon two standards espoused by the child's social milieu that are inconsistent. One standard demands, "Get the answer quickly," while the second exhorts, "Do not make a mistake." When the problems are difficult, as in MFF or HVM, these standards are mutually exclusive. It is suggested that the impulsive child places a greater value on "quick success" than he does on "avoiding failure." Phrased somewhat differently, each child is pulled by two forces, or, if you wish, each child is in an approach-avoidant conflict situation. If the strength of the approach gradient is stronger (seek quick success), he will be impulsive; if the strength of the avoidant gradient is stronger (i.e., anxiety over making a mistake), he will be reflective.

This argument suggests that the reflective child is a low-risk child who avoids situations that are potentially dangerous and productive of failure, humiliation, or harm. The impulsive child prefers a high-risk orientation. In an effort to determine if signs of this temperamental disposition were discernible early in development we examined the corpus of behavioral observations available on a group of 75 Fels children who had been studied from birth through preadolescence. These children had been administered the MFF and HVM when they were between seven and thirteen years of age. Using norms for MFF and HVM responses gathered on large numbers of independent samples, we categorized a small group of Fels children as either extremely impulsive or extremely reflective. In order to be classified as reflective, the child had to be above the median (for children of his age range) on response time on MFF and HVM and below the median on errors on these two tests. The child classified as impulsive was fast on both HVM and MFF but above the median on errors on both tests. These criteria for classification yielded eleven reflective boys and nine reflective girls, eight impulsive boys and eight impulsive girls, about one-half of the original group of subjects. The remaining Ss were neither clearly impulsive nor clearly reflective. The behavioral observations on these children were obtained primarily in the home and in the Fels experimental nursery school or day camp to which the children came once or twice a year for a three-week session. The descriptions of the children's behaviors in these situations are being quantified (seven-point rating scale) for a small set of well-defined variables for two age periods—the preschool and early school years. Preliminary analyses suggest that during both the preschool and early school years there are striking differences in the behavior of the children who later become impulsive or reflective. This differentiation hinges on three major classes of behavior. First, the reflective child demonstrates higher standards for mastery of intellectual tasks and greater persistence with such tasks during the early school years ($p < .05$, Fisher exact test). He chooses more difficult tasks to work on (hard puzzles, various kinds of hand crafts) and works on them for a longer period of time. Second, the reflective child has a strong tendency to avoid peer group interaction and to be initially phobic in a strange social situation with peers or adults ($p < .01$, Fisher exact test). The reflective child typically stands on the sidelines the first few days at the Fels nursery school and watches the group vigilantly before joining them. The reflective child often withdraws from peer group interaction and retreats to solitary, sedentary tasks. The impulsive child, on the other hand, typically enters the nursery school or day camp situation with zeal and appears to enjoy active social participation. Finally, the reflective child of three to five years of age shows a strong avoidance of activities that are physically dangerous ($p < .05$, Fisher exact test). He is reluctant to climb high on gym apparatus, to walk a narrow plank, or to ride a tricycle fast. When the peer group becomes "wild," the reflective child is likely to withdraw to a quiet corner. These differences obtain for both boys and girls and suggest that the reflective child avoids "risky" situations that are potential sources of physical harm or social rejection.

RELATIONSHIP OF REFLECTION-IMPULSIVITY TO PERSISTENCE
WITH DIFFICULT TASKS

The data on the Fels sample suggested that reflective children showed higher standards of performance with intellectual tasks and persisted longer with difficult tasks than impulsive youngsters. This association is intuitively attractive, for it has been postulated that a child who wanted to avoid failure experiences would be likely to adopt a reflective strategy with difficult problem tasks.

A recently completed cross-sectional study with fourth- and fifth-grade Ss demonstrated a positive association between a reflective disposition and the tendency to choose to work on difficult tasks and to persist with these tasks. A brief summary of this experiment follows.

Subjects

The Ss were children in Grades 4 and 5 who had been seen for the past several years and had been administered MFF and HVM. There were 26 boys and 28 girls in the fourth grade and 30 boys and 24 girls in the fifth grade, yielding a total sample of 108 children. Initially, each child was brought to the Institute by a female examiner with whom he was very familiar. The examiner told the S she had to test another child, and that the S was to do what he wanted for 40 minutes. The E then left the child in a room containing an array of tasks and coded the child's behavior through a one-way vision screen for 40 minutes. The room contained 13 different games arrayed on two tables. The tasks had been selected to contain seven hard tasks (four-piece pyramid puzzle, a Chinese ball puzzle, seven plastic pieces that could be made into various shapes, five difficult crossword puzzles, magic arithmetic squares, a 63-piece jigsaw puzzle, and a set of stencil designs). These tasks were seen as difficult by the child for they were appropriate for high-school youths or young adults. The remaining six tasks were either easy or had undefined goals (four puzzles designed for second graders, pages from a Grade 2 work book, easy arithmetic problems appropriate for primary school children, a word square, dice that contained letters, and a simple pegboard with pegs). The examiner coded each task that S started, the length of time spent with each task, the time spent uninvolved with any task, and the tasks completed.

Results

There were no dramatic age or sex differences in the major dimensions extracted from this 40-minute play session. The fifth graders spent a bit more time with the harder tasks and returned more frequently to uncompleted difficult tasks. The subjects spent an average of 14 minutes with the difficult tasks, and a mean of 6 minutes not involved with any task.

Each of these subjects had been previously classified as reflective or impulsive using a complex criterion that combined both errors and response time on MFF and HVM as described above. There were no dramatic differences between reflective and impulsive children with respect to time not involved or average time per task. However, the critical variable of "total time spent with the seven hard tasks" revealed that reflective boys spent more time with the hard tasks than the impulsives and this difference was greater for low-verbal than for high-verbal boys. When the reflective and impulsive boys were compared on total time spent with hard tasks the resulting t was 3.15 ($p < .01$). Among girls, verbal skill was a more critical variable in determining free play performance, and the brighter girls spent more time with the hard tasks. As with boys, the impulsive girls with low verbal ability spent less time on the hard tasks, but the impulsive bright girls spent the longest time on the difficult tasks. For both sexes, therefore, the most dramatic difference between reflective and impulsive children on time spent with hard tasks occurred among children of average or slightly below average verbal ability. Correlations were computed between the index of reflection-impulsivity and time spent with the seven difficult tasks for children of high and low verbal ability. The coefficients were $-.31$ and $-.49$ ($p < .10; p < .01$) for boys and girls of average verbal ability and $-.17$ and $-.12$ for the boys and girls of above average verbal ability. These data give more objective statistical support for the earlier statement that reflective children tend to have higher standards of performance and persist longer on difficult intellectual tasks. This finding strengthens the developmental data described earlier from the longitudinal Fels population.

IMPLICATIONS FOR EDUCATIONAL PRACTICE AND RESEARCH

There are two obvious implications of this work for everyday practices in education. The first set involves a plea for an appreciation of the pervasiveness of the child's conceptual tempo. Most teachers are not attuned to this behavioral aspect of the child. Teachers are apt to categorize the child as bright or dull, obedient or disobedient, timid or outgoing; but rarely do they notice whether the child is impulsive in his conceptual approach to problems. When they do acknowledge this dimension there is a tendency to classify the reflective child as "slow" and less bright than the impulsive, quick child with the same intelligence test score and social-class background. As stated earlier, reflective children have slightly higher verbal skills than impulsive children so that a belief in the stereotypic association "slow = dull" is both a distortion of reality and a gross disservice to the child.

Since there is minimal appreciation of this dimension, teachers are not apt to regard this variable as relevant in their attempts to influence the quality of the child's cognitive products. The data presented suggest that impulsive children make more errors in reading textual material. Many teachers assume that this behavior is the consequent of low motivation, poor visual acuity, or "brain damage." This essay urges the teacher to consider the relevance of the reflection-impulsivity dimension and to experiment with it where appropriate. It may be wise to institute special training in conceptual reflection for a selected group of primary school children. Reading difficulties can be the sequelae of an impulsive conceptual tempo, and remedial work might well include explicit practice in reflection.

A related implication deals with the teacher's tendency to punish incorrect answers. If, as suggested earlier, a disposition toward impulsivity has a long developmental history and is not the result of current apathy or hostility, it is fair to conclude that the impulsive child should not be subjected to severe negative sanctions for offering incorrect answers. If peers and teachers react to incorrect answers with sarcasm, laughter, or rejection the impulsive child will eventually become anxious, angry, or apathetic and desist from offering any answers. In time he will become alienated from the educational process. I have seen too many teachers respond with harsh sarcasm to the child who offers incorrect answers quickly but praise the child who offers correct answers quickly. This attitude communicates to the child the value the teacher places upon speed of response and handicaps the impulsive child with average ability. This assumption is supported by a recent finding with fourth- and fifth-grade children who were doubly classified as reflective or impulsive and as below or above average on verbal ability. During an interview session each child was asked to rate himself on his intellectual ability with respect to peers of the same sex in his immediate classroom. Among the below-average ability group, the reflective children regarded themselves as more capable than the impulsives ($p < .05$). Even though measured ability was similar, the impulsive child regarded himself as *less* adequate than his reflective counterpart. It is suggested that the impulsive child of below average ability experienced more frequent overt failures in the classroom because of his tendency to blurt out ill-considered answers, and his poorer self concept resulted from this negative experiential history. Among the bright children, the impulsives regarded themselves as more capable than the reflectives. This finding agrees with the earlier statement that the school and community view the child who can be correct quickly as highly intelligent. It is suggested that teachers inhibit their tendency to punish the incorrect immediate answer and help to prevent apathy from growing in the temperamentally impulsive child of average ability.

A final implication concerns the tempo of the teacher. Some teachers have a rapid tempo. They hurry through presentations, remind the children that there are only a few minutes left to complete an exercise, encourage speed, speak fast, and offer a rapid flow of ideas. Reflective teachers unconsciously encourage consideration of alternatives in their presentations, urge the child to "think about" his answers, and do not place a premium on speed. It is likely that the teacher's tempo influences that of the child, and some preliminary evidence from our laboratory supports this statement. Perhaps the school of the future will tailor the tempo of the child to that of the teacher in order to maximize the productivity of the learning enterprise.

SUGGESTIONS FOR RESEARCH

The above discussion suggests three interesting classes of experiments. First, it is important to assess the differential effect on the child's learning and performance of programs of instruction that are predominantly reflective or impulsive, for there may be an interaction between tempo of presentation and tempo of child. Does a two-year exposure to a reflective or impulsive classroom atmosphere have differential effects on the mastery of reading and arithmetic skills, and what are the characteristics of the children who benefit most from each procedure? A second question asks whether specific training in reflection has a long-lasting effect on the child's behavior and whether it facilitates acquisition of reading skills in impulsive children who are retarded in reading mastery. Finally, what is the deleterious effect of matching an impulsive child with a reflective teacher or vice versa? Is there a benefit to matching child and teacher on conceptual tempo? These three related questions are all testable and of considerable import. We have the instruments to initiate the work and can obtain the cooperation of the educator. All that is required are imagination, energy, and a commitment to the problem.

REFERENCE

Kagan, J., Rosman, Bernice L., Day, Deborah, Albert, J., & Phillips, W. Information processing in the child: Significance of analytic and reflective attitudes. *Psychol. Monogr.*, 1964, **78**, No. 1 (Whole No. 578).

Chapter 7

SEQUENCE OF SPEAKING
AND LISTENING TRAINING
IN BEGINNING FRENCH

EVAN R. KEISLAR AND LARRY MACE,
University of California, Los Angeles

The interaction of speaking and listening is not well enough understood to permit any judgment regarding the optimum sequence of teaching these two skills to students beginning a second language. A major purpose of this chapter is to clarify the definitions of the terms first by relating listening and speaking to the processes of stimulus discrimination and response differentiation and then by specifying in some detail the various measure-

The research reported in this chapter was performed under two contracts with the United States Office of Education, NDEA, Title VI, DHEW: SAE-8950 and OE 3-14-022, for which the senior author was principal investigator. The junior author participated as a research associate in both projects. He was primarily responsible for the planning and execution of the second investigation, carried out while the senior author was away on leave as a Fellow at the Center for Advanced Studies in the Behavioral Sciences, Stanford, California. The second project constituted the junior author's doctoral dissertation under sponsorship of the senior author. The authors wish to express their indebtedness to Paul Pimsleur who was a foreign language consultant for both projects.

ment procedures which have been used to describe these terms. Two major investigations were carried out to study questions relating to the optimum sequence of listening and speaking in beginning French instruction.

Sequence of instruction enters into learning a second language in many ways. The student's native language influences the learning of the new language. The student's other prior experiences with language offer a host of sequence variables which might be studied. In the present research one aspect of the problem of sequence was emphasized. The question dealt with how learning to "listen" to foreign-language utterances affects subsequent learning to "speak," or produce such utterances vocally, as well as the effect of speaking on subsequent listening. An important concern, therefore, has been the problem of teaching the phonology of a second language, i.e., how students should learn the sound system of the foreign tongue.

In his excellent review of the field of foreign-language learning, Carroll (1963) distinguishes four problems in the learning of phonology:

1. the problem of *discrimination,* i.e., hearing the differences between phonemes which are not distinguished or used in one's native language;
2. the problem of *articulation,* i.e., learning to make the motor movements adequate to proper production of the foreign phonemes;
3. the problem of *integration,* i.e., learning to assemble the phonemes of a connected discourse with the proper allophonic variations and "smearing"; and
4. the problem of *automaticity,* i.e., making correct production so habitual that it does not need to be attended to in the process of speaking (pp. 1069-1070).

The first problem in Carroll's list deals with discrimination or listening. The last three problems, articulation, integration, and automaticity, are all involved in speaking.

Carroll has noted that linguists are divided regarding the relation between sound discrimination and sound production. Some maintain, on the one hand, that careful listening to speech sounds in the second language leads directly to an adequate production of these sounds. On the other hand, others maintain that the ability to distinguish among phonemes results from sound production coupled with attention to articulatory phonetics.

A leading representative of the view that listening should precede speaking is Nelson Brooks (1960), who has stated:

> The learner's activities may be briefly summarized as follows: . . . he is to hear much more than he speaks, he is to speak only on the basis of what he has heard, he is to read only what has been spoken, he is to write only what he has read . . . (p. 50).

In support of this position, Brooks maintains that

> . . . it is the ear that dominates the learning and use of speech sounds. Ear training must come first. The second objective is the reproduction by the tongue and adjacent organs of the speech sounds the ear has learned to recognize (p. 107).

Morton (1960) has similarly adopted the principle that listening must precede speaking. In his development of an instructional program in Spanish, he has utilized a procedure of "phonematization" in which the individual "learns first to 'hear' and to 'discriminate' all significant classes of sounds in the new language before a conscious effort is made to reproduce them." Only after the individual has mastered this discrimination task is he permitted to proceed to sound production. Valdman and Mueller (cited by Lane, in press) also place listening training first; in their instructional program in French, discrimination training precedes training through echoic responding.

On the other hand, Lane (in press) in his careful review of the literature summarizes experimental evidence which "suggests that discrimination training ideally should follow response differentiation." In his own work (Lane & Schneider, 1963) he has shown that even after fine discriminations of Thai tonemes have been established there is inadequate production of such sounds.

Liberman (1957) has given evidence in support of the position that articulation serves an extremely important role in speech perception. He concludes that discrimination between auditory stimuli is facilitated by vocal responses which function as mediating behavior to add distinctiveness to these stimuli. This "motor theory of speech perception" has been further elaborated by Lane (1964). There is a considerable body of evidence (e.g., Norcross & Spiker, 1957) which suggests that the learning of verbal labels also adds to the distinctiveness of nonauditory cues.

DEFINITIONS OF LISTENING AND SPEAKING

One reason for the current confusion regarding the sequence of listening and speaking in foreign-language learning is that there is little agreement regarding the meaning of the terms. For example, the term "listening" has been used by Hamilton and Haden (1950) to include training in which students repeated aloud the utterances they heard. Even when "listening" is supplanted by the more technical word "discrimination" it is still given a variety of meanings. Discrimination sometimes refers to a comparison test to see if the student, by his verbal report, can "tell the difference" between two speech sounds in the foreign language (e.g., Suppes et al., 1962, cited by Lane, in press). Elsewhere, discrimination means that the student is able to tell whether a given sound is properly pronounced so that it "belongs to" the language in question. Or, discrimination may mean being able to classify sounds appropriately into proper phoneme categories, perhaps by supplying an appropriate name or phonetic symbol for such a category (e.g., Morton, 1960). Lastly, discrimination may imply that a student is able to "understand" an utterance when he hears it; that is, to "listen" means to "comprehend" (vide Brooks, 1960).

"Speaking" also has received a number of different definitions. It sometimes includes echoic responding, although most would not limit the definition to vocal mimicry. Speaking sometimes refers solely to the adequate native-like pronunciation of foreign-language words. Lastly, it may mean producing utterances which are appropriate to a given situation.

Some investigators have related the terms "listening" and "speaking" to the more technical concepts of "stimulus discrimination" and "response differentiation" respectively. Applied to the acquisition of a second language, stimulus discrimination has been used to refer to the process of learning to respond in a distinctive fashion to an utterance which is spoken to the learner, while response differentiation has referred to the process of learning to emit vocal responses which are similar to those of native speakers. As noted above, however; a difficulty is that even these technical terms have not been used in a consistent fashion by different investigators and writers in second-language learning. The technical terms have been given almost as great a diversity of meanings as have the more popular words "listening" and "speaking."

Rather than engaging in further discussion about what the terms should mean, it may be useful to look at the ways in which student competencies in speaking and listening may be assessed in purely operational terms. This can be done by specifying the tasks which constitute useful training and testing procedures. Expanding on Gagné's definition of a task in Chapter 1, we shall refer to a task as a single unit of instruction aiming toward a limited instructional objective. A task should be described in terms of the general instructions given to the student, the particular stimulus provided, and how the student may be expected to respond.

Listed in Table 1 are some of the tasks which have been used for instruction in foreign language by different investigators. The table is restricted to speaking and listening; to include additional competencies, such as composition, the list would have to be extended. Throughout the table, the word "utterance" refers to the same specific utterance in a foreign language. The sentence *C'est un chat* could, for example, appear as the stimulus or part of the stimulus for every task involving listening and as a response term for every task involving speaking. On this basis a separate table, like Table 1, could be constructed for each utterance in the language.

The tasks have been arranged in two general classes: those which stress listening and those which stress speaking. In the first class, *listening*, the process of discrimination is emphasized. Here all of the stimulus terms involve spoken French utterances.

TABLE 1

LISTENING AND SPEAKING TASKS IN SECOND-LANGUAGE LEARNING

Category	Task No.	Task description	Instructions	Stimulus	Response
I. Emphasis upon listening					
A. Discrimination indexed by sample comparison	1	Sample comparison	"Are these utterances the same or different?"	Two utterances. Two identical or two different but similar utterances in foreign language.	Says "same" or "different" OR presses one of two buttons.
	2	Model-to-sample comparison	"Is the sample like the model?"	Two utterances. A model pronunciation of the same word(s).	"Yes" or "No."
B. Discrimination indexed by evaluation	3	Matching to sample evaluative comparison	"Which pronunciation is correct?"	Two utterances. One correct, one poor.	"First" or "Second."
	4	Utterance	"Is this good pronunciation?"	A single utterance.	"Yes" or "No."

C. Discrimination indexed by writing	5	Dictation	"Write down the utterance (using the notation previously acquired)."	A single utterance.	Writes utterance (conventional spelling or phonetic alphabet).
	6	Utterance-to-writing matching	"Select the correct written form of the utterance (or part of utterance)."	A single utterance (plus two or more written forms as choices).	Chooses one of the alternatives (e.g., circles word, pushes button).
D. Discrimination indexed by listening comprehension	7	Utterance-to-picture matching	"Select the picture to which the utterance refers."	A single utterance, plus two or more pictures as choices.	Selects one of the pictures.
	8	Following instructions	"Do what the utterance requires."	A single utterance, plus objects and physical setting.	Individual performs some action (e.g., closing door).
	9	Utterance-to-English	"Select the English expression corresponding to the utterance."	A single utterance.	Selects English word corresponding to the utterance.
	10	Oral true-false test	"Indicate whether statement is true or false."	A single utterance.	Selects "true" or "false."

TABLE 1 (CONTINUED)

LISTENING AND SPEAKING TASKS IN SECOND-LANGUAGE LEARNING

Category	Task No.	Task description	Instructions	Stimulus	Response
II. Emphasis upon speaking					
A. Differentiation indexed by echoic responding	11	Echoic responding	"Repeat what you hear."	Utterance.	Speaks utterance.
B. Differentiation indexed by oral reading	12	Oral reading (texting)	"Read these words out loud."	Printed French words.	Speaks utterance.
C. Differentiation indexed by comprehension	13	Oral description	"Describe the picture (in a way in which pictures have been described)."	Picture.	Speaks utterance.
	14	Oral translation	"Translate into French."	Utterances in English.	Speaks utterance.

While response differentiation may be part of the task, the major concern is "listening to utterances," and not producing them. The different responses are simply various ways of indexing discrimination. The individual must learn *when* (i.e., to what utterance) to respond in a given fashion.

In the second class, *speaking*, response differentiation is emphasized. The learner must articulate the response using a pattern which approximates native speech. Although the learner must have learned when to produce this utterance, the emphasis of these speaking tasks is upon *how* he responds. The different stimuli are merely various ways of evoking the spoken response.

In Table 1, ten tasks are presented in the first major division, *Emphasis on Listening*. These ten tasks have been grouped into categories, each category representing one meaning of discrimination or listening. It is assumed that the tasks within the same category are mutually facilitative, or, to some extent, equivalent. In other words, it is assumed not only that two tasks within the same category are correlated but also that improvement on one will effect an improvement on the other. For example, if the student has mastered Task 5, i.e., to write a French word when he hears a certain utterance, he should be able to do quite well on Task 6 for that same utterance, i.e., to identify the aurally presented word by selecting the correct written form. Task 6 will, in turn, facilitate learning in Task 5. In the present formulation, given in Table 1, all tasks within the same category have either similar stimulus terms or similar response terms. However, the facilitation is not simply a case of primary stimulus or response generalization; the transfer which results from one task to others within the category occurs on the basis of prior learning, a process of secondary or mediated generalization.

Turning to the tasks in the individual categories, the tasks in Category IA, "Discrimination Indexed by Sample Comparison," represent the kind of tests which would probably be used by investigators who wish to see if students can "hear the difference" between sounds in the foreign language.

Learning to discriminate among utterances also involves learning to classify utterances, that is, learning to respond in the same way to different utterances belonging to the same phoneme class. Not only must the student learn to disregard differences on irrelevant dimensions, but he must disregard differences on critical dimensions as long as the utterances fall within acceptable limits of the same phoneme. The tasks in Category IB, "Discrimination Indexed by Evaluation," require this kind of classification. Here the student is instructed not merely to note whether the sample is like the model, but whether it belongs to the same class of allophones as the model. A closely related task is an evaluation of pronunciation in which presumably the individual is required to indicate whether the utterance belongs in a class within the foreign language or falls outside of any acceptable class.

The tasks in Category IC, "Discrimination Indexed by Writing," require the learner to write or identify the written label for a class of utterances using either the orthography of the second language or a phonetic alphabet. The fact that a student can perform these tasks does not necessarily mean that he "understands" what he is writing.

Category ID, "Discrimination Indexed by Comprehension," includes a number of tasks which involve a single utterance as a stimulus but which require varying kinds of responses. For any person skilled in the English language these tasks should be roughly equivalent. With mature students, it makes little difference whether the task calls for selecting a picture of a dog or the word *dog* when the French utterance *le chien* is given.

Within the second major division of the table, *Emphasis upon Speaking,* all the tasks involve producing the same utterance; it is the stimulus for this response which differs from one task to the next. The most central task for speaking training is Task 11, "Echoic Responding," in which a learner repeats the utterance he hears. The primary purpose of this imitative task is to evoke an approximation of native-like pronunciation efficiently. While it is true that some discrimination is involved in "hearing" the model utterance, response differentiation (speaking) is most important. With Task 12, "Oral Reading," the utterance is evoked by the printed French word with no necessity for comprehension. For Tasks 13 and 14 there is evidence not only that the individual can pronounce French words acceptably, but that he can speak appropriately for the occasion; that is, he understands what he is saying.

This list of tasks does not include other more important and more advanced tasks introduced in beginning French. For example, pattern practice frequently requires the student to produce French utterances which are transformations of the expressions he hears. He may be required to change a spoken French statement into a question, or to alter the person or number of the utterance; most of the tasks involved in what language teachers call "facility in language" would involve responding in a more complex fashion to more complex stimuli than are described here. Further investigation is required to determine the value of analyzing French instruction at these more advanced levels in terms of a stimulus-response approach.

It has not been the purpose here to provide a single definition for each of the terms, "speaking" and "listening," but rather to clarify the way in which these words are currently used in language research and teaching. Our approach has been to define the terms according to the tasks, i.e., the training and testing procedures which appropriately identify "speaking" and "listening" for each study carried out.

The problem of sequence of listening and speaking in the learning of French was attacked in two major investigations. The question faced in the first investigation involved only one sequence, the effect of preliminary training in listening upon a subsequent speaking task. Two major experiments, I and II, each adopting a different definition of the term "listening" (Tasks 4 and 6, respectively, in Table 1), were carried out in the first investigation. Other sequences of listening and speaking were studied in the second investigation, which also included two major experiments. Experiment III dealt with the study of two sequences, speaking upon listening, and the opposite, listening upon speaking. Experiment IV dealt with an extension of the notion of sequence to tasks in addition to speaking and listening. All the experiments in both of the investigations were conducted under modified language laboratory conditions which permitted the controlled presentation of slides, sound recording, and printed materials.

THE FIRST INVESTIGATION:
EFFECT OF PRIOR DISCRIMINATION TRAINING
ON SPEAKING[1]

The original question grew out of the fact that a student usually learns to produce an utterance echoically, i.e., by echoing back or repeating what he has heard (Task 11). This is possible presumably because he is able to "tell the difference" (Task 2) between his pronunciation and that of the model. Under ordinary classroom conditions the teacher is, of course, able to correct the student who may be unable to evaluate himself realistically.

In the language laboratory, however, a student may think that his performance is satisfactory and continue to produce a response which is actually inferior to that of the model. Lane (1961), for example, found that students who were engaged in such self-shaping echoic behavior leveled off in their pronunciation at a point somewhat different from that of the model. However, discrimination training similar to Task 5, in which subjects were required to identify a particular Thai toneme, resulted in improvement in the pronunciation of that toneme under continued self-shaping.

The major hypothesis of the first investigation was that, if a student is given preliminary training in a discrimination task in the learning of French, subsequent pronunciation training will be more effective.

DEVELOPING TESTS OF DISCRIMINATION

In our initial attempt to develop a discrimination training task, we tried to duplicate as closely as possible the conditions a student might encounter in a language laboratory setting where he was trying to evaluate his own pronunciation. On each item of the first test the student heard the voice of a native speaker followed by an American saying one of four French words containing the phoneme /u/ as in *la flute*. This phoneme, which is

---

[1] A fuller description of this investigation will be found in Pimsleur, Mace, and Keislar (1961).

not present in English, was judged to be difficult for Americans to pronounce. For each item, the subject was to rate the pronunciation of the American as "acceptable" or "unacceptable." This Task 2 test, given before and after a training program, yielded disappointing results. Other native speakers agreed neither with the original criterion of acceptability nor among themselves. Furthermore, our training program had raised the standards of many subjects so high that their performance on the test dropped; they learned to rate as unacceptable many pronunciations which our judges called acceptable.

In a second test, subjects were required to "tell the difference" between minimal pairs involving distinctions which are present in French but not in English. The task involved eight French words constituting four minimal pairs, e.g., *banc—bain*. In one version of the test, for each item, the student heard a French word and had to respond by circling one of two English words printed on his answer sheet. The two words were always the equivalent English words for the members of the minimal pair. For example, the subject might hear the French word *but* (meaning "goal") while he saw on his answer sheet the two English words: MUD—GOAL. On some subsequent item he might hear the other member of this French minimal pair, *boue* (meaning "mud"), and would see the same two English words randomly rearranged.

One difficulty we encountered with this Task 9 test was that students seemed to be able to "tell the difference" between the words of a minimal pair but they were unable to remember which English words "went with" the French word. Consequently, we used the same words to develop a sample comparison test, Task 1. Here the student heard two French words on each item. Half the time the words were identical and half the time they constituted a minimal pair. The student responded by circling SAME or DIFFERENT on his answer sheet. Unfortunately, even though we had picked phonemic differences which do not appear in English, the test was too easy for secondary school students. Subjects with no prior second language experience did entirely too well on this test to permit much improvement as a result of training.

To make this Task 1 discrimination test more difficult, therefore, we incorporated each of these words into a phrase and a sentence to make much longer utterances. On the revised test we had items consisting of minimal "phrase pairs" and items with minimal "sentence pairs," for example, *Le pont est tombé dans l'eau* and *Le peau est tombé dans l'eau*. Although the test now was quite difficult we realized two serious drawbacks: (1) in a pilot study, we found that it took an exceedingly long time to teach naive subjects to discriminate between such utterances, and (2) subjects unfamiliar with French could not use context to aid in discrimination and were, therefore, being asked to perform a more difficult job than that faced by a native French speaker!

Although our studies with these tests were not definitive, the use of sample comparisons (Tasks 1–3) seemed to be a blind alley; we could not find phonemic discrimination tasks in French which were both difficult and important for secondary school students. We are not prepared to say that there is no value in a certain amount of this type of training at the secondary level in the teaching of French, but the problem itself seems to be a minor one. In their most recent publications, Carroll (1963) and Lane (in press) report similar findings; they suggest plausibly that experience in the native language may provide considerable transfer to performance of phonemic discriminations in a foreign language within the same language family.

Faced with these difficulties, the previous tests of discrimination were abandoned and new tests were developed for the two major experiments of the first investigation. In Experiment I, discrimination was assessed by having subjects evaluate the pronunciation of an utterance (Task 4). In Experiment II, students were required to discriminate among different French phonemes by identifying the written form of the phoneme (Task 6). For both of these experiments the criterion of speaking consisted of oral reading (Task 12). The design for each experiment was the same: preliminary discrimination training for an Experimental Group and exposure for a Control Group, speaking training for both groups, followed by a speaking test as the criterion. As stated above, the hypothesis tested for each experiment was that the Experimental Group, with preliminary discrimination training, would profit more from its subsequent pronunciation training, and thereby would excel the Control Group in the final speaking test.

EXPERIMENT I. TRAINING IN EVALUATING PRONUNCIATION OF UTTERANCES

In the first experiment the subjects were required to learn the pronunciation of a phoneme, the French /o/ as in *chaud* versus the incorrect dipthongized /oᵘ/, as in the English word *show*. For this study, 144 eleventh-grade students were tested in a language laboratory, as many as 36 at a time. After a group of students took seats they were assigned randomly, in equal numbers, to either the Experimental or Control Group.

As discrimination training, the Experimental Group was presented with a list of the following words: *chaud, sauts, beau, faux* and *chaux*—each word appearing at random several times. For each item, the same word was pronounced by a native Frenchman and an American. The experimental subjects were required to circle either F or A to indicate whether, for that word, the pronunciation was French or American; then they were told which choice was correct. The same printed words pronounced only by a native speaker were presented to the Control Group, with no arrangement for the French-American discrimination training.

During pronunciation training, all subjects first heard a word pronounced by a native speaker while they looked at the printed word in their booklets. Each subject immediately said the word out loud and listened back at frequent intervals to hear both the model pronunciation and his own.

The posttest required the student to read out loud a list of French words as he heard the number spoken for each word. The test tapes were scored independently by two native judges who gave ratings on a seven-point scale for each subject; the score on the test was the sum of the two ratings. The correlation between the judges' ratings was .84, indicating a very satisfactory interjudge reliability.

The difference between the mean pronunciation scores for the two groups was not reliable. However, on a discrimination test given after the experiment the Control Group was highly superior to untrained subjects from the pilot studies. It appeared, therefore, that this discrimination task, which required identifying good and poor pronunciation (Task 4), was learned relatively well without the special discrimination training received by the experimental subjects.

Our experience with this experiment and the previous studies had led us to reject discrimination tests of the same comparison type (Category IA) first, then tests involving translation or comprehension (Category ID), and finally tests requiring pronunciation evaluation (Category IB). Therefore, for the next experiment we adopted a discrimination task requiring a student to identify an utterance by selecting its correct written form (Category IC).

EXPERIMENT II.   TRAINING IN IDENTIFYING WRITTEN FORMS OF UTTERANCES

In the second experiment, instead of learning good and poor pronunciation, the experimental subjects were taught to discriminate among French words containing different nasal vowels: when they heard a French utterance they had to identify the corresponding printed word (Task 6). Like Experiment I, the criterion test consisted of reading these words aloud (Task 12). The subjects were 196 eleventh-grade students.

The phonemes among which discriminations were to be taught consisted of the nasal vowels /ɛ̃/, /õ/, and /ã/. The experimental subjects circled the correct printed forms of words containing the phonemes (e.g., *pend, pont, pain*) when they heard the words pronounced, and then received immediate confirmation. Control subjects heard the same words but saw only the correct printed forms; they were simply told to listen carefully. During speaking training all subjects looked at a list of printed words as they repeated the model utterances of a native speaker, recording their pronunciation attempts and listening back as in Experiment I.

On the posttest, each subject read out loud each word listed on a test booklet. In scoring the recordings of this test, each of the two judges listened to the word a subject uttered and decided which one of the three phonemes /ɛ̃/, /õ/, or /ã/ had been uttered. This was recorded on the scoring sheet, the total score for each subject being the number of correct items the judge could recognize?

The results showed that the Experimental Group obtained a mean score of 36 and the Control Group 29 with standard deviations of 11 and 9, respectively, a significant difference. It was concluded that the discrimination training among these phonemes, in comparison with mere exposure to the materials, resulted in superior speaking performance.

DISCUSSION OF EXPERIMENTS I AND II

In attempting to assess the effect of discrimination learning upon subsequent pronunciation training, one should notice that in Experiment II it made no difference how poorly a student pronounced the words as long as they were comprehensible to the judges. In fact, students could have given a version of the sound which was completely lacking in any nasal quality and still have made a perfect score, as long as the judges identified which one of the three phonemes the student was trying to say. Students need not have learned to differentiate the responses (pronouncing the nasal vowels), but only to give some approximation; for this purpose, well-differentiated responses from the familiar English phonemes would have been adequate.

During the preliminary discrimination training of Experiment II (Task 6) the student learned to identify a written form when he heard an utterance. In the subsequent pronunciation training and on the criterion test the student did the opposite; he produced a given utterance when he saw a printed word (Task 12). The fact, therefore, that the experimental subjects did so well on the criterion test may be seen as an example of the reversibility of paired-associate learning in which a stimulus term in one training period becomes the response term in a later session (Mace & Keislar, 1965).

Such an effect has been previously demonstrated by Murdock (1956) and Feldman and Underwood (1957). McCormack (1961) refers to the phenomenon as an R-S, or backward association, as opposed to S-R, or forward association. On the other hand, in Experiment I where the preliminary discrimination training was not shown to be effective, the discrimination task was not the reverse of the speaking task; students in this experiment identified not the printed form of the word (which they later had to read) but a letter to indicate good or poor pronunciation.

In interpreting the results of the two experiments, the negative findings in Experiment I and the substantial differences in Experiment II, one should note two major differences. First, unlike Experiment I, the discrimination task in Experiment II was the reverse of the speaking task. Second, the speaking responses in Experiment II were evaluated not in terms of quality of pronunciation but in terms of comprehensibility, that is, in terms of rough approximation to the desired speech. In Experiment II, therefore, emphasis was placed on associative learning, not on response differentiation as in Experiment I.

THE SECOND INVESTIGATION:
THE EFFECTS OF DIFFERENT SEQUENCES IN
LEARNING FRENCH VOCABULARY[2]

The first investigation dealt with the effect of preliminary discrimination training, or "listening," upon subsequent training in sound production, or "speaking." In the second investigation the problem was extended to include this study of the effects of this order of training as well as the reverse, the effects of speaking on listening.

A number of changes were made in this continuing study of sequence. First of all, pupils in the primary grades were used instead of secondary school students. In a pilot study carried out at the beginning of the second investigation, it was found that early primary school children were much less competent than older children in learning to say seven-word French utterances after being taught these utterances through echoic training procedures. Second-grade and third-grade children on the average could repeat only 1.8 of the seven words satisfactorily, while

---

[2] A detailed report of this investigation has been presented by Mace (1964).

sixth-grade and seventh-grade children, by the same standards, averaged 3.4 words. From this evidence it was concluded that, contrary to many opinions, young children do not echo foreign utterances as well as older children; with these younger subjects the effects of sequence training might be more pronounced.

A second major difference concerned the definition of discrimination adopted in this new investigation. Experiment I and the previous pilot studies had shown the lack of utility in defining discrimination either by sample comparison or by evaluation of pronunciation; our subjects found these tasks so easy that there were no measurable training effects. In Experiment II, the learner not only had to discriminate among three similar phonemes by identifying the corresponding written form, he also had to learn when to produce the correct pronunciation for each one. As discussed earlier, the critical feature of Experiment II was the requirement of paired-associate learning. However, in neither of these experiments were subjects told the English equivalents of these words; the task did not involve comprehension or "meaning." In the second investigation, on the other hand, since the paired-associate terms consisted of different forms of the French utterances and the corresponding pictures, subjects had an opportunity to learn the meaning of the utterances.

Experiment III. Effects of Different Listening and Speaking Sequences

In the first experiment of the second investigation, Experiment III, the major emphasis was placed upon *speaking*, learning to make a particular utterance in the presence of the appropriate picture (Task 13), and *listening comprehension*, learning to identify the appropriate picture in the presence of the utterance (Task 7). The question was "Which will have the greatest facilitative effect upon speaking and listening performance, speaking training first, listening training first, or concurrent training in the two tasks?"

A ten-day program was prepared for the teaching of beginning French, consisting of five daily lessons of speaking training and five lessons of listening training. The subjects learned to speak and to comprehend utterances which were short sentences composed from a group of approximately a dozen words (e.g., *Le grand chien est debout* and *La petite fille est assise*). Each lesson, lasting about ten to fifteen minutes, consisted of 60 "frames" of programed instruction in which six children, each in an individual booth, saw slides projected on a screen while they heard a commentary over earphones. Through duplication and rearrangement of the 600 frames, four sequences of materials were created, one for each of four experimental groups. These sequences were composed of identical frames arranged in different orders.

The subjects, 108 children from the first, second, and third grades, were assigned to the four treatment groups, 27 in each group. The first group received five daily lessons of speaking training, followed by five days of listening training. The second group received five daily lessons of listening training followed by five days of speaking training. The third and fourth groups received these two types of training concurrently. The third group received a 15-frame segment of speaking training followed by a 15-frame segment of listening training. Two more segments in the same order completed the 60 frames of instruction for the day. Consequently, each day the third group was given 30 frames of speaking instruction and 30 of listening comprehension. The training was the same for the fourth group, except that each day the listening training segments came *before* their speaking counterparts. For the first and third experimental groups, therefore, speaking training came first; for the second and fourth groups, listening comprehension training came first.

Following the ten days of instruction all subjects were given a listening comprehension test twice, once at the conclusion of the instructional program and again two weeks later as a retention test. During this two-week interval all subjects were given an individual speaking test. These tests included only the terminal frames of the respective programs.

The results of the listening comprehension test showed that the groups which had received speaking training first (the first and third groups) excelled the two groups which received listening training first. This difference was also significant on the same listening test given two weeks later as a retention test. The difference on the speaking test, which also favored the groups which had speaking training first, was not reliable.

On the listening comprehension test, the first group (with five days of speaking training first) was significantly superior to the second group (with five days of listening training first). The means were 45 and 35 with standard deviations of 14 and 16, respectively. The difference was maintained on the retention test where the means were 48 and 35 with standard deviations of 12 and 17, respectively. No differences were established between the two concurrent groups whose means were 42 and 41 on the listening test and 45 and 41 on the retention test.

One major interpretation of the results is that speaking training provides a student with a vocal response which permits greater progress during subsequent listening training. This vocal response may constitute a mechanism which increases the distinctiveness of the utterances heard (cf. Norcross & Spiker, 1957; McNeil & Keislar, 1963).

If this interpretation is correct, it would suggest that training in beginning French, at least where materials like those in the present study are used, might well require the child to learn to speak very early in the instructional program. It appears that the child's ability to comprehend spoken French is greater than if speaking is delayed.

Another interpretation of the findings is possible in terms of recency. The group with five days of speaking training first might have done better on the listening test simply because they had just concluded their training on this type of task. While this interpretation appears weakened by the fact that, after two weeks, the obtained differences on this test were even greater, further evidence is called for on this question.[3] It is also desirable to investigate the relation of the features of the program itself to the experimental findings. For example, program revisions to lower the error rate might lead to different conclusions.

[3] Since this chapter was written, another experimental study of the same hypothesis has been completed by the senior author and Carolyn Stern using modified versions of the ten-day program. Not only was the superiority of the speaking-first group supported, but the experimental design of the new study provided a strong basis for arguing against the "recency" explanation.

EXPERIMENT IV.   VARIATION IN NUMBER OF RELATED TASKS
WHICH ARE MASTERED

In the previous experiments, the tasks involved a number of different kinds of stimulus and response combinations. Since our primary interest up to this point has been in speaking or listening, all of these tasks have involved a French utterance, either in the stimulus term or in the response term. For example, on certain occasions students selected a picture from among alternatives when they heard a French word spoken; on other occasions, they said the word aloud when they saw its printed form. However, many other combinations are possible. Students, for example, might write the appropriate word in French when they see a picture, or they might select a picture which corresponds to a given printed word. It is clear that these combinations are not independent of each other for a given vocabulary item; for example, it has already been noted that mastery of one task facilitates the learning of its opposite, illustrating the reversibility of stimulus and response terms. Experiment IV of this series dealt with the facilitation of one task as a result of learning another related task for a given French word. Moreover, it explored whether learning *several* such tasks will further facilitate the mastery of certain others. The central question raised in Experiment IV was, therefore, whether the performance on certain tasks of a vocabulary item is related to the *number* of other tasks for this same item which have already been mastered.

In Experiment IV, the tasks for a vocabulary item were viewed according to the following stimulus and response paradigm:

S_1 picture presented R_1 subject selects picture
S_2 word presented aurally R_2 subject says word
S_3 written word presented R_3 subject writes word

Since each stimulus in the left-hand column may be associated with any response in the right-hand column, there are nine different stimulus-response combinations of these terms. Three of these combinations were called *formal tasks* since the stimulus resulting from a response was of the same physical form as a model stimulus. Referring to the paradigm, these three formal tasks were S_1R_1 or picture matching, S_2R_2 or echoic responding, and S_3R_3 or transcription. The remaining six tasks, S_1R_2, S_1R_3, S_2R_1, S_2R_3, S_3R_1, and S_3R_2, were called *associative tasks* since there was no physical correspondence between the stimulus and response forms; the learning here is analogous to paired-associate learning.

The formal tasks represent primarily response learning. The acquisition of such a response repertoire is prerequisite to the associative learning involved in foreign language instruction. Perhaps most important is the development of vocal responses which ordinarily require a good deal of training through echoic responding (S_2R_2). The writing responses also may require considerable training in transcription (S_3R_3), especially if the orthography used is quite different from that of English.

Mastery of the three formal tasks provides the student with the responses which are necessary for learning the associative tasks for a vocabulary item; the individual may now learn to associate these responses with stimuli other than the model stimuli. This "hooking up" of stimuli and responses, to use the expression of Underwood and Schulz (1960), is the central feature of Experiment IV. The problem may be restated as follows: For any given vocabulary item, following the mastery of the three formal tasks, will the ease of learning certain associative tasks depend upon the number of the other associative tasks that have already been mastered?

The subjects for this experiment were 100 third-grade children assigned to five treatment groups of 20 subjects each. For three French vocabulary items (*le garçon, la fille,* and *le chien*), all subjects were first given equal training in the three formal tasks. Then training in an additional number of associative tasks was varied for each of the five treatment groups who were given training in no, one, two, three, and four additional associative tasks, respectively. These additional tasks were as follows: speaking or "tacting" (picture presented, subject says word), dictation (word presented orally, subject writes word), texting (written word presented, subject says word), and reading comprehension (written word presented, subject selects picture).

In Table 2, the tasks which each of the five groups were taught are listed in the column below the group number. In addition to the particular training for each group shown in Table 2,

TABLE 2

TASKS LEARNED BY FIVE TREATMENT GROUPS IN
EXPERIMENT IV

Group I	Group II	Group III	Group IV	Group V	
S_1R_1	S_1R_1	S_1R_1	S_1R_1	S_1R_1	Picture identification
S_2R_2	S_2R_2	S_2R_2	S_2R_2	S_2R_2	Echoic responding
S_3R_3	S_3R_3	S_3R_3	S_3R_3	S_3R_3	Transcription
	S_1R_2	S_1R_2	S_1R_2	S_1R_2	Speaking (tacting)
		S_2R_3	S_2R_3	S_2R_3	Dictation
			S_3R_2	S_3R_2	Texting
				S_3R_1	Reading comprehension
S_2R_1	S_2R_1	S_2R_1	S_2R_1	S_2R_1	Listening comprehension test
S_1R_3	S_1R_3	S_1R_3	S_1R_3	S_1R_3	Composition test

each group received enough additional practice with the materials so that the total amount of sheer exposure to the stimulus term as well as practice on the response term was the same for all subjects. Finally, two test tasks were administered. These tests required learning, for each of the three French words, the final two associative tasks which were not taught previously: listening comprehension (word presented orally, subject selects picture) and composition (picture presented, subject writes word).

The means for the five treatment groups on the listening comprehension test indicated a statistically significant linear function between the number of associative tasks taught during training and the ease of learning the listening comprehension task. On one test, consisting of the number of trials to master listening comprehension to a criterion, the mean scores for the groups receiving no, one, two, three, and four additional associative tasks were 31, 20, 20, 21, and 14, respectively. There was no analogous finding for the results of the writing test.

Often it has been claimed that vocabulary learning proceeds better in a "meaningful context" than under "rote" conditions of learning. Experiment IV suggests one way of attacking this problem. If the number of related associative tasks is used as a measure of "meaningful context" for vocabulary learning, this experiment supports the position that speed of mastery of a listening comprehension task is a function of meaningful context assessed in this fashion. Which of the tasks should come first in order that competence in the others will proceed most efficiently? On the basis of these studies, it seems likely that tacting (a picture as a stimulus, speaking as a response) is one task which should come early in the instructional sequence.

CONCLUSIONS AND IMPLICATIONS FOR RESEARCH

Our studies of sequence have focused on only one kind of problem in the teaching of French, the sequence of listening and speaking for a limited set of utterances. Although the central question of optimum sequence of different utterances was largely ignored, there may be value in the method we have used for broader research questions. We have found it helpful to discuss listening and speaking by specifying the particular task involved for each term. Four different definitions of listening and three of speaking have been presented in the form of task categories. It may be desirable to pose questions of sequence by specifying the order of such tasks.

For our purposes the best test of speaking was oral reading; echoic responding seemed to supply the subject with too much guidance, while the translation task seemed to be too dependent on the mastery of other associative tasks. Two different methods of scoring speaking tests were developed. Where pronunciations varied in a limited fashion, along what seemed to be a single continuum, high reliabilities were obtained from a rating scale. Where pronunciations varied in many ways, satisfactory ratings were not obtained from judges; instead the responses were evaluated by a simple test of "comprehensibility," that is, whether or not the judges could identify the utterance. The question of which of these scoring methods should be used involves a value judgment regarding the objectives of foreign language teaching: Should students acquire a native-like pronunciation or is it enough that they be easily understood by native speakers?

We could not find any value in French instruction, at least at the secondary level, in teaching students discriminations involving sample comparisons or pronunciation evaluation (Tasks 1–4). Even after trying out a number of utterances, we were unable to find discrimination tasks which, by this definition, seemed difficult enough to require much training. However, there may be some advantage to introducing the learner to similar-sounding utterances in French, especially with young children. This may be analogous to simultaneous discrimination training where the confusing sounds are presented in close proximity to each other before being presented in successive discrimination fashion (cf. Lipsitt, 1961).

The results of the first two experiments indicated that where discrimination learning involved an associative task which was the reverse of the subsequent speaking task, facilitation was clearly in evidence. The student responded in the listening or discrimination task by producing a term (circling a word) which was similar to the stimulus of the speaking task; the discrimination training therefore affected subsequent speaking behavior through what appears to be simply associative learning.

The study of facilitation of one task through the mastery of a reverse task was broadened in the final experiment to include many other kinds of related associative learnings. By extending the scope of tasks beyond simply listening and speaking, there was introduced the possibility of dealing with certain aspects of the problem of "meaningful context" for vocabulary learning under these experimental conditions. Within the limits of the experiment it was demonstrated that the ease of learning for one particular associative vocabulary task was a function of one characteristic of "context," the number of related associative tasks already taught.

If questions of sequence are posed by specifying the order of the formal and associative tasks, there are a large number of permutations, and the selection of an experimental treatment involving a task sequence will need to be guided by theoretical considerations. For example, echoic responding and tacting might be undertaken simultaneously rather than separately. It might also be possible to evaluate the usefulness of having students learn the formal phonetic features of the second language by introducing discrimination tasks involving writing in phonetic notation. The effect of such training upon subsequent listening and speaking with comprehension could then be assessed.

The results of the third experiment suggest that, at least with the type of instructional materials used, having pupils in the primary grades learn to speak these utterances with comprehension before they learn to listen and understand them is a more efficient sequence than the reverse, learning to listen before learning to speak. Acquiring appropriate vocal responses very early in foreign language instruction appears to facilitate subsequent learning of listening comprehension tasks. However, because the experimental procedure also permits a plausible interpretation of the results in terms of the effects of recency, further study to control for this factor is desirable. Furthermore, generalization to a greater variety of teaching situations calls for confirmation of these results with other types of instructional materials.

A serious weakness of much educational research has been the fact that instructional treatments of any appreciable length have not been used. Only through gross extrapolation may conclusions regarding a course of study lasting months or years be made from experiments an hour long. Together with studies of a highly limited and controlled nature, it is essential that research in this field give more attention to the development of instructional problems which deal with the cumulative effect of one day's learning upon the next. It was this problem of sequence that was the major concern of the investigations just reported.

Long-term studies have been avoided in education partly because they usually involve uncontrolled variables. In the experiments which have been reported, the modified language laboratory situation, using both slides and tape recordings, provided a fairly realistic and yet highly controlled condition for the study of instructional variables for a two-week period. In the development of such instructional programs, we found it was useful to try out brief tape-recorded materials with one or two individual subjects. After revision, an expansion of the program was tested with small groups. This procedure of improving and enlarging the program, as well as incréasing the number of subjects at each stage, was a relatively efficient method of producing materials for a week or two of instruction. It should be noted that even two weeks of instruction is too short to provide an adequate test for major questions of sequence.

The strategy of behavioral analysis adopted in this series of investigations may prove helpful in clarifying the problems of instruction in phonology for foreign language teaching. By specifying in behavioral terms different definitions of listening on the one hand and speaking on the other, fairly precise research questions may be formulated. It remains to be determined whether this approach will produce the kind of research that will result in actual improvement of classroom instruction.

REFERENCES

Brooks, N. *Language and language learning. Theory and practice.* New York: Harcourt Brace, 1960.

Carroll, J. B. Research on teaching foreign languages. In N. L. Gage, (Ed.), *Handbook of research on teaching.* Chicago: Rand Mc-Nally, 1963.

Feldman, S. M., & Underwood, B. J. Stimulus recall following paired-associate learning. *J. exp. Psychol.*, 1957, **53**, 11–15.

Hamilton, D. L., & Haden, E. F. Three years of experimentation at the University of Texas. *Mod. Lang. J.*, 1950, **34**, 85–102.

Lane, H. Self-shaping of vocal behavior. In Experimental analysis of the control of speech production and perception. Progress Report I, under contract with the Language Development Section, United States Office of Education, Contract No. SAE-9265, 1961.

Lane, H. Programmed learning of a second language. In Robert Glaser (Ed.), *Teaching machines and programmed learning. Data and directions.* Washington, D.C.: National Education Association, in press.

Lane, H. The motor theory of speech perception. A critical review. *Amer. Psychol.*, 1964, **19**, 530. (Abstract)

Lane, H., & Schneider, B. A. Methods for self-shaping echoic behavior. *Mod. Lang. J.*, 1963, **47**, 154–160.

Liberman, A. M. Some results of research on speech perception. *J. acoust. Soc. Amer.*, 1957, **29**, 117–123.

Lipsitt, L. Simultaneous and successive discrimination learning in children. *Child Develpm.*, 1961, 32, 337–347.

Mace, L. L. Response differentiation and stimulus discrimination in learning French. Unpublished doctoral dissertation, Univer. of California, Los Angeles, 1964.

Mace, L. L., & Keislar, E. R. Reversibility of stimulus and response terms following discrimination learning of French phonemes. *J. educ. Psychol.*, 1965, 56, 46–49.

McCormack, P. D. Backward mediated positive transfer in a paired-associate task. *J. exp. Psychol.*, 1961, 61, 136–141.

McNeil, J. D., & Keislar, E. R. Value of the oral response in beginning reading. An experimental study using programmed instruction. *Brit. J. educ. Psychol.*, 1963, 33, 162–168.

Morton, F. F. The language laboratory as a teaching machine. Ann Arbor: Publ. Univer. of Michigan Lang. Lab. Series Preprints and Reprints, 1960, Vol. 1.

Murdock, B. B. Backward learning in paired-associates. *J. exp. Psychol.*, 1956, 51, 213–215.

Norcross, Kathryn, & Spiker, C. C. Effects of type of stimulus pretraining on discrimination performance in preschool children. *Child Develpm.*, 1957, 28, 80–84.

Pimsleur, P., Mace, L. L., & Keislar, E. R. Preliminary discrimination training in the teaching of French pronunciation. Final Report: Under contract with Language Development Section, United States Office of Education, Contract No. SAE-8950, 1961.

Underwood, B. J., & Schulz, R. W. *Meaningfulness in verbal learning.* New York: Lippincott, 1960.

Chapter 8

SOME THEORETICAL AND EXPERIMENTAL APPROACHES TO PROBLEMS IN WRITTEN INSTRUCTION

ERNST Z. ROTHKOPF, *Bell Telephone Laboratories, Incorporated*

The current work on written instruction started with a series of experiments on how humans learn equivalences from written sentences. These studies were originally prompted by questions about the role of student responses in programed instruction. Partially as a consequence of these studies, an informal conceptual model was formulated which appeared to integrate some known facts about verbal learning and written instruction. This model, which makes no special distinction between the most common forms of autoinstruction and other written instruction, then led to further research.

In order to provide suitable context for the experimental work, the conceptual model will be described in considerable detail. The conceptualization is restricted to learning from written sentences, but it fastidiously avoids certain classes of phenomena that should be included in a comprehensive account of sentence learning, e.g., the bases of generalization among grammatical transformations. While it is not sufficiently formal to permit rigorous deductive elaborations it has nevertheless served usefully as a guide for phrasing experimental questions and interpreting results.

A CONCEPTUAL MODEL

The model is in several respects similar to that proposed by Cook and Kendler (1956) for paired-associate learning. The learning of a subject matter is measured by observing associations (constraints) among certain words or phrases in test-like situations. Subject matter learning is assumed, in the main, to depend on temporal contiguity. For literate Ss, written letters, words, or groups of words are *previously conditioned* stimuli which can elicit appropriate articulatory responses, i.e., if they are read. These responses may be of a fractional, or representational, character. When S is exposed to a sentence and makes articulatory responses, the stimulus consequences of such responses (or any other internal representation of these) may gain control of other articulatory responses which were made in close temporal contiguity. The process is illustrated in Figure 1. The sentence segment "The offspring of a male horse and a female donkey is called" results in the articulatory response r_{a1} which in turn produces stimulus consequences s_{a1}. The stimulus s_{a1} occurs in close temporal contiguity with the previously conditioned stimulus "a hinny" and therefore r_{a2}. In this way the association s_{a1}–r_{a2} may be established, and the stimulus object "The offspring of a male horse and a female donkey is called" can become conditional for the response "hinny."

FIGURE 1. Paradigm of learning from a written sentence. Articulatory responses are indicated by r_{a2}. Stimulus consequences of articulatory responses are marked s_a. Solid lines with arrows indicate a previously conditioned connection. Dotted lines with arrows indicate a connection being formed.

The sentence fragment "The offspring of a male horse and a female donkey is called" played the role of conditioned stimulus in this illustration. But the segmentation of the sentence into stimulus and response components in Figure 1 was quite arbitrary. Conditioning may be backward or circular in that words occurring near the end of a sentence may become effective cues in a test situation for words that occurred near the beginning of the sentence. Nor is it assumed that backward associations are necessarily weaker constraints than forward associations. The structure of the sentence probably does impose some constraints on the likelihood of various associative pairing. There is some evidence (Rothkopf, 1962; Rothkopf, 1963) that words occurring early in the sentence in training are better stimuli for words toward the end of the sentence, rather than vice versa. But this effect appears weak, and the conditions under which the phenomenon occurs are poorly understood (see Anderson, 1963).

The associative model which was described above also is appropriate to learning from certain incomplete sentences, such as test-like items, or certain kinds of frames that are used in autoinstructional programs. For example, it is a common practice in autoinstructional programs to require Ss to make written responses to a frame sentence from which one or more words have been deleted. S attempts to supply the missing term(s) and is then provided with the correct answer. In the early stages of learning, some prompting stimulus is generally supplied that is capable of inducing S to respond with the word that has been deleted from the sentence. The prompt can be supposed here to act as a previously conditioned stimulus. The prompting stimulus may be part of the sentence in which the deletion has been made. Alternatively it may have been in some other part of the instructional frame, or it may have been presented to S in one of the frames that has just preceded the individual item in question. The prompting stimulus plays a similar role in learning as the deleted word would, were it still part of the sentence, i.e., it evokes the appropriate articulatory response. This is illustrated in Figure 2. The stimulus word *smaller* acquires stimulus control over the articulatory response *hinny* in the first sentence of the frame. In the second sentence, the word *smaller* brings about temporal contiguity between s_{a1} and r_{a2} (i.e., *hinny*) by evoking r_{a2}. If the prompt is inadequate or absent and the appropriate articulation response, r_{a2}, does not occur, then the correct answer which is supplied to S evokes r_{a2}. However, this eventuality may, in some circumstances, result in increased temporal delay between s_{a1} and r_{a2}.

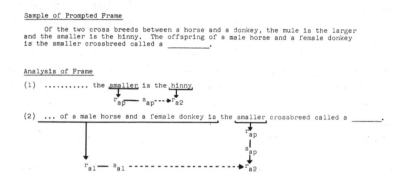

Sample of Prompted Frame

   Of the two cross breeds between a horse and a donkey, the mule is the larger and the smaller is the hinny. The offspring of a male horse and a female donkey is the smaller crossbreed called a _____.

Analysis of Frame

(1) .... the smaller is the hinny,

(2) ... of a male horse and a female donkey is the smaller crossbreed called a _____.

FIGURE 2. Analysis of a prompted autoinstructional frame. The notational system is the same as in Figure 1.

Temporal contiguity among articulation responses may be a necessary but is certainly not a sufficient condition for the formation of appropriate associations among sentence components. Consider for example the demonstration training series described by Woodworth and Schlosberg (1954, p. 711) "John Smith is a psychologist. Henry Jones is an astronomer. Walter Hodge is a biologist." Following exposure to this series, the majority response to the question "Who is the psychologist?" is "John Smith." This is found despite the fact that "John Smith" is more remote from the word "psychologist" with respect to other interposed words than "Henry Jones." Thorndike (1932, pp. 64–73), who obtained results that were consistent with this demonstration, thought that these observations illustrated the principle of "belongingness." This principle, in effect, implies that the *period* and other grammatical features act as a kind of psychological barrier, which reduces the likelihood that temporally contiguous terms, on opposite sides of this barrier, become associated with each other. Any adequate theory of learning from strings of sentences must account for these "belongingness" effects. It is conjectured here that "belongingness" depends on the prosodic or rhythmic patterns in which S emits articulatory responses when reading a passage. The patterns are thought to occur regardless of whether the articulatory responses are readily observable. The intonation or timing that underlies these patterns is under control of syntactic and probably semantic cues. The fact that stress and temporal patterning influence the formation of associations has been demonstrated experimentally. It has been shown, for example, that when lists of nonsense syllables are read in trochaic rhythm (i.e., feet consisting of one long or accented and one short or unaccented syllable), associations between adjacent syllables within the same foot are more strongly formed than between syllables that were also adjacent but were not within the same trochee (Müller & Pilzecker, 1900; Müller & Schumann, 1894). Of course we cannot observe these intonation patterns directly when S is reading silently. However we can conjecture that these hypothetical intonation patterns occur in a way similar to what they would if sentences were read aloud. For simple sentences an adequate intonation pattern may be achieved after a single inspection of the sentence. Difficult sentences probably involve repeated scanning of the stimulus sentences and repeated changes in intonation patterns. Such changes have been observed by Miller (1962) when extremely difficult sentence structures were repeatedly read aloud. The behaviors that lead to stable intonation patterns are probably acquired by Ss during childhood attempts at learning from written materials. If the process is successfully completed for a given passage, S arrives at patterns of intonation or timing that functionally separate sentence from sentence and that differentiate and group the terms within a sentence. By observing how Ss intone when reading a given passage aloud, we can infer what the characteristics of the covert intonation pattern would be for that passage. If this assumption is correct, experimental investigations of the relationships between sentence structure and intonation pattern, on the one hand, and learning, on the other, are feasible.

MATHEMAGENIC BEHAVIOR

It is clear from the conceptual model which has been described that the formation of associations appropriate to the training objectives depends critically on the character of the stimulation which results from exposure to the written training materials. For written stimulus material, this stimulation depends in turn on the activities that S engages in when confronted with the written document. This matter is related to a classical problem in psychology—the discrepancy between *nominal stimulus* (or, as it sometimes is referred to, *stimulus object*) and *effective stimulus*. *Nominal stimulus* refers to the stimulus source as specified by some objective physical measurement. *Effective stimulus* refers to the psychological consequences of stimulation and cannot be directly observed.

It appears intuitively obvious that the distinction between stimulus object and effective stimulus is useful. This distinction is commonly made in psychophysics, e.g., frequency and pitch, or frequency difference and just noticeable difference, but has also been made in connection with learning problems (Hovland, 1937; Hull, 1943, pp. 183–190; Rothkopf, 1957; Underwood, 1963). It is well known that the relationship between nominal and effective stimulus is generally complex, even with simple stimulus dimensions such as frequency and pitch. This complex relationship becomes crucial in the case of learning from written material because of the complete degree to which effective stimulation depends on activities of the experimental subject. The effective stimulation that results from exposing a written passage to an illiterate subject is likely to be quite different from that of a literate student exposed to the same stimulus object. Nor is the effective stimulation that results from "skimming" a page quite the same as that which results from careful, slow reading.

The activities in which S engages when confronted with an instructive document determine the character of the effective stimulation that results from this confrontation and so, in turn, determine what will be learned. They play such an important role in learning from written material that I have given them a special name: *mathemagenic behavior*, i.e., behaviors that pro-

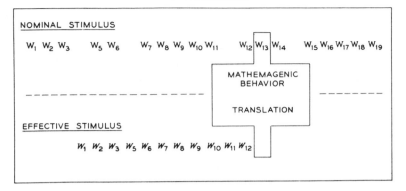

FIGURE 3. Schematic representation of the translation function of mathemagenic behavior. The nominal stimulus consists of a string of written words $W_1 W_2 \ldots W_n$ in syntactic segments. The effective stimuli resulting from translation may not be segmented in an analogous manner.

duce learning. The name is derived from the Greek roots *mathema* (that which is learned) and *gignesthai* (to be born).[1] Mathemagenic behaviors include gross postural adjustment of the head and body toward the printed page and the movement of the eyes over the page. It is assumed that there are other mathemagenic activities that cannot be observed directly and which must be inferred. These inferred activities are in many respects more interesting than the directly observable aspects of mathemagenic behavior.

We can make some conjectures about the function that the inferred mathemagenic behaviors may perform. They certainly include translation of the written symbols into internal speech. This is schematically illustrated in Figure 3. The second function is the segmentation of internal speech through intonation and rhythmic organization into phrases, sentences, and other syntactic components. This function, which is diagramed in Figure 4,

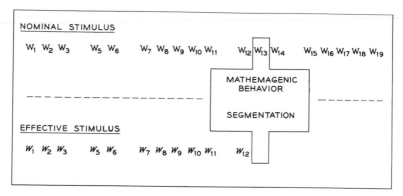

FIGURE 4. Schematic representation of the segmentation function of mathemagenic behavior. The effective stimulus string is actually a result of both translation and segmentation.

may seem to violate the principle of parsimony. Segmentation is useful, however, in accounting for otherwise puzzling empirical facts such as Thorndike's "belongingness" effect, which was referred to earlier (Thorndike, 1932), and also observations such as those on the relationship between rhythmic meter and recall (Müller & Pilzecker, 1900; Müller & Schumann, 1894).

Another inferred function of mathemagenic responses involves the augmenting of the effective stimuli by responses that are evoked by them. These include the echoic responses sometimes referred to as rehearsals or review (see Figure 5), mediating response chains of various kinds such as arithmetical calculation or deduction, and the invention of mnemotechnic devices (schematically represented in Figure 6).

The critical assumption about each of these functional classes of mathemagenic responses is that it has topography, rate characteristics, and persistence and that these attributes can be modified or altered by certain environmental events. The character of these important environmental events is not well known, and much of the current research in our laboratory concerns itself with the identification of environmental controls of mathemagenic responses. There are also strong grounds for suspicion that some of the most interesting changes in mathemagenic be-

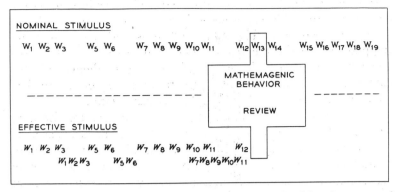

FIGURE 5. Schematic representation of a review-like function of mathemagenic behavior. The effective stimulus string is augmented by echoic responses in segments based on syntactic units.

havior involve changes in the stimulus control of this behavior. These stimulus controls functionally resemble attention.

Not all attributes of mathemagenic responses are consistent with the attainment of the training objectives. One of the most obvious cases of mathemagenic behaviors that are not consistent

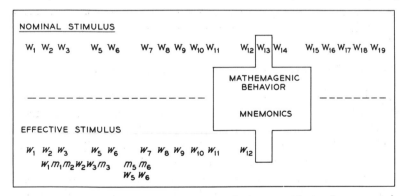

FIGURE 6. Schematic representation of mnemotechnic (mnemonic) devices as part of the processing function of mathemagenic behavior. Verbal constructions (m_1, m_2, etc.) are incorporated in echoic responses to the effective stimulus string.

with training objectives is the progressive changes in reading behavior that resemble experimental extinction. Fewer and fewer words are read on each page. Paragraphs and even pages are skipped. Eventually the reader may begin to inspect the room about him or become sleepy. But frequently mathemagenic behavior becomes inconsistent with training objectives in less obvious ways. Some of these will be discussed later.

Consistency with training objectives is measurable because we can subject S to various tests after he has been exposed to the instructive document. This is the logical key to our experimental procedures. Since topography, rate, and persistence of mathemagenic responses cannot be observed directly, we have concentrated on determining the effect of various antecedent variables on the consonance of the resulting mathemagenic responses with training objectives. This in fact devolves to finding out how these variables affect retention test performance.

EXPERIMENTAL PROCEDURES AND FINDINGS

It may be instructive to consider experimental findings that have contributed toward the adoption of the mathemagenic behavior concepts. Recent experiments on the effect of repetition interval on retention provide a good illustration and also serve as an example of the use of sentence materials in our research.

SPACING THE REHEARSAL OF ATTRIBUTIVE SENTENCES

The following procedure was used. Subjects read an informative fictional passage about eight supernatural beings to which a primitive tribe makes food sacrifices. Besides standard introductory and closing materials (see Rothkopf & Coke, 1963), the instructive passages contained for each of the eight supernatural beings one definition-like sentence (referred to as a translation rule) that stated an equivalence between the name of the being and a clause descriptive of its function. The passages also included for each supernatural being a sentence that specified the food sacrifice made to it (to be referred to as an attributive sentence). The attributive sentences were repeated exactly once later in the passage. An example of a translation rule (*ND*) linking a descriptive clause (*D*) and a name (*N*) was: *The ghosts who shield the men in war are the Kirbys*. An example of an attributive sentence (*NF*) was: *The Kirbys are offered melons*. The experimental treatments differed in the character of the second presentation (rehearsal) of the attributive sentences with respect to both type and variety of types. They also differed with respect to the average magnitude and variations in the interval between the two presentations of *NF*.

Four kinds of repetition or rehearsal of the attributive sentences were used. These were: (1) reading of the sentence; (2) response anticipation, i.e., presentation of the sentence with that term (food or name) deleted, which would be required as response on the posttraining retention test; (3) stimulus anticipation, i.e., presentation of the sentence with that term (food or name) deleted, which would be used as stimulus on the postacquisition retention test; and (4) no rehearsal. When a term was deleted from a sentence during practice, a line was substituted in its place and Ss were under instructions to try to write the missing term over the line. The correct response was in all cases provided immediately after S attempted to supply the missing word.

Two methods for determining repetition interval were used. In one of these, referred to as the 0-condition, the rehearsal followed immediately after the initial presentation of any attributive sentence (*NF*), i.e., the repetition interval was zero. Ss might see the sequence *DN, NF, NF*. In the second method, a number of other experimental items were interposed between the initial presentation of *NF* and its rehearsal. The exact number of interposed items was determined by a random method. It could be as small as zero and as large as 21. This method will be referred to as the R-condition. An example of an experimental sequence generated by this method might be *DN, NF, X, Y, Z, NF*, where *X, Y, Z* could be other *DN, NF* sentence pairs or rehearsals of other *NF* sentences.

The experimental design was implemented by an IBM 7094 computer program, which also generated the card decks that served as experimental materials. The use of the digital computer was especially convenient because of the complex experimental

204 Learning and the Educational Process

design. This design was necessitated by the fact that learning difficulty was not precisely the same for all sentences and that mixed-list experimental treatments were sometimes used. For any given S, mixed-list treatments involved assigning subgroups of the experimental sentences to different treatments. The procedure for producing these materials as well as the group procedure for their experimental use have been described in detail elsewhere (Coke & Rothkopf, 1963; Rothkopf & Coke, 1963). Comparison among treatments was based on a retention test which was administered approximately five minutes after acquisition.

The experiment yielded several findings that are consistent with the mathemagenic behavior hypothesis. One of these was an observation made when an anticipation method was used, i.e., when S was directed to supply a missing word during the repetition of the attributive (NF) sentence. Under that rehearsal condition consistent immediate repetition (0-interval) resulted in considerably less retention on the postacquisition retention test than delayed repetition (R-interval).

This can be interpreted to indicate that consistently short repetition intervals result in Ss providing the required rehearsal responses from cues other than the incomplete attributive sentence. Perhaps the response term is supplied from short-term memory. As a consequence the required stimulus controls over the response are not well established. While S has given the response *melons* correctly, he has done so because it was the last food term which was read, *not* because he has attempted to link it to Kirbys. It can be hypothesized that anticipation method rehearsal or immediate repetition of the sentence material has resulted in the shaping of mathemagenic response topographies that were not consistent with training objectives. It is also likely that the fact that all the required response terms are of the same class (i.e., names or foods), and hence predictable, also plays an important role in the shaping of inappropriate mathemagenic responses.

PREDICTABILITY OF THE RESPONSE CLASS

Information about the last conjecture can be obtained by comparing the treatments that differed in the predictability of the response terms that had to be anticipated. In two treatments, the same term (in one case the name term, in the other the food word) was deleted for all eight sentences. In another treatment, four of the sentences had the food term deleted, while the name term was deleted in the remaining four sentences. Finally, in one of the treatments, the food and the name term were deleted for two sentences each, while the remaining four sentences involved either simply rereading the sentence when it was repeated or no repetition at all. It can be seen that for the first two treatments, Predictability of the Response Requirement (PRR) was highest ($PRR = 1.0$), and PRR was progressively less for the other two treatments (i.e., $PRR = .5$ and $.25$). The response term that was to be supplied during repetition could be cued by instructionally irrelevant processes since for all four of the treatments referred to above repetition was immediate and the response requirement could be satisfied from short-term memory. Performance on a recall test, administered five minutes after the completion of training, supports the prediction that PRR interfered with learning. This is shown in Figure 7. Percentage correct recall for relevant items was 13.7 per cent for the treatment where $PRR = 1.0$, 16.3 per cent for the case where $PRR = .5$, and 22.5 per cent for the $PRR = .25$ condition. The difference between $PRR = 1.0$ and $PRR = .25$ was significant beyond the .01 level (as estimated from an analysis of variance, $d.f. = 300$). For the $PRR = .5$: $PRR = .25$ comparison, p was just at .05. The remaining difference was not reliable.

Additional indications that suggest the need for postulating general learning factors such as mathemagenic responses come from several other observations on the effect of list composition on the learning of particular list members. For example, the so-called stimulus recall decrement (reversal of direction of association) appears when *all* the sentences are rehearsed by stimulus anticipation. It does not appear or is very small (for items rehearsed by stimulus anticipation) provided that only half the sentences in the set are rehearsed that way while the remainder are rehearsed by response anticipation.

Similar observations were made in comparing the training effectiveness of the anticipation method with simultaneous presentation in sentence learning. Here again the effect of an anticipation rehearsal, when *only* anticipation rehearsal was used, was

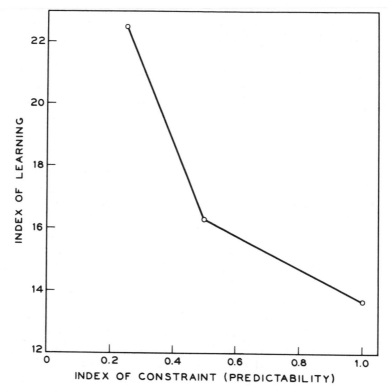

FIGURE 7. Learning as a function of the predictability of the response requirement. The index of constraint is the largest proportion of required responses which belong to any given word class.

markedly different than when anticipation rehearsal was mixed with simultaneous presentation. Anticipation rehearsal resulted in higher retention scores in the second case.

The fact that mixed-list experimental designs yield different results for given variables than pure-list design suggests that some general learning factor influences performance in these situations. Mathemagenic behavior is such a factor. Another illustration of the importance of variations in the sequence of learning conditions was provided by Keislar and Mace in Chapter 7.

VARIATIONS IN THE PHRASING OF ATTRIBUTIVE SENTENCES

A subsequent experiment (Rothkopf & Coke, in press) has confirmed earlier findings about the poor retention test performance that results from consistent immediate repetition and active rehearsal. This experiment closely followed the procedure of the first study except for one important detail. In the first experiment repetition of an attributive sentence was always verbatim except for the possible deletion of one of the major terms. In the second experiment the phrasing of the attributive sentence was varied at times. Sometimes the second presentation of any attributive sentence was a syntactic transformation and sometimes a semantically equivalent translation of the first presentation of the sentence. It could also be both or neither. Semantically equivalent translation involved changing the reference term for the fictional supernatural being, e.g., from the name of the ghost to a phrase describing its function or vice versa. For example, a semantically equivalent translation of an attributive sentence is the change from: *The Kirbys are given melons.* to: *The ghosts who shield the men in war are given melons.* An example of a syntactic transformation is the change from: *The Morgans are offered walnuts.* to: *Walnuts are offered to the Morgans.* For some Ss the style of phrasing was the same for each of the eight supernatural beings. For others, a mixed phrasing style was used. For that condition the pair of attributive sentences was phrased in a different way for each of the Gruanda ghosts.

Immediate repetition resulted in poor retention test performance even when the phrasing of the attributive sentence had been changed on repetition. It can therefore be assumed that the variations in phrasing that were used in the present study did not substantially alter the conditions that led to the shaping of inappropriate mathemagenic responses.

It should not be concluded from these experiments, however, that repetition interval is a simple variable, nor that short repetition intervals should always be avoided in training. First of all, the experiment yielded evidence (see Rothkopf & Coke, in press) that the poor retention test performance associated with immediate repetition is due to at least two factors. One of these can be identified with inappropriate mathemagenic responses. The other appears to be an adaptation or satiation effect that is of considerably smaller magnitude than the first. The adaptation effect is observable for immediate repetition items in treatments that employ a random distribution of repetition intervals, and is presumably additive with the mathemagenic response effect.

Another complication associated with immediate repetition is pertinent to performance in transfer situations. The second experiment that has been described (Rothkopf & Coke, in press) involved some treatments in which Ss were exposed to sentence sequences consisting of a translation rule followed by two identically phrased presentations of the attributive sentence. Some of these Ss were presented in the retention test with an attributive sentence that was a semantically equivalent translation of the attributive sentence seen in acquisition. For example, the acquisition sentence sequence might have been: *The ghosts who shield the men in war are the Kirbys. The Kirbys are offered melons. The Kirbys are offered melons.* In the retention test, S might be required to respond to: *The ghosts who protect the men in war are offered* ————. Such translated test items result in poorer test performance than sentences that have not been changed. This can be understood as a generalization or transfer decrement. However, it was observed that less generalization decrement was associated with consistent 0-interval between the two presentations of attributive sentences than for random repetition interval. It seemed safe to conclude from the available data that consistent immediate repetition results in substantially *less learning* than delayed repetition but also in *more generalization* to test items that differ in translation phrasing from the original study materials. It is almost certain that repetition must be immediate for *all* items in the sentence set in order for the generalization effect to occur. The reason for greater generalization with short repetition interval is not known.

MATHEMAGENIC BEHAVIOR AND TEST-LIKE EVENTS

The results of the experiments that were just described strongly suggest that one of the environmental controls of mathemagenic responses is test-like events. There is also evidence in the literature that tends to confirm this observation.

EFFECTS OF TESTS ON PERFORMANCE

By illustration, eye-movement studies (Carmichael & Dearborn, 1947, pp. 358–371) suggest that testing provides a state of affairs which maintains eye movements in reading at an efficient level. They interposed short quizzes throughout the experimental period and in this way maintained reading behavior with little loss in efficiency throughout a six-hour reading period. By contrast, Hoffman (1946), who had Ss read equivalent materials for four hours but did not use quizzes, observed decrements in number of fixations after only 30 minutes. The quizzes administered by Carmichael and Dearborn did not afford knowledge of results for S, and yet they appeared to have been instrumental in maintaining certain mathemagenic behaviors. There is some suggestion that knowledge of results probably enhances the effectiveness of tests in shaping mathemagenic responses under some circumstances. The observations of Angell and Lumsdaine (1960) have some bearing on this hypothesis. They found that the use of periodic anticipation trials (i.e., testing with knowledge of results) in a paired-associate training sequence consisting otherwise of all prompted trials resulted in generally higher recall performance than a training series that was composed entirely of prompted presentations. Both treatments also included testing trials *without* knowledge of results, and so it is unlikely that the "test" character of the interposed anticipation trials is sufficient to account for the obtained differences. It is also interesting to note that while the prompting-with-interspersed-anticipation-trials treatment produced better results than the pure prompting condition, the prompting treatment was found to be in turn better than training consisting *only* of anticipation trials (Cook, 1958; Cook & Kendler, 1956; Cook & Spitzer, 1960).

A recent series of experiments by Hershberger and associates (Hershberger, 1963; Hershberger & Terry, 1964; Hershberger & Terry, in press) are also relevant. Using a more realistic experimental task, they have shown convincingly that Ss learn more from written passages if they are periodically tested on the material that they are reading. This is in itself an interesting finding, but it cannot be decided from these studies whether tests shape effective mathemagenic behaviors, i.e., have a general rather than a specific facilitative effect on learning. In the Hershberger studies, as in other related studies in the literature, the subject matter on which Ss were tested while reading the passage was identical or closely related to the material on which the final criterion examination was based. It is difficult to interpret the Hershberger findings because it is well known that test-like events, with knowledge of results, are like practice events and produce improvement in recall performance on the material tested, e.g., the anticipation method in paired-associate learning. There is also evidence that test questions improve subsequent recall performance even when no knowledge of results is available during testing (Estes, 1960; Estes, Hopkins, & Crothers, 1960; Levine, Leitenberg, & Richter, 1964). It was therefore not clear whether the facilitated criterion test performance that was reported by Hershberger and associates was due to the specific, practice-like effects of the experimental questions or, alternatively, whether the test questions resulted in the shaping of appropriate mathemagenic responses and consequent general facilitation of learning. In short, answering questions while reading may result in improved postreading recall because: (*a*) the questions are in themselves instructive, and (*b*) they strengthen mathemagenic behaviors that generally facilitate learning.

EFFECT OF VARIATIONS IN TEST QUESTION SEQUENCE AND LEARNING DIRECTIONS

An experiment was recently completed for the purpose of obtaining more direct evidence as to whether test-like events had a general facilitative effect on learning (Rothkopf, unpublished paper). In order to do this, experimental test questions were constructed that were based on material that had little or no transfer of specific training on the material covered in the criterion examination.

Subjects were asked to read the chapter, entitled "The Sunless Sea," in Rachel Carson's book *The Sea Around Us*.[2] This

---

[2] Permission for the experimental use of these copyrighted materials

chapter was about 5,200 words long and described marine life at the greater ocean depths. Although the entire content of the chapter was topically related, many adjacent paragraphs dealt with relatively independent factual domains. The chapter was divided into seven sections. Two questions of the fill-in type were constructed from the material in each of the seven sections. The resulting set of 14 questions (to be referred to as *EQ*s—Experimental Questions) were used in the main experimental manipulations of this study. The *EQ*s were selected so as to minimize transfer of training from the portions of text underlying the 14 *EQ*s to the material underlying a 25-item criterion test on which the main experimental comparisons were based.

Five experimental treatments and two control groups were used. These differed mainly in the location of *EQ*s in the textual sequence and in whether knowledge of results (correct answers) were provided for *EQ*s. The experimental treatments were as follows:

SBA (*EQ*s shortly before, with answers). Just before starting on any section, S read the two *EQ*s for the section and was instructed to guess the correct answer for each. After writing his guess S obtained the correct answer.

SB (*EQ*s shortly before, no answers). Same treatment as *SBA* except that the correct answers were not provided after S made his guess.

LBA (All *EQ*s given before starting the chapter, with answers). Just before starting to read the chapter, Ss were given all 14 *EQ*s en bloc. They were instructed to guess the answer to each *EQ* and write it into the appropriate space. The correct answer was then provided as in *SBA*.

SAA (*EQ*s shortly after each section, with answers). Immediately after reading each section, S was asked to respond to each of the two *EQ*s appropriate to the section he had just read. The correct answer was provided as soon as S responded to each question.

SA (*EQ*s shortly after each section, no answers). Same as *SAA* except that the correct answers were not provided after S responded to questions.

was kindly granted by the publishers, Oxford University Press, 417 Fifth Avenue, New York 16, N.Y.

Control A. No *EQ*s were given in this treatment, and Ss were simply exposed to general directions that were composed of portions of those used in other treatments. These stressed that Ss should try to remember as much of the experimental chapter as they could and that they would be tested later.

Control C (Care). Same as *Control A* except that the general directions included statements that the reading materials contained a good deal of detailed information and that they should read the chapter carefully and slowly.

The final 25-item criterion test (*GT*) was administered immediately after S had completed reading the chapter. After the criterion test, all Ss were given another test consisting of the 14 *EQ*s.

The main experimental results are summarized in Figure 8. *Control C* and the two treatments in which *EQ*s were administered immediately after each section (*SAA, SA*) resulted in better general (*GT*) test performance than the other treatments. This facilitation of performance, which may be attributed to the strengthening of appropriate mathemagenic responses, amounts to a rise of approximately 10 per cent correct responses. An analysis of variance showed the between-treatment effects to be significant ($F = 2.44$, $d.f. = 6$, 139, $p < .05$). The *SA* treatment ($t = 2.21$, $d.f. = 139$, $p < .01$) and *Control C* ($t = 2.09$, $p < .05$) resulted in significantly higher *GT* scores than the *Control A* condition. The difference between *SAA* and *Control A* did not reach the conventional significance level ($t = 1.59$, $p < .20$).

The superior performance of *Control C,* *SAA,* and *SA* on the general test (*GT*) cannot be ascribed to the transfer of specific skills from the experimental questions because we were able to obtain experimental evidence that no transfer of specific skills has occurred from *EQ*s to the general criterion test. Also, three of the treatments that were exposed to *EQ*s, namely *LBA,* *SBA,* and *SB,* did not result in facilitated performance on the criterion test.

The results of this experiment therefore support the view that when a written passage is studied, Ss not only learn the specific content but also may acquire some more general and

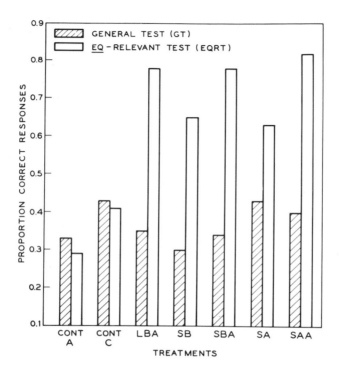

FIGURE 8. Proportion of correct responses on a retention test as a function of various arrangements of test-like events during acquisition. The various treatments are described in the text.

sometimes facilitative skills. These have been identified in the present experiment with mathemagenic behaviors consistent with the training objectives.

Two environmental controls of these mathemagenic behaviors were observed in the study. These were (1) written directions to read slowly, read with care, and pay attention to detailed facts; and (2) short tests, on material which had *just* been read, which were self-administered approximately every 1,000 words. It was clear that these short tests worked even when feedback as to the correct answers was *not* supplied after the student made a response. As a matter of fact, in the present experimental sample the SA treatment without feedback produced somewhat better performance on the general test (*GT*) than the equivalent treatment for which correct answer feedback was supplied after responding.

The experiment also provides evidence that there are some reasonably persistent respondent-like controls (see Skinner, 1957, pp. 357–362) of mathemagenic responses. *Control C* differed from *Control A* only in that it contained five additional short sentences in the general directions that were read by the student before starting on the experimental passage. These five sentences were enough to cause Ss to inspect the passage in a different manner from Ss in the *Control A* condition, and this difference was sufficient to produce more learning.

The evidence with respect to instrumental control of mathemagenic behavior is inconclusive. It could be assumed that some instrumental control existed if some consequences of effective mathemagenic responses could be shown to have improved general test performance. Finding out the right answer after having made the right response on an *EQ* is such a consequence. The fact that a right response has been made increases the likelihood that effective mathemagenic behaviors may have been used. There are, however, grounds for the belief that supplying S with the correct answer after responding is not the only way S finds out whether he has made a correct response. It is quite possible that the improved performance following the *SA* treatment is due to instrumental control of inspection behavior even though no formal error feedback was supplied. Nor can the possibility be disregarded that the improved criterion test performances of both *SA* and *SAA* are due to respondent-type control.

There are also some grounds for concluding that inspection time is under marked control of test-like events. Median reading time per page in seconds tends to be higher immediately after the administration of *EQs* and then falls off on subsequent pages of each section. These data are illustrated in Figure 9. It is impossible to reach a definite conclusion in this matter, however, because reading time was not balanced between pages in the present experiment.

The study just described increases confidence in the usefulness of the concept of mathemagenic behavior. Other studies are now under way to bring the characteristics of mathemagenic

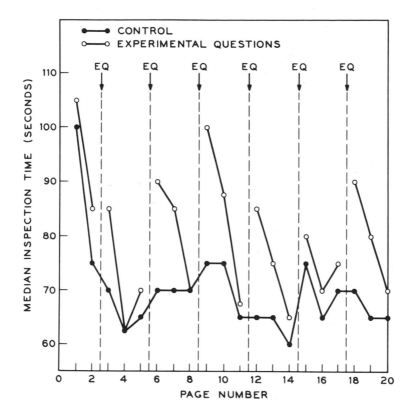

FIGURE 9. Median inspection time per page in seconds as a function of page number. The lines marked *EQ* indicate the administration of two experimental questions. The hollow circle data is from the *SA* treatment.

responses into sharper focus and improve our understanding of its effective environmental controls.

PROBLEMS FOR FURTHER RESEARCH

The present conceptual model of sentence learning has not been stated precisely enough to be directly vulnerable to empirical criticism. An attempt to describe aspects of the model in a more rigorous fashion is now under way. But even if this attempt is successful, it will almost certainly be a very incomplete account of written sentence learning and this account will be partially wrong. Nevertheless, even now the model is useful in thinking about the general problem of written instruction and in phrasing experimental questions.

The most interesting feature of the conceptual model is the notion of mathemagenic behavior. It divides the domain of written instruction into two related classes of problems. The first of these is how the instructive material must be arranged to produce efficient learning. The second problem concerns itself with mathemagenic behavior, i.e., what must be done to assure that the content of an instructive document is effectively used.

Many efforts have been made to apply the results of laboratory experiments to the first class of problems (e.g., Gagné & Bolles, 1959; Lumsdaine, 1964; Orbison, 1944; Rothkopf, 1958). The approach to the problem has been in general to look for a calculus of practice. Such a calculus of practice, on the basis of what we know about factors such as acquisition, generalization, or interference, attempts to arrive at a set of rules for the optimal arrangement of various practice events. In general, these attempts have not been successful. From a practical point of view the mathemagenic behavior problem is more likely to yield fruit. It is a commonplace observation that, given certain circumstances, humans will learn from instructive documents which are very badly prepared. What is necessary is that all the needed information is in the document in some form and that the student studies until he has achieved the desired training objectives. Hence it would seem that discovering the conditions that will keep the student working and teaching the student how he should study are the most practical approaches toward making written documents useful instructive tools. This is the problem of the environmental control of mathemagenic behavior. The work of Berlyne reported in Chapter 3 on stimulating curiosity may be interpreted as an approach to maintaining mathemagenic behavior.

Mathemagenic behavior needs to be understood better. The problem of its persistence seems particularly important. If tests are reinforcement-like events for certain desirable mathemagenic responses, what density of tests is likely to maintain these responses for the longest period? This may be an opportunity to bring some of the laboratory work on the relationship between reinforcement schedules and resistance to extinction to bear on an educational problem.

Another interesting set of problems is concerned with the characteristics of mathemagenic responses. At present we infer some of these characteristics from the kind of test questions which Ss are able to answer on a retention test. It is not yet known whether events which affect mathemagenic responses change performance on all possible test questions or just a few subclasses. Such subclasses might be questions about historical dates, magnitudes, technical names, relationships, etc. Can Ss learn to learn the exact population of cities in a geography passage? Probably! But what are the categories of test questions which can be manipulated in this manner? If certain procedures result in learning to learn city populations, are city altitudes, or freight car loadings, similarly affected?

If Ss can learn to learn certain associations, it must be assumed that this skill is controlled by some set of stimuli either in the written passage or in the study situation. If the stimulus control of mathemagenic responses is in the written passage, it would be useful to discover the character of possible stimulus controls. For example, a particular questioning procedure in connection with reading material on the *benzene ring* may result in mathemagenic responses which are inconsistent with training objectives. Will these inadaptive mathemagenic behaviors transfer to a passage on the *synthesis of urea*? On *photosynthesis*? How important is the time interval between reading the two passages in question, etc.?

It is apparent that a large number of experimental questions follow from the conception of mathemagenic behavior as responses which convert the nominal stimuli of a written page into effective stimulation. The two key problems are probably (*a*) the classes of environmental events which modify and shape mathemagenic responses and (*b*) the kind of stimulus controls (occasions for occurrence) which are feasible for mathemagenic responses. Both of these key issues involve some measurement problems which should prove a challenge to the ingenuity of the investigator.

SOME GENERAL REMARKS

The experiments which have been partially described here demonstrate, if nothing else, that fundamental verbal learning problems can be investigated with prose materials. This can be done without loss of precision even in an instructional context. The use of sentences as experimental material may not be as novel to Ss as it is to the Es of the verbal learning laboratory, since it is not unlikely that many Ss deal with paired word associates as if these were in fact presented in a sentence context.

The increased use of sentence materials in verbal learning studies is likely to yield results that would contribute directly to our understanding of the processes that underlie written instruction. This is a worthwhile purpose because written instruction is of great practical importance. American education consumed nearly 900 million dollars' worth of instructive written material in 1963 (Booher, 1964). Research on how humans learn from written material offers an unusual opportunity of fruitful interaction between the psychological laboratory and the practical needs of man. This is because written instruction is probably more responsive to laboratory findings than any other educational procedure.

The characteristic of written instructive material that makes it particularly well suited for the utilization of fundamental research findings is that written material can be *edited*. This makes it possible to cope with complex recommendations from the laboratory more readily than, for example, a live teacher can. Suppose it was observed that some particular ratio of impersonal pronouns to nouns resulted in more learning than other ratios. A teacher, speaking directly to a class, would have a good deal of trouble in trying to implement such a finding. On the other hand, routine editorial procedures such as those used in producing textbooks that conform to readability measures or in programed instruction would readily handle the pronoun-to-noun ratio findings. On the other hand, a particular instructive document can be repeatedly examined to see if it meets, in some measurable aspect, requirements that theory or empirical laws may place upon it in order for it to be an effective instructive document. It can then be edited and modified in relative leisure until it meets requirements. This makes it possible to incorporate reasonably complex characteristics into an instructive document, and this is an important source for optimism about the future of a technology of written instruction.

REFERENCES

Anderson, B. The short-term retention of active and passive sentences. Unpublished doctoral dissertation, Johns Hopkins Univer., 1963.

Angell, D., & Lumsdaine, A. A. Prompted plus unprompted trials versus prompted trials alone in paired-associate learning. Report AIR-314-60-IR-219, Pittsburgh: American Institute of Research, 1960.

Booher, E. E. Challenge of the future. *Book Production Mag.*, 1964, 44–47.

Carmichael, L., & Dearborn, W. F. *Reading and visual fatigue.* Boston: Houghton Mifflin, 1947.

Coke, E. U., & Rothkopf, E. Z. Electronic data processing machines in the preparation of materials for verbal learning studies. *Psychol. Rep.*, 1963, 13, 536.

Cook, J. O. Supplementary report: Processes underlying learning a single paired-associate item. *J. exp. Psychol.*, 1958, 56, 455.

Cook, J. O., & Kendler, T. S. A theoretical model to explain some paired-associate learning data. In G. Finch and F. Cameron (Eds.), *Symposium on Air Force human engineering, personnel, and training research.* Washington, D.C.: National Academy of Science, National Research Council, Publ. No. 455, 1956. Pp. 90–98.

Cook, J. O., & Spitzer, M. E. Supplementary report: Prompting versus confirmation in paired-associate learning. *J. exp. Psychol.*, 1960, 59, 275–276.

Estes, W. K. Learning theory and the new "mental chemistry." *Psychol. Rev.*, 1960, 67, 207–223.

Estes, W. K., Hopkins, B. L., & Crothers, E. J. All-or-none and conservation effects in the learning and retention of paired associates. *J. exp. Psychol.*, 1960, 60, 329–339.

Gagné, R. M., & Bolles, R. C. A review of factors on learning efficiency. In E. Galanter (Ed.), *Automatic teaching: The state of the art.* New York: Wiley, 1959. Pp. 13–54.

Hershberger, W. A. Learning via programmed reading and cue versus response in programmed reading. Palo Alto, Calif.: American Institute for Research, July, 1963. Technical Report AIR-C28-7/63-TR.

Hershberger, W. A., & Terry, D. F. Delay of self-testing in three types of programmed text. Palo Alto, Calif.: American Institute for Research, May, 1964. Technical Report AIR-C28-5/64-TR.

Hershberger, W. A., & Terry, D. F. Typographical cuing in conventional and programmed texts. *J. appl. Psychol.*, in press.

Hoffman, A. C. Eye movements during prolonged reading. *J. exp. Psychol.*, 1946, **36**, 95–118.

Hovland, C. I. The generalization of conditioned responses: I. The sensory generalization of conditioned responses with varying frequency of tone. *J. gen. Psychol.*, 1937, **17**, 125–148.

Hull, C. L. *Principles of behavior.* New York: Appleton-Century, 1943.

Levine, M., Leitenberg, H., & Richter, M. The blank trials law: The equivalence of positive reinforcement and nonreinforcement. *Psychol. Rev.*, 1964, **71**, 94–103.

Lumsdaine, A. A. Educational technology, programmed learning, and instructional science. *Yearb. nat. Soc. Stud. Educ.*, 1964, 371–401.

Miller, G. A. Some psychological studies of grammar. *Amer. Psychol.*, 1962, **17**, 748–762.

Müller, G. E., & Pilzecker, A. Experimentelle Beiträge zur Lehre vom Gedächtniss. *Z. Psychol.*, 1900, Supplementary Vol. 1.

Müller, G. E., & Schumann, F. Experimentelle Beiträge zur Untersuchung des Gedächtnisses. *Z. Psychol.*, 1894, **6**, 1–190.

Orbison, W. D. The relative efficiency of whole and part methods of learning paired associates as a function of length of list. Unpublished doctoral dissertation, Yale Univer., 1944.

Rothkopf, E. Z. A measure of stimulus similarity and errors in some paired-associate learning tasks. *J. exp. Psychol.*, 1957, **53**, 94–101.

Rothkopf, E. Z. Stimulus similarity and sequence of stimulus presentation in paired-associate learning. *J. exp. Psychol.*, 1958, **56**, 114–122.

Rothkopf, E. Z. Learning from written sentences: Effects of order of presentation on retention. *Psychol. Rep.*, 1962, **10**, 667–674.

Rothkopf, E. Z. Learning from written sentences: Within-sentence order in the acquisition of name-class equivalences. *J. verb. Learn. verb. Behav.*, 1963, **2**, 470–475.

Rothkopf, E. Z. Some conjectures about inspection behavior in learning from written sentences and the response mode problem in programmed self-instruction. *J. progmd Instruct.*, 1963, **2**, 31–46.

Rothkopf, E. Z. Learning from written materials: I. An exploration of the control of inspection behavior by test-like events. Unpublished paper.

Rothkopf, E. Z., & Coke, E. U. Repetition interval and rehearsal method in learning equivalences from written sentences. *J. verb. Learn. verb. Behav.*, 1963, 2, 406–416.

Rothkopf, E. Z., & Coke, E. U. Variations in phrasing, repetition interval, and the recall of sentence materials. *J. verb. Learn. verb. Behav.*, in press.

Skinner, B. F. *Verbal behavior.* New York: Appleton-Century-Crofts, 1957.

Thorndike, E. L. *The fundamentals of learning.* New York: Teachers College, Columbia Univer., 1932.

Underwood, B. J. Stimulus selection in verbal learning. In C. N. Cofer & B. S. Musgrave (Eds.), *Verbal behavior and learning.* New York: McGraw-Hill, 1963. Pp. 33–47.

Woodworth, R. S., & Schlosberg, H. *Experimental psychology.* New York: Henry Holt Co., 1954.

Chapter 9

MODEL THE
MASTER TEACHER
OR MASTER THE
TEACHING MODEL

LAWRENCE M. STOLUROW, *University of Illinois*

The educational psychologist probably does not think that he works at a weaver's trade, but in many ways he does. He is concerned with the fabric of behavior. In fact, some of the real problems he faces are those of planning its warp and woof and of determining its pattern. He works with conceptual tools and experimental devices to determine the threads and the weave. He is concerned with the loom, and with the way it is used to develop a behavioral fabric that suits a teacher's taste and a student's needs.

The educational psychologist who not only is concerned with achieving an understanding of teaching as a psychological process but also wants to help in the weaving is faced with a dilemma. Either he must begin by looking at the craftsmen who

Reproduction in whole or in part is permitted for any purpose of the United States Government. Research was sponsored by the Office of Naval Research Contract Nonr 3985(04), Authority NR 154-239/9-30-64; Office of Naval Research Contract Nonr 1834-36; and Air Force Contract No. AF 33(616)-5965.

have been weaving by tradition and intuition, or he must think of the design and engineering problems necessary for automation. He either looks at teachers and extracts a list of characteristics, or he manipulates variables which he thinks are important factors for improving the process. The former is essentially a passive approach; the latter, an active approach.

The passive approach is insufficient (e.g., Ryans, 1960; Ryans, 1963). If the objective is to understand teaching rather than teachers, and to find ways of redesigning education, then the educational psychologist needs to study the process of teaching by analyzing and then synthesizing. Traditionally, the research on teaching has been passive and analytical and has consisted of describing teacher characteristics rather than specifying the necessary and sufficient teaching behaviors and the way in which the behaviors are interrelated with one another. Often, research has attempted to study an unarticulated, incompletely defined, and poorly controlled set of activities which were called a "method." Furthermore, the so-called method was used as if it were a replicable variable that was derived from a unidimensional theory.

It is now possible for the research on teaching to be an active scientific process which does not involve the nominalism just mentioned. Experiments can be conducted in which the variables are derived from a model and are replicable. Models of the teaching process can be formulated (see Gage, 1963), and their variables can be studied both individually and jointly. In addition, it is possible to study the variables in conceptual isolation while operating *in situ*. There are many problems that must be dealt with in using this approach, but with it there is the possibility of advancing the knowledge about teaching by several orders of magnitude. One of the first problems is the laboratory capability that permits work with complex variables under conditions that can be replicated. This is now technologically possible by means of a computer-based teaching machine system, at least for the study of tutorial instruction. This technological capability alone is a necessary step and an important advance toward the solution of old and persistent problems, but it is not sufficient (see Stolurow & Davis, 1965).

MODELING THE MASTER TEACHER

Once the laboratory hardware is obtained, there is the problem of mastering the software. The question is how to get a grasp of this problem. One suggested answer is to model the master teacher.

This idea of modeling the master teacher has not worked. When this solution to the problems of instruction is examined, many reasons for its failure become apparent. One potentially important factor working against this approach is the complexity of the behavior being observed and the associated difficulties of controlling behavior so that it can be studied. Observations of teaching produce an effect which can be associated with the Rorschach and other projective tests in that different factors are identified by different observers and each observer interprets what he sees in a different way. The experimental demonstration by Skinner (1948), that superstitious behavior is readily learned, presents a related point. Skinner showed how irrelevant but correlated events can become the cues for behavior. This is especially possible in view of the fact that the conditions for learning about teaching are typically so highly variable, and the critical result (student learning) is not readily relatable to particular teacher behaviors.

Since there probably are fewer ways to teach effectively than there are to teach ineffectively, it is more likely that ineffective teaching behaviors would be identified in observational studies of teaching behavior. Even master teachers are likely to engage in ineffective behavior, and these ineffective correlates of master teacher performance would be misleading to investigators and students who are unguided by validated concepts of what to look for. Thus, they would be more likely to learn the wrong ways to teach than the right ways.

The Myth of the Single Method

While there has been a vain search for a single effective method of instruction, there also has been a widespread practice of recommending the virtues of variety. An excellent example of the fruitless search for the one grand method is that which sought to show that learner-centered instruction was superior to teacher-centered instruction (see Anderson, 1959). Like many other efforts to locate the instructional pot of gold, the learner-centered method turned out to be an ill-defined, unspecified, and unreplicable collection of methods. The results of its use show a normal distribution of outcomes. Intimately involved in the search for the single but undefined method are the deception of nominalism and the treacheries of reification.

An alternative is to dissect the psychological threads of a teaching fabric so that particular operations can be individually related to their effects on learning. In this way, useful relationships can be identified and effective combinations of them formed to produce an efficient teaching method.

The most significant conclusion that can be drawn from efforts to use teachers as a basis for information about teaching is that effective instruction can be produced by a variety of combinations of characteristics and conditions rather than by one unique combination. If this were not the case, efforts to enumerate the characteristics of good teachers would have resulted in the identification of at least one or two critical characteristics. However, neither the observation of master teachers nor that of a large number of effective teachers (e.g., Ryans, 1960) has led to findings that are either substantial or sufficient for the understanding of teaching as a process. Thus, an alternative approach is needed.

GOING BEYOND DIRECT OBSERVATION

It seems reasonable to consider the possibility that it is undesirable to limit one's attention to only those factors which have been revealed by observations of teachers. Doing so might impose unnecessary restrictions upon an effort to understand teaching as a process, although it might add to an understanding of individual teachers.

There are several points to be made here. It may be possible to do a better job of teaching than that which has been observed. This may not be a popular position, but it is one that an objective analysis of the situation suggests. If this is tenable, then it is unwise to *restrict* one's concern to what teachers are doing now. There would be little point to the study of teaching if we did not want to improve it. Another possibility is that many of the things which teachers are now doing may be accomplished more effectively by other means. An efficient combination of resources must be found if effectiveness is to be improved.

MASTERING THE TEACHING MODEL

The Process of Modeling

It is important to consider the appropriate use of models in the solution of teaching problems. The term "model" is used a great deal, and although it is assumed to have only one meaning, there are different kinds of models and different reasons for developing models. Some models are built to predict, while others are designed to describe. These are very different purposes, although they may not appear to be at first.

While a descriptive model also should predict at least one dimension of a system's output, it is not the case that the predictive model also describes the real phenomena. Adequacy of prediction often is confused with accuracy of description. Although a watch can predict time very adequately, it cannot accurately describe the solar system. A mathematical model of a mechanical system may provide an adequate basis for predicting an outcome, but it does not necessarily tell us the position of each of the parts at any point in time. Similarly, mathematical models of learning provide an adequate basis for the prediction of a set of outcomes but may not give an accurate description of the processes going on within the learner.

Another example relates to the molar and molecular relevance of models. A model such as a chemical formula does not describe what any particular set of ions is doing at a particular point in time; rather it describes the mode or median effect. Thus while it is perfectly useful on a statistical basis, it is not useful for predicting what an individual molecule is doing. It seems useful therefore to distinguish models designed to predict individual cases from those designed to predict group outcomes.

An algorithm is a procedure for accomplishing a transformation. Many people have learned algorithms to accomplish such arithmetic operations as long division and the extraction of square roots. However, the algorithms learned in the past are not the only means by which these transformations can be accomplished. In fact, a large number of new algorithms are being developed so that modern computers can perform these very operations. Certain algorithms are efficient for one computer, but not for another. Similarly, while an algorithm may be efficient for a computer, the same algorithm does not permit children or adults to accomplish the same operations. Thus, algorithms differ in their suitability to the system using them. Models that are equivalent in one respect are not equivalent in all other respects. For example, one model used to predict a particular outcome or class of events may be as accurate in its prediction as another model, but it may not do other things that the first one will do. Obviously, the more outcomes a model accounts for, the more useful it is.

RESOURCES FOR MODELING

The modern computer is capable of rapid performance of a large number of tasks that would require considerable mental energy if performed by humans. This is not to say that machines think, but rather that they do tasks which are said to involve thinking when accomplished by living systems. While teaching is an activity which involves thinking when accomplished by a live teacher, it may be possible to achieve the same effect by the use of a computer. Since computers can only do as they are told, the various directions put into the computer can be experimented with to see which produce the most effective combinations.

IMPLICATIONS OF MODELING

What are the implications of modeling for the process of mastering the teaching model as contrasted with the modeling of a master teacher? Assume that we set out to develop a teaching model which has the prediction of a set of learning outcomes as its objective. It does not also follow that the model will describe the behavior of a master teacher. If the model is built to predict learning outcomes, it may not describe the procedures that a teacher might use to accomplish the same objective. If, however, one is attempting to develop a descriptive model of instruction, then the procedures used could be the prototype of those employed by a teacher.

The constructed model may focus on the development of a set of elements sufficient to achieve a particular objective; however, the set of elements used may not be a necessary set. Other models using other elements may be just as effective. Just as different models of internal combustion engines can be used to convert chemical to mechanical energy, so a variety of different teaching models can be used to convert teacher activities into student learning. Consequently, the relationship between a model of teaching and a model of learning is not a one-to-one correspondence. On the other hand, knowledge about the critical variables in learning would affect the design of a model of teaching. Nevertheless, different teaching models might be developed to account for the same set of dependent variables used to measure learning.

If there is no unique solution, then why use models? An important reason is to make explicit the elements and relationships needed to account for the phenomenon in which we are interested (e.g., a student's performance on a learning task). A model is a commitment to a position and can be tested if properly formulated. It is not a loosely assembled, inarticulated set of statements that some theorists can point at with pride in their eclecticism.

Why build a model for teaching? There seem to be a number of reasons in addition to those already mentioned. Each time research is done to study conditions that affect students' performance on a learning task, five or six factors are suggested that were not taken into account as possible reasons for the results. In short, there is a widely held belief that teaching is a complex process, and that a large variety of variables affect what students do, even in a tutorial situation. If this is the case, a model of teaching must be developed that will do at least two basic things. First, it must make the large set of relationships explicit. Second, it must permit the correction of mistakes made in trying to find out about teaching and indicate the nature of the required cor-

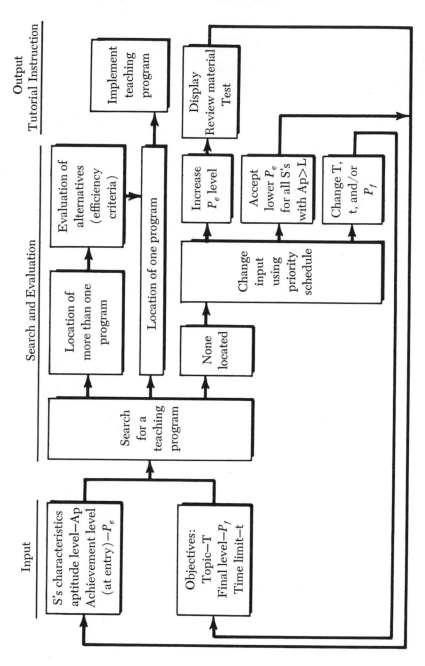

rections. To achieve these things, either lists can be developed and the loose state of the eclectic maintained, or a set of factors can be articulated to see how much explanatory power can be obtained from a model. In this latter way, clarification and continuity can be increased, while control is gained over nominalism and reification.

SOCRATES

SOCRATES (System for Organizing Content to Review And Teach Educational Subjects) is a system for modeling teaching and for doing research that tests the models (see Stolurow & Davis, 1965). In developing SOCRATES, it was assumed that there are two basic processes constituting instruction. One is the sampling or selection of content (e.g., concepts, principles, facts). The other is the processing of response data and the implementation of sets of decision rules about the content so as to accomplish stated instructional objectives with a particular student.

SOCRATES was designed with the assumption that, at the present time, the teaching process can be divided into two phases. The first is the *pretutorial phase.* Its objective is the selection of an initial teaching program that will achieve a desired minimum outcome. The second is the *tutorial phase.* Its objective is twofold: one is to implement the teaching program; the other is to monitor the student's performance. The monitoring process enables the system to change programs if the student exceeds certain expected limits (above or below) in his performance level. The pretutorial decision process is shown in Figure 1.

Pretutorial Process

Three sets of variables figure in the pretutorial phase of instruction: the objectives or outcomes, the entry behaviors (P_e), and the teaching program.

Outcomes. The outcome considered in the pretutorial decision is the minimum level of performance (P_{min}) to be achieved in a given topic of a subject matter (T) within a given

FIGURE 1. The pretutorial decision process.

232   *Learning and the Educational Process*

maximum amount of time (t). The attainment of specific outcomes for a particular student requires an instructional program.
Each teaching program is designed to accomplish a stated minimum objective for a particular entry behavior level.

Entry behaviors. There are three critical characteristics of
the student's entry behavior. The first is his level of performance
on a specific list of tasks or pretest performance; it is the quality
of his performance at the beginning of the instruction. The second is his aptitude level (A) which is the relatively stable set
of transferable skills which are not necessarily tied to particular
subject matter but can be elicited by a large class of materials
(see Ferguson, 1956). The third is his personality, which is considered as the perceived needs of a student (see Frase, 1963).
One of the critical problems in making efficient decisions about
teaching is that of specifying the inclusive set of relevant entry
behaviors. Gagné and Paradise (1961) describe one procedure
for identifying the set. They ask the question, "What does the
student have to know in order to do X?" Here, X is a variable
that changes as the question is asked. Through the sequential use
of this question, more and more basic levels of behavior are
identified; the process is stopped when the programer has enu-
merated the levels of student performance assumed to be present
when the program is used.

The basic problem with entry behavior measurement is the
inclusion of all relevant ones. Once the relevant set has been
specified, it is possible to decide upon the content of the program to be used in getting the student to the terminal performance level. The content is determined by two sets of rules: one
set determines the sequence of concepts to be presented; the
other set determines the remaining contingencies that depend
upon the student's responses.

Instructional programs. Instructional programs should produce the desired transformations of pretest behavior to posttest
achievement. To do this, programs have two critical components:
the content units to be learned, and the decision rules that are
applied to the student's performance. At this point, tutorial and
classroom instruction part company. At the minimum level in a
tutorial situation, the decision rules specify the performance that
is sufficient to provide knowledge of results; however, the deci-

sion rules can do more than that. For example, a decision rule might specify that the response must be correct before the student is allowed to go on to the next item or concept. In experimental studies, this is called the correction procedure. In some previous research where correction procedure was used, it was found to be more effective than a noncorrection procedure (Briggs, 1949; Irion & Briggs, 1957). The importance of some decision rules seems to depend, at least in part, upon the age of the learner, and the decision rule that the student must make the correct response before he goes to the next step is a case in point. It seems to be a significant factor in making decisions about teaching children (Suppes & Ginsberg, 1962) but does not seem to be significant in teaching older students (Merrill, 1964). The effectiveness of correction procedure may depend to some extent on the nature of the task in relation to the learner. There are many other contingencies that can be associated with a student's responses. Each rule that specifies a contingency is an aspect of the complex process called teaching; a complete set of rules defines a particular teaching program.

The nature of the initial teaching program that will meet the objectives can be specified once the student's characteristics are known. Estimation of possible outcomes in terms of the student's achievement level and time requirements can be estimated for every topic at the beginning of instruction. This set of estimates can be used to estimate the total time required to see if a suitable set of programs is available for use with each student.

There are three possible outcomes of the pretutorial decision (Figure 1): first, more than one program may work; second, none may work; and third, only one may work. For the first two of these possibilities, it is necessary to make some additional decisions. The set of possible programs must be reduced by some criteria relating to the relative efficiency of the possible alternatives. However, if no program is found, either the student is to be rejected and considered for some other kinds of training or the objectives are to be changed. Among the student changes that can be considered, some are more feasible than others. For example, the student's entry level may be raised by a review exercise. High-aptitude students would be good risks to be given pretraining if their entry level on prerequisite knowledge and skills is below the minimum originally set. Another, but more risky decision, would be to include students whose entry behavior is greater than a minimum level. Each of these decisions represents a change in objectives since the objectives include achievement level on particular topics within maximum time. If the decision were to give the student more practice, then the maximum time would be increased. Other changes in objectives such as reducing the required set of tasks or reducing the level of proficiency required on the tasks also might be considered.

Student's entry level	Teaching programs A	B	C
a	1	3	2
b	2	1	3
c	3	2	1

FIGURE 2. An hypothetical matrix (3 × 3) relating S's entry level (row) to teaching program (column) in the accomplishment of objectives (numerical entries).

If the pretutorial decision is made by relating each of the different levels of student entry behavior (row in Figures 2, 3, and 4) to one of the teaching programs (column in Figures 2, 3, and 4) to determine a scaled value of the outcome (numerical entry in Figures 2, 3, and 4), a variety of different matrices can be generated. One of these is illustrated in Figure 2. In this example, the teacher's position is ideal since he can achieve any one of the possible objectives by selecting a program for each level of entry behavior.

It is possible, however, for a very different set of conditions to occur as illustrated in Figure 3. For some objectives there are several programs for a particular entry behavior that will produce the desired outcome. For example, at level *c* there are three ways of achieving outcome 1. However, if outcome 2 were the objective, no program would accomplish it for students at levels *a* or *c*. If this were to happen, then it would be necessary either to change the objective or to reject students at levels *a* or *c*.

Since programs are the means by which students of a given entry level are moved to a particular final level (within a stated maximum amount of time), then the established levels of entry

Student's entry level	Teaching programs A	B	C	D
a	1	4	1	4
b	2	4	1	1
c	4	1	1	1
d	4	2	1	2
e	4	1	2	4

FIGURE 3. An hypothetical matrix (4 × 5) relating S's entry level (row) to the teaching program (column) and resulting outcomes (numerical entries) when not all objectives are achieved.

behavior make a difference in the outcome. This means that duplications of the values representing the outcome would not be found within any particular column representing a teaching program. Figure 4 shows a matrix that meets this requirement by means of a 3 × 9 representation of the pretutorial prediction about instructional outcomes which presumably would be based upon normative data.

One interesting implication of this analysis is that it is necessary to use a different program for each student entry when only one outcome is accepted for all students. For example, if we wanted to achieve outcome 3, then in Figure 2, B would have to

Student's entry level	Teaching programs A	B	C
a	1	16	9
b	2	2	2
c	3	17	3
d	6	6	11
e	8	8	13
f	10	4	4
g	11	5	6
h	12	14	8
i	13	11	1

FIGURE 4. An hypothetical matrix (3 × 9) relating S's entry level (row) to the teaching program (column) and resulting outcomes (numerical entries) when no two outcomes in any column are identical.

be used for level *a*, C for level *b*, and A for level *c*. If more than one outcome is acceptable (for example, all students above a certain entry level might be required to achieve outcome 1, whereas those below that level might be required to achieve outcome 2), then several different programs may still be required, but the number of programs may be smaller than that required of the system when only one outcome is sought for all of the students who represent a wide distribution of entry levels. In Figure 4, for example, the teacher must use one of three programs to achieve outcome 11, i.e., for level *g* he must use A, for level *i* he must use B, and for level *d* he must use C. Another implication is that it is impossible for every level of entry behavior to reach the same objective unless the teacher has available as many programs as he has levels of entry behavior (Stolurow & Davis, 1965).

This analysis indicates several things. First, as an illustration of the effects of a model, it reveals the constraints imposed by our assumptions regarding relationships. At a more substantive level, it indicates that teaching systems limited to a single teaching program (a strategy and set of content units) will produce as many outcomes as there are student levels at entry. It might be said that this implication is unacceptable in that a linear program could be used with a variety of students, all of whom may answer all the questions on the test after completing the program. If the achievement test is accepted as valid, the original distinction among the levels is invalid and needs to be changed, or the entry levels were irrelevant to the decision about the teaching program. In addition, time is a factor. While it may be possible for students who are different in entry behavior to achieve the same score on the final test, they may not complete the program in the same amount of time, and time is one of the factors determining the value of the outcome. If the number of different outcomes is not at least equal to the number of valid entry behavior classes, then either the categories of individual differences in entry behavior are invalid, the test of the attainment of objectives does not provide the degree of discrimination required, or the programs are not really different. Whichever of these seems most plausible should then be re-examined.

Tutorial Process

Figure 5 concerns the basic elements and relationships in the tutorial process (Stolurow, 1964b; Stolurow, in press). Basically, it is a recognition and extension of the S-O-R model of Woodworth (1947). The addition of feedback includes the idea of reinforcement and, therefore, is an explicit recognition of the need to make selected events contingent upon response. Feedback is recognized as a stimulus event that follows response, as distinguished from the cue and eliciting stimulus functions. Feedback is a more descriptive term since school situations involve both informational contingencies and reinforcement contingencies.

The performance standard (Figure 5) is a critical function in the making of decisions in experimental studies of learning. Teaching can no longer allow performance standards to go unnoticed as a critical part of the definition of the learning task; their function needs to be made explicit.

Performance standards are the various principles used to

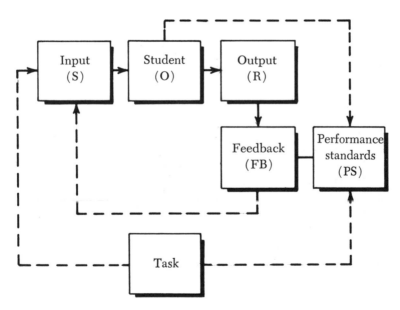

FIGURE 5. The tutorial instructional system.

generate the criteria employed in making decisions about the correctness of each response. Standards vary with school grade and often with a student's ability. Teachers impose different standards upon different students in a class and in this way define different tasks for these students.

Performance standards used by the teacher at an early period can be taught to students at later periods. This makes performance standards a part of the material covered in a course and thus available to the students who can later use them to evaluate their own performance. The student who is taught rules of grammar, for example, can apply these to his own writing. Once he does this, he becomes his own teacher by supplying himself with knowledge of results and, if he verbalizes the rule when he corrects his own work, even with information feedback. This links the rule to the cues of the material and establishes an even more effective association for later use.

Idiomorphic programing. Idiomorphic programing is a special case of tutorial instruction in which decisions are made regarding the next instructional experience of the student in terms of entry behavior data and sets of responses made during learning. In idiomorphic programing, the repertory of the teaching system is more extensive than it is when teaching is conducted using other models. The four types of options (repeat, remediate, skip, or pace) are decided upon in terms of a larger base of information about the student than is used in other branching programs such as intrinsic programing (see Crowder, 1960). The following considerations are included in idiomorphic programing: (1) displaying (presenting cues and prompts to the student); (2) accommodating student responses; (3) pacing (control of timing for displays and responses); (4) comparing student response with performance standard; (5) reinforcing response by providing knowledge of results; (6) collating the record of students' responses with relevant displays; (7) selecting displays according to rules that use student response information; (8) storing information that may be displayed to any student using the system; (9) generating programing rules for frame selection so that they can be changed when the student's responses do not meet criteria; and (10) computing forecasts of student performance on criterion tasks based upon entry data and responses made to selected frames of the program in terms of both time and correctness.

The tutorial model relates the various classes of events that are presumed to be necessary and sufficient for teaching. This aspect of the total model, which includes the pretutorial and the tutorial processes, has been used in the development of SOCRATES. This computer-based teaching system is now being used to study specific variables relating to the teaching process.

DATA AND DIRECTIONS

SOME IMPLICATIONS OF THE MODEL

The teaching system must have the capability of handling either a broad range of relevant content, a variety of decision rules, or both, so that by selective combinations the number of different programs is at least equal to the number of different levels of entry behavior to be taught. Thus, *the wider the range of student ability to be taught by the teaching system, the larger the requirement for different programs if all students are to achieve the same objective.* It would seem that a large number of limited teaching systems must be used if each one is capable of presenting only a single program. However, a complex computer-based instructional system can be used to cope with the wide range of individual differences because of its capacity to generate a variety of programs selectively for different students depending upon ability levels, personality, etc. The computer-based system appears to be the most efficient way of coping with the task of individualized instruction. It can store the requisite information and the various decision rules that are differentially called upon to produce the program which each student requires.

INTERACTION BETWEEN ABILITY AND METHOD OF INSTRUCTION

One type of data that relate to the model consists of interactions between ability level and method of instruction. Several studies provide this type of evidence. For example, Little (1934) found that the immediacy of KR (knowledge of results) was more critical for students in the lower half of the ability range than it was for those in the upper half. Related is the finding by Eigen (1962) that IQ and method interacted, since there was a critical difference in the immediacy of KR for the methods he used. When KR was most immediate, there was no correlation between ability (IQ) and performance or between reading level and performance; but when KR was less immediate, both of these variables correlated with performance on the immediate and delayed posttest.

Porter (1961), on the other hand, reported that under conventional instruction the greatest gains occurred with the lower half of the IQ distribution, whereas with programed instruction the greater gains were made by the upper half of the IQ distribution.

When methods differed in terms of the type of student response required, McNeil (1962) found that an overt (oral) reading response was more effective for children in the lower IQ range than for those in the upper range. Burton and Goldbeck (1962) also found that response factors produced an interaction with ability. Gropper and Lumsdaine (1961) found that the upper half of their IQ distribution performed significantly better than their counterpart in ability when they learned from a programed television lesson in physics. The delayed retention test findings were even more significant. Not only did the *high*-ability students (programed TV course) do better than their counterparts (conventional course), but the low-IQ group achieved *lower* scores when they saw the programed TV course than they did when they saw the conventional course. Reed and Hayman (1962) also found that high-ability students performed significantly better with a program while low-ability students performed significantly better when they received conventional instruction.

Ability also seems to interact with method of instruction when the students are allowed self-direction (Berliner, Bivens, & Campbell, 1963; Bivens, 1964; Bivens, Campbell, & Terry, 1963; Campbell, 1963a; Campbell, 1963b; Campbell & Bivens, 1963; Campbell, Bivens, & Terry, 1963; and Silberman et al., 1961).

These studies showing method and ability interactions suggest that it is possible to design a program that disproportionately benefits either the high- or low-ability group. Therefore, they suggest that both extremes of ability can be differentially affected by a method of instruction. The problem is to find out which method best suits each level.

APTITUDE AND ACHIEVEMENT TEST CORRELATIONS

Cartwright (1962), Smith (1962), and Dick (1963) report that different methods of instruction result in different patterns of correlation between specific abilities and performance on an achievement test following learning. These data suggest that the sequence of the experience may be a potentially important variation in instructional programs that could be manipulated so as to make use of different student aptitudes. Thus, the sequence in which a set of instructional steps is assembled could determine the optimum match with ability.

INTERACTION BETWEEN MOTIVATION AND TASK DIFFICULTY

The data relating to interactions with motivation are less substantial. Spence and Taylor (1951) have reported an interaction between task difficulty and level of motivation. This form of interaction was originally suggested by Yerkes and Dodson (1908) and is sometimes referred to as the Yerkes-Dodson law. It identifies another potentially significant factor in achieving an optimum match with ability, since one can assume that difficulty would vary inversely with ability with a given task, as defined by Stolurow (1964a; 1964b). Atkinson reported further evidence of interaction between motivation, task difficulty, and other variables in Chapter 2.

INTERACTION BETWEEN INTELLIGENCE, INFORMATION, AND EFFECTS OF REWARDS

Abel (1936) reported that "the effect of rewards dependent upon improvement with a group of average intelligence does not seem to be as great as that of reward administered at every trial with a group of superior intelligence" (p. 50). This suggests that reward contingencies might have a different effect depending upon age or ability of the learner. Stacey (1949) found an inter-action between amount of reward, information, and ability. Children with high ability performed better than those of average or low ability when given minimum information. Furthermore, when the amount of information was just above the minimum, rewarded children of average ability again performed significantly better than those of high or low ability. When maximum information was available, the children with high ability performed significantly better than those of average ability. These findings suggest that in optimizing learning it may be necessary to make both information and reward contingencies depend upon student ability. These interaction effects with the conditions of feedback suggest the potential significance of factors other than the simple schedule of reinforcement as important variables relating to learning. Reinforcement schedules might be optimized by making the contingencies depend upon what is being taught and who is learning.

SOME IMPLICATIONS OF THE INTERACTION FINDINGS

These findings not only indicate the importance of ability factors for the model but also indicate ways in which ability information could be used discriminately to optimize learning. These data suggest specific ways in which teaching could be made more effective and efficient if modeled as a differential decision process (see Cronbach & Gleser, 1964).

The model suggests that learning can be optimized by rules that guide the contingencies employed to present materials to different ability levels. For example, they suggest that the optimizing teacher would select procedures that would give priority to the minimization of the interval between response and KR in teaching low-ability students. They suggest that the optimizing teacher would use procedures that allow self-directed study only with high-ability students. They suggest that various means be used to raise the motivation level of the students according to their ability levels so as to maintain an equilibrium between motivation and task difficulty. They suggest that more information feedback should be used with high-ability students and that minimum information feedback should be used with students of average ability.

PERSONALITY AND EVALUATIVE FEEDBACK

Frase (1963) related personality scores to performance on a logic program under different conditions of evaluative feedback. Four groups studied the program. One group was simply told they were right or wrong whenever they made a response; the other three groups, however, had their responses evaluated. Students in one of these groups had their responses evaluated whenever they were correct but *not* when they were incorrect; another group was evaluated whenever they made incorrect responses but not when they made correct ones; and the last group had all responses (right and wrong) evaluated. Negative evaluative feedback was more effective than positive evaluative feedback in changing student performance, and there was evidence of differential reaction to the different evaluative statements depending upon the student's personality. Aggressive students, for example, liked the program that "fought back" (negative evaluation).

EVIDENCE FOR MIXED STRATEGIES

There are data accumulating which suggest the need of a mixed strategy, i.e., the use of more than one set of decision rules with students at a particular level of ability. Reference is made here to the use of two sets of decision rules which are related to each other in such a way that only one of them can be used at a time, e.g., differently organized frames, prompting and confirmation.

For example, Cartwright (1962) used two different sequences of the same set of frames and found that while immediate achievement was the same, one sequence of frames led to significantly better retention, whereas the other led to significantly better transfer effects. The question that this result raises is whether the students might be given both sequences so as to improve both retention and transfer. If this were done, the question which arises is that of the order of the two sequences to use in order to optimize retention and transfer effect.

In a study by Stolurow and Lippert (1964) using mentally retarded children, the prompting sequence led to faster learning, but with a high degree of overlearning the confirmation sequence led to better retention. Several combinations of the two were used in a later study, and these data showed that the number of words recalled by the mentally retarded children was greatest when the proportion of confirmation trials was greater than the proportion of prompting trials. This suggests that mixed strategies might be used to an advantage but that the rule used to develop the mixture can make a difference in the resulting learning effects. For example, for the group ranging in MA from 5–6 to 6–5, the best sets of conditions were those in which the number of confirmation trials exceeded the number of prompting trials (see Stolurow, 1964a).

SUMMARY

The implications of individualizing instruction are far from clear. The threads that relate ability, prior knowledge, and personality to the decisions made in selecting a set of teaching conditions and in implementing a complex set of rules to optimize learning are still not clear. We have only begun to tease out relationships by tracing them through the complex fabric of behavior.

The computer program used to make a decision about the contingencies of various events upon the different responses of individual students is an explicit model of teaching. It relates data about individuals such as test scores and performance during learning to each of the decisions made during the instruction of every student. In this sense, it uses the results of the study of individual differences and those of the learning laboratory to produce a testable model of teaching. Hopefully, mastering the teaching model will prove to be more useful than previous efforts at modeling the master teacher.

REFERENCES

Abel, L. B. The effects of shift in motivation upon the learning of a sensory motor task. *Arch. Psychol.*, 1936, **29**, 205.

Anderson, R. C. Learning in discussions: A resumé of the authoritarian-democratic studies. *Harvard educ. Rev.*, 1959, **29**, 201–215.

Berliner, D., Bivens, L., & Campbell, V. Memory span and self-direction in serial learning of a name list. Palo Alto, Calif.: American Institute for Research, AIR-D10-12/63-TR, 1963.

Bivens, L. Feedback complexity and self-direction as factors in programed instruction. Palo Alto, Calif.: American Institute for Research, 1964.

Bivens, L., Campbell, V., & Terry, D. Self-direction in programed instruction: Effects on learning in low-ability students. Palo Alto, Calif.: American Institute for Research, AIR-D10-7/63-TR, 1963.

Briggs, L. J. The development and appraisal of special procedures for superior students and analysis of the effects of "knowledge of results." *Abstr. Doctoral Diss.*, Ohio State University Press, 1949, **58**, 41–49.

Burton, B. B., & Goldbeck, R. A. The effect of response characteristics and multiple-choice alternatives on learning during programed instruction. San Mateo, Calif.: American Institute for Research, Contract No. Nonr-3077(00) Tech. Rep. No. 4, 1962.

Campbell, V. Learning. From R-M theory to educational planning. Palo Alto, Calif.: American Institute for Research, AIR-D10-11/63-TR, 1963. (a)

Campbell, V. Self-direction and programed instruction for five different types of learning objectives. Palo Alto, Calif.: American Institute for Research, AIR-D10-12/63-TR, 1963. (b)

Campbell, V., & Bivens, L. Self-direction in programed geography instruction. Palo Alto, Calif.: American Institute for Research, AIR-D10-11/63-TR, 1963.

Campbell, V., Bivens, L., & Terry, D. Effects of mathematical ability pretraining and interest on self-direction in programed instruction. Palo Alto, Calif.: American Institute for Research, AIR-D10-10/63-TR, 1963.

Cartwright, C. P. Two types of programed instruction for mentally retarded adolescents. Unpublished master's thesis, Univer. of Illinois, 1962.

Cronbach, L. J., & Gleser, Goldine. *Psychological tests and personnel decisions.* (2nd ed.) Urbana, Ill.: Univer. of Illinois Press, 1964.

Crowder, N. A. Automatic tutoring by intrinsic programming. In A. A. Lumsdaine and R. Glaser (Eds.), *Teaching machines and programmed learning. A source book.* Washington, D.C.: National Education Association, 1960. Pp. 286–298.

246   *Learning and tre Educational Process*

Dick, W. Paired vs. individual study of programed instruction in contemporary algebra. In C. R. Carpenter and L. P. Greenhill (Eds.), *Cooperative research methods and media for presenting programed courses in mathematics and English.* University Park, Pa.: Pennsylvania State Univer., Univer. Division of Instructional Services, 1963.

Eigen, L.D. A comparison of three modes of presenting a programed instruction sequence. *J. educ. Res.,* 1962, **55**, 453–460.

Ferguson, G. A. On transfer and the abilities of man. *Canad. J. Psychol.,* 1956, **10**, 121–131.

Frase, L. T. The effect of social reinforcers in a programed learning task. Urbana, Ill.: Univer. of Illinois, Training Research Laboratory, ONR Contr. Nonr 1834–36, Tech. Rep. No. 11, September, 1963.

Gagné, R. M., & Paradise, N. E. Abilities and learning sets in knowledge acquisition. *Psychol. Monogr.,* 1961, **75**, No. 14 (Whole No. 518).

Gage, N. L. Paradigms for research on teaching. In N. L. Gage (Ed.), *Handbook of research on teaching.* Chicago: Rand McNally, 1963. Pp. 94–141.

Gropper, G. L., & Lumsdaine, A. A. An experimental comparison of a conventional TV lesson with a programmed TV lesson requiring active student response. Pittsburgh: Metropolitan Pittsburgh Educational Television Station WQED-WQEX and American Institute for Research, Studies in Televised Instruction, Rep. No. 2, 1961.

Irion, A. S., & Briggs, L. J. Learning task and mode of operation variables in use of Subject Matter Trainer. Lackland Air Force Base, Texas: Air Force Personnel and Training Research Center, AFPTRC-TR-57-8, October, 1957.

Little, J. K. Results of use of machines for testing and for drill upon learning in educational psychology. *J. exp. Educ.,* 1934, **3**, 45–49.

McNeil, J.D. Programed instruction as a research tool in reading. An annotated case. *J. progmd Instruct.,* 1962, **1**, 37–42.

Merrill, M. D. Transfer effects within a hierarchical learning task as a function of review and correction on successive parts. Urbana, Ill.: Univer. of Illinois, Training Research Laboratory, Contr. No. Nonr 3985(04), Tech. Rep. No. 5, September, 1964.

Porter, D. An application of reinforcement principles to classroom teaching. Cambridge, Mass.: Harvard Univer., Graduate School of Education, Laboratory for Research in Instruction, 1961.

Reed, J. E., & Hayman, J. L., Jr. An experiment involving use of English 2600, an automated instruction text. *J. educ. Res.,* 1962, **55**, 476–485.

Ryans, D. G. *Characteristics of teachers, their description, comparison and appraisal: A research study.* Washington, D.C.: American Council on Teaching, 1960.

Ryans, D. G. Assessment of teacher behavior and instruction. *Rev. educ. Res.*, 1963, **33**, 415–441.

Silberman, H. F., Melaragno, R. J., Coulson, J. E., & Estaban, D. Fixed sequence vs. branching auto-instructional methods. *J. educ. Psychol.*, 1961, **52**, 166–172.

Skinner, B. F. 'Superstition' in the pigeon. *J. exp. Psychol.*, 1948, **38**, 168–172.

Smith, Leone M. Programed learning in elementary school: An experimental study of relationships between mental abilities and performance. Urbana, Ill.: Univer. of Illinois, Training Research Laboratory, USOE Title VII, Proj. No. 711151.01, Tech. Rep. No. 2, August, 1962.

Spence, K. W., & Taylor, Janet. Anxiety and strength of the UCS as determiners of the amount of eyelid conditioning. *J. exp. Psychol.*, 1951, **42**, 183–188.

Stacey, C. L. The law of effect in the retained situation with meaningful material. In Esther J. Swenson, G. L. Anderson, and C. L. Stacey, *Learning theory in school situations.* Minneapolis: Univer. of Minnesota Press, Univer. of Minnesota Studies in Education, No. 2, 1949. Pp. 74–103.

Stolurow, L. M. A model and cybernetic system for research on the teaching-learning process. Urbana, Ill.: Univer. of Illinois, Training Research Laboratory, ONR Contract Nonr 3985(04), Tech. Rep. No. 4, 1964.(a)

Stolurow, L. M. A taxonomy of learning task characteristics. Urbana, Ill.: Univer. of Illinois, Training Research Laboratory, Contract No. AF 33(616)-5965, Proj. No. 1710, Task No. 171003, Tech. Doc. Rep. No. 64-2, January, 1964.(b)

Stolurow, L. M. Programed instruction and teaching machines. In P. H. Rossi and B. J. Biddle (Eds.), *The impact of new media on education and the society,* in press.

Stolurow, L. M., & Davis, D. J. Teaching machines and computer-based systems. Urbana, Ill.: Univer. of Illinois, Training Research Laboratory, Contr. Nonr 395(04), Tech. Rep. No. 1, August, 1963. In R. Glaser (Ed.), *Teaching machines and programmed learning: Data and directions,* 1965. Pp. 162–212.

Stolurow, L. M., & Lippert, H. Prompting, confirmation, and overlearning in the automated teaching of a sight vocabulary. In J. P. DeCecco (Ed.), *Educational technology: Readings in programmed instruction.* New York: Holt, Rinehart and Winston, 1964. Pp. 187–197.

Suppes, P., & Ginsberg, R. Application of a stimulus sampling model to children's concept formation with and without overt correction responses. *J. exp. Psychol.*, 1962, **63**, 330–336.

Woodworth, R. S. *Experimental psychology.* New York: Holt, 1947.

Yerkes, R. M., & Dodson, J. D. The relation of strength of stimulus to rapidity of habit formation. *J. comp. Neurol. Psychol.*, 1908, **18**, 459–482.

Chapter 10

SCHOOL LEARNING
OVER THE LONG HAUL

JOHN B. CARROLL, *Harvard University*

Educational psychology is the study of the school learning process in all its aspects. Efforts to expand its research base are intensifying. One can point to literally thousands of studies recently published or now in progress dealing with such detailed problems as the role of reinforcement and feedback of results in learning, the influence of the child's social environment, the optimal conditions for the formation of concepts, the nature of teacher-pupil interaction, and many other interesting and useful topics. Let me get immediately to the essential point: Research programs that contain these studies will remain fragmented, unintegrated, and largely inapplicable to school problems unless they are set in the context of broad, longitudinal perspectives on the course of school learning. Most educational research studies are what we may call "snapshot" studies of school learning: they look at particular aspects of the school learning process for a relatively brief moment. We need also "panoramic" studies that would examine all interrelated aspects of educational growth over a major part of the years spent in school by significant numbers of pupils.

LONG-TERM LEARNING OUTCOMES

Even if one could not arrive a priori at this need for longitudinal research, it would have been forced upon us by the advent of contemporary curriculum reform movements (Heath, 1964). In contrast to curriculum reforms of thirty and forty years ago, concerned as they were with the nature of the learner and his problems of adjustment in a given stage of development—and thus with how the school is to be conducted from moment to moment, as it were—the current reforms are concerned with the content of the curriculum over fairly long stretches of a pupil's experience in school. By a "fairly long stretch" I mean any period of a year or more. The PSSC (Physical Science Study Committee) curriculum was intended to absorb the interest of a high-school student for a year's course; the new chemistry and biology programs are likewise oriented around a year's course at some time in the high-school experience. Now let me point out that the work of a year's course in a high school would on the average amount to something like 150 hours of instruction, or even more if laboratory work is done in addition to regular classroom hours. If we consider the amount of homework and outside study the average student might do, this figure might be increased to, say, something like 300 or 400 hours that a high-school student might spend learning the fundamentals of physics or biology or chemistry in the course of a school year.

What psychological experiments in learning can one cite that would compare with such settings in amount of time that the student devotes to them? Is it safe to generalize to such courses the findings of the typical psychological learning experiments that demand no more than, say, four or five hours of the subject's time? Now obviously, it is hardly feasible to develop highly controlled psychological experiments that would compare in length with a year's high-school course, and it could be argued that such experiments would be pointless and unnecessary even if they were to be carried out. Agreed, but I would insist then that the learning behavior encountered in a typical high-school course ought to be studied and described with something of the care and precision one exercises in the typical psychological experiment. Such studies would be useful, desirable, and in fact urgently necessary if we are to understand better the process of school learning.

For the moment, however, let me amplify my remarks on the emphasis that the new curricula put upon long-term learning experiences. When we turn our attention to such subjects as English, social studies, and mathematics, we find that the thrust is toward revamping almost the total sweep of the child's experience with these subjects—for these are subjects that have traditionally been introduced in the first grade or certainly early in the elementary school and that figure in the curriculum of most children right through the senior high school and often beyond. Foreign language curricula are a special case. The trend is toward both increasing the amount of time spent, for example from two years to four or five years on a given language, and starting language instruction at earlier grades, say at the third grade rather than the traditional eighth or ninth grade. What do we have in psychological investigation that compares with such educational ventures in terms of the amount of time devoted to them by the student? It is almost ridiculous to raise the question.

Even if we seek parallels in psychological investigation that cover approximately the same amount of the life span, one can think only of such unusual psychological enterprises as the Terman studies of gifted persons, the Fels Institute growth studies (Sontag, Baker, & Nelson, 1958), and a few others. Long-term studies of *educational,* as opposed to *intellectual,* growth have been extremely rare, despite the fact that the raw data for such studies have been gathering dust in school records for years upon years. The major study of educational growth that seems appropriate to cite is the almost forgotten work of Learned and Wood (1938), conducted over a span of years in the schools and colleges of the state of Pennsylvania and resulting in the monograph *The Student and His Knowledge.* Despite the paucity of long-term studies of educational growth, as educational psychologists we are called upon to guide the planning, carrying out, and evaluation of long-range curricular efforts. Our "snapshot" studies of learning in the laboratory help us very little when we are asked questions like the following: Will foreign languages taught in the elementary school facilitate the learning of new languages in the high school? How well will natural science concepts taught in the elementary school transfer to the learning of biology in the high school? What are the advantages of introducing elementary set theory in the second grade, in terms of later understanding of mathematics?

CURRICULUM EVALUATION

The evaluation of curricula that are designed to carry a child through a major part of his school years entails, it seems to me, nothing less than a very large-scale, long-term psycho-educational experiment. This conclusion, at any rate, forces itself on me even though I see tremendous theoretical and practical difficulties standing in the way of acting upon it. These difficulties, and some possible solutions to them, are the central concern of this paper.

One difficulty, particularly obvious to the experimental psychologist, is that any research that attempts to "evaluate" a curriculum cannot be an experiment in the usual sense of the term. At least, if we think of the process of "evaluation" as answering the question, "Is the curriculum under consideration better or worse than any other?" it would seem that the curriculum itself is the major independent variable. Starting from this kind of assumption, one is immediately tempted to contrast the curriculum under study with some *other* curriculum. This "other curriculum" is presumably a "rival" curriculum, like one of the colors (Green, Yellow, Blue) of the Biology series (BSCS), or some so-called "traditional" or "conventional" curriculum. Either way one runs into a problem not unlike the "nth-country" problem discussed by those concerned with the control of nuclear armaments. How many "rival" curricula does one have to evaluate? Can one generalize from any comparison between a given "new" curriculum and a traditional curriculum? Probably not. One is reminded of the discussions that one hears nowadays concerning the possibility of comparing a "programed course" in some subject-matter with a "conventional" classroom presentation of the same subject matter. As Lumsdaine (1963, p. 594) points out, "The severe restrictions on interpretation of such a comparison arise from the lack of specificity of the instruction with which the instrument is compared." We may apply Lumsdaine's remark also to the comparison of curricula. But we still do not have an answer to the question of how one evaluates a curriculum.

I would define curriculum evaluation as a process of determining whether a given curriculum attains the ends it seeks, or, rather, of determining which objectives it can attain, under what conditions, and for what kinds of pupils. The particular ends sought by a curriculum must be regarded as an unquestioned *given* in the situation, provided only that they are specified adequately enough to permit an empirical determination of whether those ends are achieved. Under some conditions, it might make sense to compare two curricula with respect to the extent to which they achieve particular objectives, for example, the attainment of adequate grapheme-phoneme "code-breaking" habits in elementary reading (Carroll, 1964). But ordinarily, curricula do not have precisely identical objectives, and it would generally be improper to compare them, because to do so would be to raise more or less philosophical questions about the comparative worth of their respective objectives.

A MODEL FOR SCHOOL LEARNING

If curriculum evaluation is defined as I have defined it above, within what kind of research model can it be accomplished if it cannot be accomplished within the classical model of the controlled experiment? I propose that an appropriate research model is one that I have discussed previously under the title, "A Model for School Learning" (Carroll, 1963). I wish to speak about this model not only as one for curriculum evaluation studies but also for long-term psycho-educational research studies that are needed to evaluate the total course of school learning. It is not a model in the sense of "learning theory," as Stolurow has proposed in Chapter 9; rather, it is a model for what might be called the "econometrics" of school learning. Taking the fact of learning for granted, it tries to explain variations in school learning success through appeal to certain gross variables in this process. Wherever it has seemed possible, I have defined the variables in terms of *time,* a physical measurement with well-known properties. The model is intended to be applicable to any defined learning task, simple or complex, long or short, except that I do not claim that it necessarily applies to affective or emotional learning; I *do* postulate that it applies to any form of cognitive or skill learning.

VARIABLES

There are three variables in the model that are defined directly in terms of time. The first of these is *aptitude,* expressed in terms of the amount of time (learning time, not elapsed time) that a person will require to attain a specified criterion of learning success on the given task *under optimal learning conditions,* i.e., when he is willing to spend enough time to reach criterion and when the quality of instruction is such that the amount of time he takes to reach the criterion is as short as it can be. The more rapid the learning, other things being equal, the higher the aptitude. Aptitude, thus defined as learning rate, may often be predictable at the outset of learning, for example by aptitude tests, although this is not necessarily the case. If perchance the individual has had prior learning on the task, or (through "transfer") on some of its components or elements, the amount of time he will take to reach criterion will presumably be lessened.

The second variable defined in terms of time is *motivation,* or what I prefer to call *perseverance,* because I conceive this simply as a matter of the amount of time the individual is willing to spend in learning. It is assumed that whatever time is actually and in some sense actively spent in learning or coping with the learning task will contribute to learning success; the model does not concern itself with the *sources* of motivation or perseverance. From the standpoint of the model, a person motivated by hope of an extrinsic reward will learn just as much as a person motivated by the intrinsic "interest" of the learning task, so long as they spend the same amount of time on this task.

A third variable is *opportunity to learn,* defined as the amount of time actually allowed for learning in the particular instructional setting. This can become a critical variable when the student is not allowed sufficient time to learn even when he is motivated to do so. In the simplest cases, opportunity (time) to learn may be limited because the inexorable school curriculum allots only a limited amount of time to a particular task or unit of the curriculum, and this may be less than needed by the student. Or, the pace of teaching may demand that every student be carried along at a certain rate, with the result that the slower learners do not have enough opportunity to learn all aspects of the materials to be learned.

The model introduces two other variables. One of them is *quality of instruction.* More precisely, this variable concerns the degree to which the content and method of teaching is structured or organized so that it is easily acquired by the student. It involves the process of communication in instruction—the adequacy with which facts, concepts, and skills are explained or otherwise imparted to the student. It also concerns the degree to which certain conditions for learning are optimal, e.g., optimal schedules of reinforcement and feedback. Whether it will be possible to measure quality of instruction in any valid way I do not know, although certainly gross variations in quality ought to be recognizable.

The final variable is what I call *ability to comprehend instruction.* Perhaps this is identifiable with verbal intelligence; perhaps it is a special type of aptitude; but in any event I find it useful to postulate that such a variable exists and that it interacts with the quality of instruction in a special way: When the quality of instruction is less than optimal, the time that a person will require to attain criterion success may be increased proportionately to his difficulty in comprehending it. His difficulty in comprehending instruction of a particular level of quality is in turn a function of that level relative to his general ability to comprehend instruction. This phase of the model stems from a number of research studies that suggest that various instructional treatment variables have little influence on learning outcomes for "bright" learners but exercise great effect on learning outcomes for "dull" learners.

The degree to which a student attains a criterion performance is viewed as some function of the amount of time he actually spends on a learning task as compared with the amount of time that would be required for him to attain the criterion in view of his basic aptitude for learning the task, the quality of instruction, and his ability to comprehend instruction. In one of my publications (Carroll, 1962) I have offered a tentative mathematical formula for computing degree of learning. As a first approximation it is convenient to think of degree of learning as a direct function of the ratio of the time actually spent on learning to the time required, a measure running from 0 to 1.

APPLICATION OF THE MODEL

How can this model be applied to actual learning situations? In general, this involves the obtaining of data on the several variables specified by the model and the analysis and representation of these data in such a way as to show the conditions under which curricular objectives are being realized. For example, I am presently in the course of conducting an evaluative study of certain aspects of the intensive foreign-language training which is given to Peace Corps trainees before they are sent to the field. The objective of the training is to give the Peace Corps Volunteer sufficient mastery of a language to enable him to perform the duties required of him in the field. The task of evaluating this curriculum is complicated by the fact that the persons who have prepared the curriculum have made assumptions about what knowledge of Spanish adequate for field service would be, but by and large I am accepting their specification of curricular objectives so that I can determine the parameters of learning within the frame of reference defined by their objectives and their training methods. By collecting rather extensive data on the foreign-language aptitudes, prior language-training experiences, and motivations of groups of Peace Corps trainees and on the content and rate of presentation of the instruction during the designated 12-week intensive course, I hope to be able to fill in the blanks in such statements as the following: For a person of age a and aptitude w, it requires x hours of training to attain level y of proficiency in language l. I have tried to select the best available tests of language proficiency, and these are being applied not only at the end of the 12-week training course but also after the Peace Corps Volunteers have been in the field

(Latin America) for a period of six to eight months, in order to gauge the effect of being in the foreign-language milieu. The attempt is being made to specify the effect of the curriculum upon students with reference to relevant characteristics of both the students and the instructional setting. This study is, of course, only a partial application of the model because not all the relevant variables can readily be measured. For example, I have no immediate way of measuring quality of instruction, nor do I have measures of students' comprehension of instruction apart from actual performance tests. Nevertheless, the study of this Peace Corps foreign-language curriculum verges upon an application of my model of the school learning process to longitudinal studies.

PROBLEMS IN LONGITUDINAL STUDIES OF LEARNING

Let us consider in a somewhat speculative vein what some of the problems of long-term learning studies might be as viewed from this conception of school learning. I shall do this under six headings.

THE NATURE OF THE LEARNING TASK

We need first a clear specification of the learning task or tasks to which the model is to be applied, as Gagné emphasized in Chapter 1. It is perhaps enough to take on the job of doing this for a specific course or unit of instruction, but, undaunted, the Russell Sage Foundation sponsored two conferences or studies that attempted to do this for the whole of the elementary and secondary school curriculum! The more successful of these, I think, was the one that concerned specifications for the elementary school curriculum (Kearney, 1953). It got right down to the detailed specification of objectives in behavioral terms—even to the maximum number of regressive eye movements in reading that were considered allowable for the well-educated child at a given grade level. The conference dealing with the secondary school (French, 1957) failed to approach the required degree of behavioral analysis and was concerned principally with "general education" aspects of secondary school education rather than with the content of particular courses of study.

Still other approaches to the specification of educational objectives need to be explored. For example, what if we were to state our educational objectives in terms of having the pupil make maximum scores on a series of cognitive tests, such as the tests of the various "factors" postulated in Guilford's presentation of the "structure of intellect" (Guilford, 1959)? What would happen if we stated educational objectives in terms of a series of generalized cognitive abilities, like verbal ability, inductive reasoning ability, planning ability, and the like?

If, of course, we are dealing with the evaluation of a particular curriculum such as the PSSC physics curriculum or a new social studies curriculum, we demand clearly stated objectives so that adequate criterion instruments for measuring knowledge and performance can be constructed. Having constructed such instruments and utilized them in the collection of data, we must push the analysis to the point that highly specific statements can be made concerning the degree to which pupils of various ability classifications have mastered this or that element of the curriculum. Such results represent what may be called "quasi-absolute" measurement in contrast to the usual relativistic measurements where raw scores are merely compared to a series of norms and are never interpreted further in terms of some standard of satisfactory knowledge or skill.

I am concerned with one additional dimension of educational objectives, namely, with what has been called the "surrender value" of the curriculum. Five or ten years after the student has successfully attained the immediate objectives of the curriculum, what is he expected to retain? Should we not construct curricula with conscious attention to their surrender value, that is, to their long-term retention benefits? We have, incidentally, very little information about what students retain from their studies long after they take them, whether or not the intervening period provides experiences that allow them to review and maintain a certain level of competence. Nor do we have any precise information about the amount of savings that would occur in relearning. For example, we spend much time and effort in teaching students foreign languages. One of the projects I have been promising myself to carry out is one in which I would select a sample of people who, say, had taken French ten years previously, test their present degree of competence in it, evaluate this in relation to the nature of their experiences with French in the intervening years, and then finally conduct a "refresher course" for them to assess the amount of savings in learning. Similar projects could be carried out for other parts of the curriculum.

APTITUDE

In "snapshot" studies, aptitude, or rate of learning, can be taken to be relatively constant over the course of the learning. That is, we can assume that whatever factors influence rate of learning are relatively constant throughout the period of learning. It should be noted, however, that I regard aptitude as specific to the task. When the task becomes complex, i.e., a series of distinct but integrated tasks, aptitudes will vary for different parts of the task. This introduces complexity into the analysis of educational learning tasks, particularly when the task is of long duration as it is when the tasks to be studied are those comprised in what is ordinarily called a course or a curriculum. But there is the additional complication that learning rate may change substantially in the course of the learning, possibly due to the acquisition of new learning sets.

And if aptitudes are viewed as subject to change, there is the exciting possibility that they are amenable to change by explicit intervention. The learning rate itself becomes the dependent variable. I have found few studies in the literature in which learning rate was an explicit dependent variable in an experiment where pretraining was introduced in an effort to modify learning rate. To give one example of an area in which I would suggest that "aptitudes" or learning rates might be changed by certain teaching procedures, I will mention foreign-language learning, where I have shown that learning rate can be predicted rather accurately (Carroll, 1962). I see distinct possibilities whereby persons' measured aptitude could be increased by instruction specifically directed to that end and whereby such increases would transfer to the foreign-language learning task, in this way facilitating it. For example, one aspect of foreign language aptitude seems to be what I have called "phonetic coding ability," that is, the ability of the individual to apprehend, reduce to some sort of implicit phonetic code, and store in memory a foreign-language word or phrase. I believe it would be possible to construct a series of exercises that would improve a person's phonetic coding ability, and I would hypothesize that a person whose phonetic coding ability had been improved by such training could enter regular foreign-language training with better chances of success than he might otherwise have had. It would be rather easy to design an experiment to test this hypothesis.

Quite apart from the possibility of improving aptitudes and thus increasing learning rates, it is interesting to speculate about what learning rates in school would be like under truly optimal conditions, that is, if over the period of his schooling each pupil were allowed to proceed at his own pace under conditions of optimal motivation and optimal quality of instruction. All the evidence suggests that under these conditions variations in learning rate would create much more pronounced differences in stage of learning after a few years of schooling than we typically find at present. Many educators have been fearful of the consequences of such a sequence of events, preferring to keep children at more or less equal stages of learning and appealing to the entirely specious argument that intellectual development should be kept in line with social and emotional development.

I have been intrigued by learning rate as an object of study of and for itself. For example, in observing students as they work on programed self-instruction in a foreign language, I have been struck by the fact that when allowed to pace themselves, the slower learners simply take more time doing, apparently, precisely the same things that a fast learner does. Where a fast learner will look at a frame and do what it tells him to do with dispatch, a slow learner will stare at the frame for a relatively long time and attempt a response only after much deliberation. Typically the fastest and the slowest learning rates differ by a factor of four or five. What is responsible for these large differences? I have no idea, only hypotheses: differential reading speeds? different learning sets? different personal tempo or degrees of impulsivity as Kagan described in Chapter 6? different attentional skills? These differences in learning rate are observed, I should mention, even when motivation is apparently high and for all practical purposes the same for all subjects.

PERSEVERANCE

In the study of a brief learning sequence, perseverance is defined as the amount of time the learner applies himself to learning or to coping with the learning task, counted up to the time when he would attain the desired criterion of learning (or, if overlearning is to be taken account of, even beyond that time). Only the actual time spent in learning is counted; "time out" for lapses of attention or the school equivalent of the coffee break is not counted.

We can apply the same concept of perseverance also to long-term learning behavior such as that in a year's course in history, or even to the learning behavior involved in the total school experience from kindergarten through Grade 16. One does not have to derive a measure of perseverance from a minute-to-minute time-and-motion study; the actual amount of time spent in learning can be estimated from records of study time, language laboratory attendance, and so on. But measurements of perseverance in longitudinal studies should allow for the possibility of variations over time. Periods of steady application, of spurts, and of motivational lapses would have to be recorded and related to variations in learning rate or measured accomplishment. Indeed, it would be interesting to determine, for a variety of settings, the relative weights of perseverance and of aptitude in learning performances. That is to say, to what extent are individual differences in educational accomplishment due to differences in the amounts of time students spend in learning, and to what extent are these differences due to differences in learning rate?

The strict application of this learning model is indifferent to the etiology of perseverance—that is, as previously stated, the "reasons" that the learner has for spending time on his learning are assumed to make no difference in the degree or kind of learning that takes place. The model postulates that a child will learn equally well whether he is intrinsically or extrinsically motivated, for example.

Nevertheless, it is probable that perseverance is rather easily subject to change by explicit intervention. Certainly we know how to *reduce* perseverance (e.g., by minimizing the value of completing a learning task or by "damaging the ego" of the learner), and we know some things about how to increase perseverance (by manipulating expectancy of reward and the consequences of failure, for example). A curriculum evaluation study should seek to determine students' manifest and latent reasons for spending or not spending time on learning, especially if these reasons are related to curricular content or methodology. For example, if certain sequences of instruction or certain teaching methods tend to arouse negative affect, these are very likely to show up as reasons for reduced perseverance in later sequences of instruction.

The notion of perseverance presented here is related to the topic of motivation which is discussed in more detail by Atkinson in Chapter 2. Motivation needs to be considered from a longitudinal perspective. Is there, for example, a developmental psychology of motivation that would be comparable, say, to Piaget's developmental psychology of cognition? Are different kinds of intervention effective in increasing motivation (and thus perseverance) at different ages? On a long-term basis, does an adaptation to certain kinds of reinforcement take place such that these reinforcements are less effective than previously? I can envision, for example, that young children would eventually get a bit jaded with toys and trinkets as reinforcers, just as older children do with kind words from adults. The variations in motivation that might be observed over time in longitudinal studies might be accounted for by changes in the effectiveness of reinforcers at different ages.

Opportunity to Learn

Recall, if you will, that we define opportunity to learn as the amount of time allowed for learning by whatever forces external to the child are relevant to the process. Most curriculum planners think in terms of definite amounts of school time to be allotted to each subject, unit, or part of the curriculum. The amounts of time that are allotted are those amounts of time that are thought to be required by the modal student, although the allotments are seldom based on accurate empirical data. They may be over-generous for some students and very much too little for some others. Some may argue that they are overgenerous for nearly all students—that the total content provided in the elementary school curriculum is so thinly strung out that most students are largely occupied in marking time while the slower students are catching up. This may indeed be true in some schools, but my own observations would suggest that the pace of instruction is quite fast enough in many other schools. If the school day or the school term could be contracted or expanded to accommodate individual differences, the miscalculation of time requirements would not have the tragic consequences it does. The pacing of instruction relative to students' actual learning rates undoubtedly leaves many students behind, with little opportunity to catch up, while it frustrates other students for being too slow. The evaluation of a curriculum, it seems to me, should specify the learning rate parameters characteristic of it so that educational planning can make appropriate allowance for them—by sectioning students according to learning rate and stage of program, and by arranging the total budget of school courses so that every student is challenged in proportion to his own ability to progress and no unreasonable demands are made on students. This, at any rate, should be the policy in the elementary school and possibly also in the secondary school. I doubt if we could ever get college faculties to agree to such a policy, much less to act in accordance with it. At a meeting of guidance counselors of Eastern Ivy League colleges, I heard talk of the concept of "selective negli-gence" that students in some of these colleges are forced to adopt in order to keep their heads above water when faced by a flood of requirements of term papers, midterm examinations, extracur-ricular responsibilities, and the like.

Certain complications are introduced in the consideration of the total school curriculum if we want to take account of inter-ference between learnings, the need for review for long-term re-tention, and the need for practice in application and transfer of learning. All these things require more time than is needed simply for original learning. Just how much time is needed is an empirical question, but it needs to be faced. I entertain the hypothesis that the American school curriculum, in contrast to the typical European curriculum, makes very little provision for the kinds of reviews that are needed to yield long-term retention. It is my belief that many of the alleged deficiencies of American education are not deficiencies in original learning and teaching as much as they are deficiencies in knowledge and skill retention caused by improper provision for periodic and meaningful reviews. In his analysis of the deficiencies of teaching in English composition, for example, Alfred Kitzhaber (1963) showed that there is not so much wrong with the teaching of English grammar and usage as with the methods used to keep the student's knowledge at a sufficiently high functional level throughout the years of secondary school and college. Students simply forget what they have been taught and are allowed to "get away with it."

Solutions to the problem of long-term retention await studies of its parameters—studies that have not yet appeared in any great quantity or quality in the literature of the psychology of learning. There is room for examining the conclusion supported by Underwood (1964, p. 149) that retention is solely dependent on degree of original learning. It is possible that individual differences in retention rate would show up more sharply than they seem to do if the periods over which retention is studied are of sufficiently long duration.

QUALITY OF INSTRUCTION

Let me review the several aspects of this variable or complex of variables. One aspect is the degree to which facts, concepts, and skills are presented to the student in a way that they can be readily comprehended and learned. Involved here are such matters as the readability level of materials, the "listenability" of oral instruction (and sometimes even its audibility!), the skill with which the structure of a sequence of concepts is utilized in a logical presentation of them, and the adequacy and faithfulness of visual demonstrations—in short, all matters having to do with the effective management of the stimulus in learning. Another aspect has to do with the effective management of the conditions of learning—the proper use of schedules of reinforcement and review, the feedback of results, and the establishment of incentive systems. People who have been developing so-called programed instruction have probably done more than any other group in recent times to improve quality of instruction, not so much because of their avowed use of operant conditioning principles as because of their insistence that the learner demonstrate understanding or skill at every step of the learning process. Their techniques of program revision force them to manage both the stimulus and the conditions of learning until learners show the desired degree of mastery.

There is need for measures of instructional quality. There is also great need for more information about what makes for quality instruction. While we have many studies of teacher-pupil interaction and "classroom climate," we have given little attention to how well teachers actually communicate instructional content to pupils.

From the standpoint of longitudinal studies of educational progress, consider an important question: What *is* the average quality of instruction? Recall that according to the model of school learning I have proposed, if instructional quality is uniformly high, educational progress does not depend on variations in the ability of pupils to comprehend instruction, but rather on other variables such as pupils' aptitude for particular learnings, the pupils' perseverance, and the pacing of instruction relative to student ability. If instructional quality tends to be low, the relevance of the pupils' ability to comprehend instruction, or let us say the pupils' intelligence, becomes accentuated. Assuming we can separate aptitude and intelligence, I would conclude tentatively that the large correlations we find between educational progress and intelligence would indicate that instructional quality tends to be mediocre in our schools. Materials of instruction tend not to be adequately organized for effective teaching, and teachers do not on the average transmit the content of instruction as effectively as they could. This conclusion, at least, would appear applicable to the instruction in the typical school curriculum across the country. Whether it would also apply to the manner in which some of the newer curricula are being taught is an interesting question that should be investigated in each case. I have no judgments to offer at this time, because I have not been associated closely with any of the newer curricular developments, and I am not familiar with any relevant research on newer curricula. The one exception to this statement I can cite is some research reported by Walter Michels (1960) on certain results of the PSSC physics curriculum. Michels reported a progressive decline throughout a year's course in correlations between intelligence and educational achievement; to me this suggests that, in this case at least, quality of instruction improved during the year, or that perhaps with instructional quality high all along, it took time to overcome the effects of poor teaching in the previous experience of the students.

There are other issues related to quality of instruction that become of particular import from a longitudinal standpoint. One of these has to do with characteristic changes in style of instruction throughout the school years. In the elementary school, group learning experiences are the rule; in the secondary school, I take it that study-recitation sequences are still much practiced; in the college, the lecture and the seminar discussion are favored methods. Is there any valid basis for these differences, or do they exist mainly through force of tradition? Probably the latter is the case. Style of instruction will become an increasingly lively issue when competing styles are presented by the various curriculum reform groups. We must find a way to compare, say, the imaginative, creative, personal teaching advocated by the University of Illinois mathematics program and the organized self-instructional procedures developed in some parts of the SMSG (School Mathematics Study Group) program. If the objectives of these two curricula can be made comparable, it is possible that comparative studies of these highly contrasting styles of instruction could be made by comparing the parameters of the two learning situations as described by the model of school learning explicated here.

Ability to Comprehend Instruction

If we take this variable as being largely identical with verbal intelligence and with the various learning sets that one needs to acquire in order to follow instruction communicated by words, pictures, and physical models, the question that arises immediately in the context of longitudinal studies is that of the stability and course of development of this characteristic of the learner. I regard "verbal intelligence" as a name for the fact of individual differences in the number and perhaps the complexity of language responses acquired through exposure to the native language milieu throughout the course of the individual's life up to the point at which the individual's ability is measured. "Learning sets" I would regard as including many of these verbal responses, but also as encompassing highly generalizable ways of perceiving and comprehending materials presented for learning. Like verbal responses, learning sets would be acquired by a process of gradual accretion through exposure to a variety of instructional settings. The rate at which verbal responses and learning sets are acquired throughout the lifetime of the individual can be described in terms of the "overlap hypothesis" first enunciated by John Anderson in 1939 (1939; 1940) and, recently, intensively studied with respect to a variety of human characteristics by Benjamin Bloom (1964). This is the notion that correlations between measures of a trait taken at any two distinct points in time in the life spans of individuals are to be explained in terms of the amount of overlap between the first and the second measure, the second measure being considered as reflecting the individual's status at the time of the first measure plus an uncorrelated increment representing gain or loss between the first and the second measure. The farther apart in time the two measures are, the lower the correlations will be. In his analysis of available longitudinal studies, Bloom finds the "overlap" hypothesis to be essentially correct. Note, of course, that these longitudinal studies are largely "naturalistic" descriptive studies of groups of individuals traced through their experiences in environments where there were no *systematic* attempts on the part of anybody to manage the environment in special ways. Thus, yearly gains were the largely random effects of a free and multifaceted environment, including schooling over a period of years.

If I assess the implications of these findings correctly, they mean that if our goal is maximal verbal intelligence for every citizen, (1) early environment is very important, because its effects continue to have great weight throughout life (e.g., according to Bloom, 50% of the variance in adult intelligence is accounted for by development from conception up to age four); and (2) maximum efforts should be made to maintain an environment that will be highly instructive in verbality throughout the child's schooling. To be sure, differences ascribable to heredity or at least to constitutional differences that appear in infancy would place certain limits on the extent to which environmental stimulation could increase verbal intelligence, but even so, a child with a continually good verbal environment would, other things equal, wind up as an adult with a significantly greater degree of verbal intelligence than a child with a continually impoverished verbal environment. The work of Strodtbeck (Chapter 4) and Loban (Chapter 5) emphasized the importance of this factor. I am very sure that the implications of the overlap hypothesis need to be carefully studied in connection with all future longitudinal studies.

CONCLUSION

And so I arrive at my closing plea, which as you might expect is one for studying all the new school curricula in the context of longitudinal research. Parametric studies of learning and educational growth that start in the first grade or even the preschool years are badly needed along with studies that would parallel, for example, the National Longitudinal Study of Mathematical Abilities that is being coordinated from the Stanford University campus. Project Talent, the long-range project initiated by John Flanagan in order to test high-school youngsters and follow them through early adulthood, needs to be replicated at a lower age level, with an emphasis upon educational growth rather than vocational placement. In all these studies, an attempt should be made to examine as well as possible—despite well-recognized difficulties—the interactions among the several kinds of variables I have postulated in my model or theory of school learning. If this can be done, we would have more exact information about the course of learning through the total school experience and a sounder basis for assessing the appropriateness and effectiveness of curricular efforts. This is what I mean by the study of school learning over the long haul.

REFERENCES

Anderson, J. E. The limitations of infant and preschool tests in the measurement of intelligence. *J. Psychol.*, 1939, **8**, 351–379.

Anderson, J. E. The prediction of terminal intelligence from infant and preschool tests. *Yearb. nat. Soc. Stud. Educ.*, 1940, 385–403, Part I.

Bloom, B. S. *Stability and change in human characteristics.* New York: Wiley, 1964.

Carroll, J. B. The prediction of success in intensive foreign language training. In R. Glaser (Ed.), *Training research and education.* Pittsburgh: Univer. of Pittsburgh Press, 1962. Pp. 87–136.

Carroll, J. B. A model of school learning. *Teachers Coll. Rec.*, 1963, **64**, 723–733.

Carroll, J. B. The analysis of reading instruction: Perspectives from psychology and linguistics. *Yearb. nat. Soc. Stud. Educ.*, 1964, 336–353, Part I.

French, W., et al. *Behavioral goals of general education in high school.* New York: Russell Sage Foundation, 1957.

Guilford, J. P. Three faces of intellect. *Amer. Psychologist,* 1959, **14**, 469–479.

Heath, R. W. (Ed.) *New curricula.* New York: Harper, 1964.

Kearney, N. C. *Elementary school objectives.* New York: Russell Sage Foundation, 1953.

Kitzhaber, A. R. *Themes, theories, and therapy: The teaching of writing in college.* New York: McGraw-Hill, 1963.

Learned, W. S., & Wood, B. D. *The student and his knowledge.* New York: Carnegie Foundation for the Advancement of Teaching, 1938.

Lumsdaine, A. A. Instruments and media of instruction. In N. L. Gage (Ed.), *Handbook of research on teaching.* Chicago: Rand McNally, 1963. Pp. 583–682.

Michels, W. C. Some lessons from high school physics. In *Proceedings, 1959 Invitational Conference on Testing Problems.* Princeton, N.J.: Educational Testing Service, 1960. Pp. 17–26.

Sontag, L. W., Baker, C. T., & Nelson, V. L. Mental growth and personality development: A longitudinal study. *Monogr. soc. Res. Child Develpm.*, 1958, **23**, 1–143.

Underwood, B. J. Laboratory studies of verbal learning. *Yearb. nat. Soc. Stud. Educ.*, 1964, 133–152, Part I.

Index

Index   273

Feldman, S. M., 179, 190
Fels Institute research, 134, 155–56, 158
Ferguson, G. A., 232, 246
Festinger, L., 28–29, 65, 74, 87
Finch, G., 219
Fiske, D. W., 73, 87
Flanagan, J., 268
Frase, L. T., 232, 243, 246
French, beginning, teaching of: effects of different sequences on, 180–84; variation in number of related tasks, 184–87. *See also* Language training, sequential; Language training, speaking and listening in.
French, Elizabeth G., 64
French, W., 257, 269
Frenkel-Brunswik, Else, 73, 88
Freud, S., 70–71
Furst, E. J., 23

Gage, N. L., 190, 224, 246, 269
Gagné, R. M., 1–24, 129, 167, 216, 219, 232, 246, 257
Galanter, E., 220
Gardner, J. W., 2, 23
Garstens, H. L., 15, 23
Ginsberg, R., 233, 247
Glaser, R., 23, 190, 245
Gleser, Goldine, 242, 245
Goals, of educational enterprises, 133–34
Goldbeck, R. A., 240, 245
Goustard, M., 88
Gréco, P., 88
Greenhill, L. P., 246
Gropper, G. L., 240, 246
Growth, educational, long-term studies of, 250–52
Guilford, J. P., 258, 269
Gurin, G., 66

Haden, E. F., 166, 190
Hamilton, D. L., 166, 190
Haptic Visual Matching Test (HVM), 136–58 *passim.*
Hayman, J. L., Jr., 240, 246
Heath, R. W., 250, 269
Hebb, D. O., 73, 88
Henry, J., 111

Herbart, J. K., 85, 88
Hershberger, W. A., 209–10, 220
Hetzer, H., 87
Hill, W. H., 23
Hoffman, A. C., 209, 220
Hopkins, B., 210, 219
Hoppe, F., 40, 65
Hovland, C. I., 198, 220
Huber, R. N., 64
Hull, C. L., 198, 220
Human performance: defined, 4; defining objectives by, 5–8; analysis of, 13–16; and stimulus processing, 18
Hunnicutt, C. D., 91n
Hunt, J. McV., 65

Idiomorphic programing, 238–39
Impulsiveness and recognition errors, 136, 139
Instruction: quality of, 255, 264–66; comprehension of, 266–68
IQs, and programed instructions, 240
Irion, A. S., 233, 246
Isaacson, R. L., 43–44, 65

Jensen, A. R., 129, 131
Jones, M. H., 75–76, 88

Kagan, J., xi, 123, 133–62
Kearney, N. C., 257, 269
Keislar, E. R., xi, 163–92, 206
Kendler, T. S., 194, 209, 219
Kitzhaber, A. R., 264, 269
Krathwohl, D. R., 23
Krawitz, Rhoda N., 65
KR (knowledge of results), 239–40, 242
Krech, D., 116, 131
Krumboltz, J. D., 41, 65
Kuhlman-Anderson measure of intelligence, 119

Lane, H., 165–66, 174, 176, 190
Langer, Susanne K., 114n, 131
Language: public and formal, 98–101; and discipline, 109–10; symbolic, growth factors in, 115–16